Netnography

Netnography

Doing Ethnographic Research Online

Robert V. Kozinets

Los Angeles | London | New Delhi
Singapore | Washington DC

First published 2010

SAGE Publications Ltd
1 Oliver's Yard
55 City Road
London EC1Y 1SP

SAGE Publications Inc.
2455 Teller Road
Thousand Oaks, California 91320

SAGE Publications India Pvt Ltd
B 1/I 1 Mohan Cooperative Industrial Area
Mathura Road
New Delhi 110 044

SAGE Publications Asia-Pacific Pte Ltd
33 Pekin Street #02-01
Far East Square
Singapore 048763

Library of Congress Control Number: 2009928780

British Library Cataloguing in Publication data

A catalogue record for this book is available from the British Library

ISBN 978-1-84860-644-9
ISBN 978-1-84860-645-6 (pbk)

Typeset by C&M Digitals (P) Ltd, Chennai, India
Printed by MPG Books Group, Bodmin, Cornwall
Printed on paper from sustainable resources

Mixed Sources
Product group from well-managed forests and other controlled sources
www.fsc.org Cert no. SA-COC-1565
© 1996 Forest Stewardship Council
FSC

CONTENTS

Acknowledgements   vi

1 Cultures and Communities Online   1

2 Understanding Culture Online   21

3 Researching Online: Methods   41

4 The Method of Netnography   58

5 Planning and Entrée   74

6 Data Collection   95

7 Data Analysis   118

8 Conducting Ethical Netnography   136

9 Representation and Evaluation   157

10 Advancing Netnography: the Changing Landscape   174

Endnotes   185
Glossary   188
Appendix 1   Online Informed Consent Form to be Used
             on Research Webpage   194
Appendix 2   A Poem/Song about the Conduct of Netnography   197
References   198

Index   213

ACKNOWLEDGEMENTS

If it takes a village to raise a child, it takes a whole network of cities to raise a book such as this. I am indebted to Patrick Brindle, my editor at Sage in London, for suggesting this book and persevering through to its completion with nothing short of unflagging enthusiasm and cheery support. When this new author seemed a little confused or overconfident, Patrick was somehow there with just the right words of advice and encouragement, or just the right interpretation of a reviewer's comments, to make things right again. This book would not have happened without him. Anna Coatman, his editorial assistant, was also there to help guide and direct me, keeping the book on track. On the support side, Harriet Baulcombe has provided patient answers to my early marketing queries, and continued support throughout the production of the book. So too has Rachel Burrows who has been a very able and friendly production editor. The text was dramatically improved by an anonymous, yet very helpful copy-editor. In addition, the writing of this book was generously supported by the Social Sciences and Humanities Research Council of Canada Standard Research Grant 410-2008-2057, 2008–2010, given for the purpose of "Developing Internet Ethnograpy for Marketing Research".

This is as good a place as any to acknowledge the many brilliant, open-minded souls whose inspiration and mentorship allowed me to develop netnography. My thesis supervisor, Steve Arnold, was consistently supportive of my web-based interest and experimentation. Without his open-mindedness and clear advice, and the encouragement of my other professors and fellow students at Queen's University in Kingston, my thesis, and the methodological work that developed out of it, could not and would not have come into being. Henry Jenkins – whose early work in this area was a foundation for my own – inspired and helped me greatly in my thesis work, and his work and advice have profoundly affected the course of my career. John Sherry has been a constant friend and mentor. John's early and sustained support of my career and its focus on high technology encouraged me to keep on working in this part of the field when very few others were there. I received a lot of assistance from my colleagues at the Association for Consumer Research, whose comments on early papers published as conference proceedings were incredibly helpful. Many ACR colleagues attended the desert 'birth' of netnography when I presented the technique in Tuscon in 1996. Among the friendly faces I remember in the room were Craig Thompson, Eric Arnould, Beth Hirschman, Jonathan Schroeder, and Stephen Brown.

Of course, this book was based on a string of conference presentations, refereed papers in proceedings, articles, and chapters. I have Russ Winer to thank for encouraging me to develop netnography as the topic of an article for the *Journal of Marketing Research*, probably the most important publication of the method thus far. I have no doubt that, had Russ not visited Kellogg and had that conversation with me, the course of the development of this method would have been very different. Wagner Kamakura took over the editorship from Russ, added his own helpful comments and suggestions to Russ's earlier comments and support and, most importantly, published the thing.

My colleagues in the field of marketing and consumer research could not have been more supportive or collegial through the years, and I feel very grateful to be working in a field with scholars that have so much intelligence, heart and soul. It has been wonderful to see a global network of fellow scholars like Ingeborg Kleppe, Pauline Maclaran, Miriam Caterall, Margaret Hogg, Markus Giesler, Hope Schau, Al Muñiz, Michelle Nelson, Cele Otnes, Bernard Cova, Russ Belk, Janice Denegri Knott, Kristine de Valck, Doug Brownlie, Jay Handelman, Andrea Hemetsberger, Johann Füller, Jill Avery, Stefano Pace, Roy Langer, Suzanne Beckman, Jennifer Sandlin and Paul Hewer become early adopters. These innovative scholars took risks by picking up and using then-new netnographic techniques in their work. And netnography benefits from the continuing development and efforts of young scholars such as Daiane Scaraboto, Handan Vicdan, Dan Weisberg, Ece Ilhan, Richard Kedzior, Leah Carter, Marie-Agnes Parmentier, Joonas Rookas, Mridula Dwivedi, Anil Yadav, Saleh Alshebil, Jeff Podoshen, Miki Velemirovich, Caterina Presi and Andrew Feldstein.

Netnography has always been an approach intended to be of practical use to companies and marketers in their marketing research. I owe a debt of gratitude to many people in Corporate American and beyond who have helped with netnography's proof of concept and worked with me in refining and developing the technique. Among the foremost of these managers and marketers whose insights, support and faith I am grateful for are Chris Yothers, Isabel Tremblay, Bob Woodard, Andrea Mulligan, Ciara O'Connell, Cindy Ayers, Martin Rydlo, Jose Carvalho, the entire brain-trust at Hyve AG, Michael Osofsky and NetBase, and Hiroko Osaka.

From around the world, to the home front. My parents, Anne and Michael, and my sister, Jennifer, have always been interested, loving, and encouraging supporters of my work. Netnography was conceived the same year as my eldest child, and my three awesome children – Aaron, Cameron, and Brooke – have patiently watched their father work away on netnographic research projects their whole life. For months, this book curtailed my participation in family activities, but my children showed nothing but interest in the book and excitement to see the final product. To my wonderful wife, Marianne, my caring sounding board and biggest source of support, go the biggest thanks of all.

Finally, to everyone who innovated, invented, invested in, created on, dreamed about, late or early adopted, jumped aboard, and made happen the Internet, I humbly offer my gratitude; and dedicate this book to all of us, in all our glorious connectedness.

1

CULTURES AND COMMUNITIES ONLINE

ABSTRACT

Our social worlds are going digital, with perhaps hundreds of millions of people interacting through various online communities and their associated cybercultures. To stay current, our research methods must follow. This book provides a set of methodological guidelines for the conduct of netnography, a form of ethnographic research adapted to include the Internet's influence on contemporary social worlds.

Key Words: community, culture, cyberculture, ethnography, Internet research, netnography, online community, research methods

INTRODUCTION

Our social worlds are going digital. As a consequence, social scientists around the world are finding that to understand society they must follow people's social activities and encounters onto the Internet and through other technologically-mediated communications. This book is a guide for this new generation of researchers. Its topic is netnography – a specialized form of ethnography adapted to the unique computer-mediated contingencies of today's social worlds.

In the field of consumer and marketing research, netnographies have become a widely accepted form of research. They have been used to tackle a large variety of topics, from applied questions of online advertising to more general investigations of identity, social relations, learning, and creativity. Netnography revealed and analysed the self-presentation strategies that people use to construct a 'digital self'

(Schau and Gilly 2003). A netnography showed how videogamers respond to product placements and brand advertising (Nelson et al. 2004). Another netnography illustrated the coping strategies used by brides to manage cross-cultural ambivalence (Nelson and Otnes 2005). Netnographies have also been used to study global ethics and perceptions of illegal peer-to-peer file-sharing (Cohn and Vaccaro 2006), to investigate consumer activism (Kozinets and Handelman 1998), and to show how knowledge creation and learning occur through a reflective 'virtual re-experiencing' discourse among the members of innovative online communities (Hemetsberger and Reinhardt 2006).

Many netnographies on a wide variety of topics have been conducted over the last decade by researchers from around the world. Given the changes in our social world, this is of little surprise. In 1996, there were approximately 250,000 sites offering published content to the online world of approximately 45 million global users, who were mainly located in North America and Western Europe. In 2009, there are over 1.5 billion users of the Internet around the world accounting for 22 per cent of the world's population. Moreover, these users are not passively consuming published content as many were in 1996 – they are actively communicating with one another. They are reaching out to form, express, and deepen their social alliances and affiliation.

Depending upon how we define our terms, there are at least 100 million, and perhaps as many as a billion people around the world who participate in online communities as a regular, ongoing part of their social experience.[1] These people are all around us. The farmer in Iowa who belongs to a soybean-growers co-operative, and actively posts to the group's bulletin board between meetings. The sociology student in Turkey who regularly uses her social networking site and posts on the fan sites of her favourite musicians. The young man with cancer who regularly turns to his online group for advice and support. The respected industry executive who dons virtual leathers and leads a secret second life in the back alleys of virtual worlds.

Netnography has been developed to help us understand their world.

Netnography has been developed in the area of marketing and consumer research, an applied, interdisciplinary field that is open to the rapid development and adoption of new techniques. Marketing and consumer research incorporate insights from a range of fields, such as anthropology, sociology, and cultural studies, selectively applying their basic theories and methods in a way analogous to the way pharmaceutical researchers might apply basic chemistry.

With some notable exceptions, anthropologists on the whole, it seems, have been rather slow and reluctant to follow social groups online (Beaulieu 2004; Garcia et al. 2009; Hakken 1999; Miller and Slater 2000). However, because information and communications technologies have permeated so many areas of contemporary social life and to such an extent, we have reached the point of no return. Social scientists are increasingly reaching the conclusion that they can no longer adequately understand many of the most important facets of social and cultural life without incorporating the Internet and computer-mediated communications into their studies. Is there a useful distinction between online social life and the social worlds of 'real life'? Increasingly, it seems like the answer is no. The two have blended into one world: the world of real life, as people live it. It is a world that includes the use of technology to communicate, to commune, to socialize, to express, and to understand.

Consider an ethnography of the work life of a professional group such as doctors or lawyers. Could we truly provide a meaningful portrayal without referencing and analysing the content of online forums, e-mails, instant messages, and corporate websites? Could we provide an ethnographic understanding of the social world of tweens and teenagers without mentioning and studying mobile phone ownership and conversations, SMS text messaging, e-mails, and social networking sites? When we come to particular topics such as the world of contemporary music, television, celebrity or motion picture fan communities, game-playing communities, amateur artists or authors, or software creators, our cultural portrayals would be extremely limited without detailed reference to the online data and computer-mediated communications that increasingly make these social collectives possible.

A decade ago, Lyman and Wakeford (1999, p. 359) wrote that 'the study of digital and networked technologies is one of the fastest growing fields of research in the social sciences', a statement that is even more apt now than it was then. There is no doubt that new research on the use of Internet and other information and communications technologies (or ICT) is adding significantly to the literature of cultural studies, sociology, economics, law, information science, business and management fields, communication studies, human geography, nursing and healthcare, and anthropology. These disciplines have generally formed their understandings in isolation from related work by scholars working in other fields and theoretical silos.

THE PURPOSE OF THIS BOOK

This book aims to provide a set of methodological guidelines, a disciplined approach to the culturally-oriented study of that technologically-mediated social interaction that occurs through the Internet and related information and communications technologies (or 'ICT'). The methods that these various fields have used to investigate these topics are still somewhat uncertain and in flux. This book will attempt to systematize these methods, recommending an approach under one umbrella term.

This book is therefore intended specifically to reward the reader who is interested in researching online communities and cultures, and other forms of online social behaviour. This reader could be a professor, an academic researcher, an undergraduate or graduate student, a marketing researcher or another type of professional researcher or consultant. The book's topics range through the varieties of online cultural experience. The netnographic approach is adapted to help the researcher study not only forums, chat, and newsgroups but also blogs, audiovisual, photographic, and podcasting communities, virtual worlds, networked game players, mobile communities, and social networking sites.

The basic principles are described and explained in this book with numerous examples. As with any type of methodological handbook, the more you engage with this text and use the examples, the greater will be your learning experience. As you read through the book, try to use the descriptions and examples for a small, rudimentary netnography project of your own. Doing netnography, you will find, is dramatically easier to begin than doing ethnography. As we are discussing research topics, focus and form your own questions. As we discuss search engines to locate appropriate online communities, start your search for them. Collect data as we discuss data collection. Analyse your data as we discuss data analysis. Read through the verbatims and examples and engage with them – if you are curious, use your search engine to go deeper. If you engage with the book in this way, you will leave it with a wealth of hands-on knowledge. The goal of this book is to enable the researcher to approach an ethnographic project focused on any type of online community and culture fully informed about what they will need to do. The more you apply the book and its examples, the more attainable you will find this goal.

After working through a few historical details, some necessary definitions, some potentially useful theory, and some methodological comparison and contrast, the book proceeds into a detailed description of the approach of netnography. The book also includes a glossary that readers may find helpful. The glossary summarizes terms and concepts used in the book and in the field of online community studies, as well as the occasional unavoidable acronym. This chapter will now provide some further elaboration upon the need for the separate ethnographic approach termed netnography.

WHY WE NEED NETNOGRAPHY

A recent set of postings on my blog debated the necessity of a separate term for ethnography conducted online. The debate benefited from the insights of a number of commenters, especially those of Jerry Lombardi, an applied anthropologist with considerable marketing research experience. Although Jerry initially questioned the need for yet another neologism, eventually he wrote about the utility of the term netnography in eloquent and historically-grounded terms.

> I recall that our dear, sacred word 'ethnography' is itself a NEOLOGISM coined in the early 19th century – which might make it an oldologism by now – to define a practice that had not previously existed in quite the form or with quite the goals that the word's coiners were trying to convey. If we were having this discussion in 1835 at the Royal Society, I might be questioning why we need that new-fangled term, 'ethnography', when, say, 'comparative moral philosophy' or 'manners and customs of the savages' still work perfectly well. (Let us try those on our business clients!) The worlds of research and intellectual innovation are strewn with neologisms that might've sounded odd or wrong when brand-new: cybernetics, psycholinguistics, software. So yes, new mappings of reality sometimes call for new names, and sometimes the names take a while to settle in.

There are a few key considerations we can think about when asking whether we need a special new designation. The first and foremost is whether we are talking about something that is actually, significantly, different. Did anthropologists over a century ago, struggling to create, legitimate, and define their new field, need the new term ethnography, or would 'manners and customs of the savages' have served their purposes equally as well? In this particular case, we need to ask of the conduct of cultural research in the contemporary world of the Internet and other ICT: is it really different?

This book suggests that it is. Chapter 4 explains in greater detail these differences, but the key assertion here is that the online social experiences are significantly different from face-to-face social experiences, and the experience of ethnographically studying them is meaningfully different. As later chapters will also explain, there are at least three differences in ethnographic approach.

First, entering the online culture or community is distinct. It diverges from face-to-face entrée in terms of accessibility, approach, and the span of potential inclusion. 'Participation' can mean something different in person than online. So does the term 'observation'. Secondly, gathering cultural data and analysing it has particular challenges as well as opportunities that are new. The idea of 'inscription' of 'fieldnotes' is radically altered. The amounts of data can be different. The ability to apply particular analytic tools and techniques changes when the data are already in digital form. The way the data need to be treated can be different. Finally, there are few, if any, ethical procedures for in-person fieldwork that translate easily to the online medium. The abstract guidelines of informed consent are open to wide degrees of interpretation.

If we can agree that these are significant differences, then we should also agree that it may be useful to provide ethnography with a different designation. That name certainly does not have to be netnography. The term 'ethnography' has been applied to online communities and culture for well over a decade. Over this time, different researchers have used different terms to describe what it was they were doing. Shelley Correll (1995) simply called her study of a bulletin board system an ethnography, perhaps signalling that the method remained unchanged whether you used it to study Trobriand Islanders or lesbians interacting through an online bulletin board. Annette Markham (1998) and Nancy Baym (1999) also used the term – although Markham and Baym (2008) appear to have opted for the more general term 'qualitative research'. The implication, perhaps, is that ethnography is already known as a flexible and adaptable approach. Ethnography is ethnography, prefixing it with digital, online, network, Internet, or web is entirely optional.

In her important and influential book, Christine Hine (2000) called her online community study a virtual ethnography, with the virtual intended to signal an effort that is necessarily partial and inauthentic because it only focuses on the online aspect of the social experience, rather than the entire experience. In recent years, I have seen many new names given to the method of online ethnography, including webnography, digital ethnography, and cyberanthropology. More neologisms can and no doubt will be invented. However, despite the many names that researchers have given their methods, *there are very few, if any, specific, procedural guidelines to take a researcher through the steps necessary to conduct an ethnography of an online community or culture and to present their work.* Although certain procedures need to be decided on a contingent basis, and extreme detail in some matters is beyond its scope, this book is specifically aimed at filling that gap.

Coming from a field where netnography is the preferred term, I have seen a number of benefits from the use of a single, distinguishing name for a technique. It is also important to note that qualitative research is blessed with an ever-growing range of techniques all related to one another and thus to ethnography. These include but are certainly not limited to such innovations as the extended case method, discourse analysis, structural ethnography, holistic ethnography, auto-ethnography, ethnomethodology, reflective phenomenology, and participatory action research (see Miles and Huberman 1994; Tesch 1990). When an approach is, arguably, significantly different from existing approaches, it gains a new name and becomes, in effect, a discipline, field, or school in and of itself. In my view, the pragmatic and applied approach to ethnography followed by corporate anthropologists is significantly different from the approach of academic anthropologists and thus merits its own guidelines and perhaps the coining of its own distinct name (see Sunderland and Denny 2007).

We need not coin these names. But we have already been doing so. Scholars producing ethnographies of online cultures and communities are rapidly minting their own names for their idiosyncratic methods. Yet, when we read a 'webnography', 'network ethnography', or a 'digital ethnography', for example, what do we know about its preferred approach or its standards of evaluation? What do we know about the way it combines online data with in-person data? Should these papers be judged in the same way or differently from other works that label themselves as 'online ethnographies' or 'virtual ethnographies'? How many different terms do we need?

In consumer and marketing research, we have generally adopted the use of the single term netnography to refer to the approach of ethnography applied to the study of online cultures and communities. Most of this type of work written after the term was coined (in 1996) uses the guidelines and techniques that have been published about the netnographic approach. Different scholars have suggested adaptations, for instance, of netnography's ethical standards. Some other scholars have opted to use those adaptations, and cited the adaptive work. Others have not.

On the whole, the system has worked quite well. This successful development of procedures and standards has led to a situation where the top-tier journals are all receptive to netnographic submissions. They know which reviewers to send it to, what citations to look for, how to evaluate it. If the method is reputable, then the reviewers and editors can concentrate on the utility and novelty of the theoretical findings. That is the role played by methodological standards in the conduct of normal science. Standards and procedures are set and, as terms regarding them fall into common usage, these standards make evaluation and understanding clearer. Social scientists build an approach that, while maintaining the inherent flexibility and adaptability of ethnography, also has a similar sense of procedural tradition and standards of quality.

For the new field of online community and culture studies, having a set of common standards will confer stability, consistency, and legitimacy. Rather than confusing those who are interested in the topic with a fallen Tower of Babel of a dozen or more different names for a perhaps-similar approach, following one technique, one set of guidelines – or explaining how one is deviating from it, improving upon it, and where this contributes to our methodological understanding – will provide much-needed clarity and consistency. If we wanted to compare different studies, we would know that, if they used closely related methods, their findings are probably comparable. The differences in them would not be due to different forms of approach. It can also help an emerging, growing field of scholarship to have a unifying stance and language. Having common terms, approaches, and a common citation base – just as I have attempted to draw on many different disciplines in my citations in this book – may also encourage the sharing of knowledge between disparate academic fields. Consistency in this area will provide much-needed clarity, less heedless replication, better theory-construction, and, in the end, greater recognition for all scholars working in this area.

DEFINITION OF NECESSARY TERMS: ONLINE COMMUNITY AND CULTURE

Netnographers grant great significance to the fact that people turn to computer networks to partake in sources of culture and to gain a sense of community. Therefore, this book must necessarily deal with two of the most complex and contestable terms in the English language: culture and community. This section of the introductory chapter is devoted to ensuring that these terms, and their application and use in netnography, are clearly defined.

Despite the prevalence of the term community to describe the sharing of various sorts of online communications, there has been considerable academic debate regarding the term's appropriateness. Early on in its development, during the period that has sometimes been called 'Web 1.0', the online experience was often more like the reading of a book than the sharing of a conversation. Originally, it was assumed that the members of online groups almost never physically met. In the original formations in which online communities manifested, participants invariably were assumed to vigilantly maintain their anonymity. Many of the interactions that members partook in seemed, at least on the surface, to be rather fleeting and often informational or functional in nature.

Yet the notion that online gatherings were somehow a form of community was present from the beginning and has persisted. Community and culture can inhere in many of the familiar forums and 'places' of the Internet. An e-mail group posting through a listserv can carry culture, and be a community, as can a forum, a blog or microblog, a wiki, or a site devoted to photo or video enthusiasts, as can podcasts and vlogs (video blogs). Social networking sites and virtual worlds carry the complex markers of many cultures and both manifest and forge new connections and communities. Newsgroups and bulletin boards, as well as chat-rooms, although 'old-style' communities, may never go out of style completely. Not only has it become socially acceptable for people to reach out and connect through this panoply of computer-mediated connectivity, but these 'places' and related activities have become commonplace. Originally heralded as the Internet's 'killer app', e-mail, it turns out, is just the tip of the communally connective iceberg.

The useful term 'virtual community' was developed by Internet pioneer Howard Rheingold (1993, p. 5), who defined virtual communities as 'social aggregations that emerge from the net when enough people carry on . . . public discussions long enough, with sufficient human feeling, to form webs of personal relationships in cyberspace'. As Rheingold notes, people in online communities

> exchange pleasantries and argue, engage in intellectual discourse, conduct commerce, exchange knowledge, share emotional support, make plans, brainstorm, gossip, feud, fall in love, find friends and lose them, play games, flirt, create a little high art and a lot of idle talk. (1993, p. 3)

We must, however, note that Starr Roxanne Hiltz (1984) studied the phenomenon, and coined the term 'online community' almost a full decade earlier, situating these communities in the realm of work, rather than leisure (for more pioneering scholarship, see also Hiltz and Turoff 1978).

BOX 1.1   DEFINING ONLINE COMMUNITY: THE FOUNDING FATHER'S WORDS

We may usefully examine Howard Rheingold's (1993, p. 3) definition of virtual communities as 'social aggregations that emerge from the net when enough people carry on . . . public discussions long enough, with sufficient human feeling, to form webs of personal relationships in cyberspace'. There are several aspects of this definition that we can develop for greater insight into netnography.

- 'Social aggregations': The use of this term makes clear that netnography is not an individualistic approach examining the personal posting of messages on the Internet, or their aggregate. Netnography's focal topic is collective. Netnography examines groupings, gatherings, or collections of people. Its level of analysis is thus what sociologists would call the 'meso' level: not the micro of individuals, nor the macro of entire social systems, but the smaller group level in between.
- 'Emerge from the net': As its name implies, netnography examines the individual interactions resulting from Internet connections or through computer-mediated communications as a focal source of data.
- 'Discussions' or communications: The element of communication is necessary to netnography. Increasingly, however, we are also seeing communities composed of people who communicate using audio information (iTunes playlists perhaps, or most certainly podcasts), visual information (Flickr), or audiovisual information (YouTube). Communication is the exchange of meaningful symbols, and all manner of human symbol systems are being digitized and shared through information networks. Each of these comprises useful data for netnography.
- 'Enough people': This implies a certain minimum number of people must be involved in order for an online group to feel like a community. We might presume

this to be about 20 people at the bottom end. There may also be a maximum number for efficiency of communication, as proposed in anthropologist Robin Dunbar's number, often held to be between 150 and 200 persons. Some online communities are, of course, much larger than this. However, we often find the larger communities splitting in order to maintain the close atmosphere of a community.

- 'Public discussions': This implies that accessibility is important to online community formation and to the conduct of netnography. Most netnographic discussions are not closed off, but open.
- 'Long enough': The concern with length of time implies that netnography examines online communities as ongoing, continuous relationships. These are not one-off meetings, but continued and repeated interactive contacts. The suggestion is that there is a minimum number of interactions and exposure over time that is necessary for a sense of community to become established.
- 'Sufficient human feeling': This concern relates to the subjective sense of authentic contact with others present in online communities. It would include such emotional matters as disclosure, honesty, reciprocal support, trust, expressions of affiliation, and expressions of intent to be social with one another.
- 'To form webs of personal relationships': This characteristic suggests that there is a social entanglement between individual members of the group, as well as the creation of a sense of the group as a discrete collection of these relationships. These relationships can, and very often do, extend beyond the online context into other aspects of people's social lives.

This foundational definition contains many key elements we find in our study of online communities and cultures, and outlines the patterns of authentic communal participation that this book will closely follow as it explains the conduct of netnography.

Complicating the description and definition, Komito (1998) carefully unpacked the various, complex notions of community, seeing virtual communities as similar to types of 'foraging society' groups of people (these were the days when people were seen to be foraging for information, see Komito 1998, p. 104), as well as bearing similarities to communities who share norms of behaviour or certain defining practices, who actively enforce certain moral standards, who intentionally attempt to found a community, or who simply coexist in close proximity to one another. Komito concluded by emphasizing the variety and dynamism of the construct:

a community is not fixed in form or function, it is a mixed bag of possible options whose meanings and concreteness are always being negotiated by individuals, in the context of changing external constraints. This is true whether group members interact electronically, via face-to-face communication, or both. (1998, p. 105)

While sharing computer-oriented cyberculture and consumption-oriented cultures of consumption, a number of these groupings demonstrate more than the mere transmission of information, but, as Carey (1989, p. 18) romantically puts it, 'the sacred ceremony that draws persons together in fellowship and commonality'. Given these definitions and appellations, the term community appears appropriate if it is used in its most fundamental sense to refer to a group of people who share social interaction, social ties, and a common interactional format, location or 'space' – albeit, in this case, a computer-mediated or virtual 'cyberspace'.

We can also locate in the term community a suggestion of some sense of permanence or repeat contact. There is some sustained social interaction and, beyond this, a sense of familiarity between the members of a community. This leads to the recognition of individuals' identities and the subjective sense that 'I "belong" to this particular group'. We would likely not say that Susan was a member of an online community devoted to breeding goldfish if she only visited that particular forum once or twice, or even if she 'lurked' on it for a half dozen occasions or so over the course of a few months. However, consider a triathlon forum in which Susan occasionally posted comments, where she was familiar with some of the main contributors, and where her preferences and interests were known by others in that group. That group would likely have more of a communal feel to Susan and it would probably be much more appropriate to suggest that Susan was a member of that triathlon online community. Clearly, a continuum of participation exists in determining what can and cannot be considered 'community membership'. Its boundaries are somewhat indistinct, but must be understood in terms of self-identification as a member, repeat contact, reciprocal familiarity, shared knowledge of some rituals and customs, some sense of obligation, and participation.

ONLINE CULTURE AND CYBERCULTURE

So what is it, exactly, that is being shared among the members of these online communities? This brings us to the equally sticky and contentious topic of culture. As Raymond Williams wrote in *Keywords:*

> Culture is one of the two or three most complicated words in the English language. This is so partly because of its intricate historical development, in several European languages, but mainly because it has now come to be used for important concepts in several distinct intellectual disciplines ... (1976, p. 87)

As Williams's erudition suggests, for there to be culture, something needs to be cultured, cultivated, or grown; the concept is intertwined with implications of civilization, socialization, and acculturation. Over time, culture tended to be viewed by anthropologists as more material and practical, concerned with continuity of behaviours and values, and by cultural studies scholars as pertaining more to languages and symbol systems, although these are currently somewhat forced distinctions.

Anthropologist Clyde Kluckhohn (1949) suggested various meanings of the term culture, including: a people's total lifeways; a social legacy; a way of thinking, feeling, and believing; a storehouse of learning; a set of orientations to problems or learned behaviours; mechanisms for the regulation of people's behaviours; techniques for adjusting to the external environment; behavioural maps; and others. John Bodley (1994) uses the term to refer to a society in its total way of life or to refer to human culture as a whole, providing a generally accepted definition of culture as socially-patterned human thought and action. He also notes that there are diverse definitions of culture that can fit into categories that are topical, historical, behavioural, normative, functional, mental, structural, or symbolic.

In *The Interpretation of Cultures* (1973), anthropologist Clifford Geertz suggested that culture is best understood from the viewpoint of semiotics, or the meanings of signs and symbols.

> Believing, with Max Weber, that man is an animal suspended in webs of significance he himself has spun, I take culture to be those webs, and the analysis of it to be therefore not an experimental science in search of law but an interpretative one in search of meaning (1973, pp. 4–5).

Culture is a public matter, Geertz suggests, because 'meaning is' – the systems of meaning through which we live are by their very nature the collective property of a group. When we look at what members of another culture are doing or saying and we cannot understand them, what we are acknowledging is our own 'lack of familiarity with the imaginative universe within which their acts are signs' and have significance (1973, pp. 12–13).

What, then, might we mean by the term cyberculture? Although it can be dangerous, or at least artificial, to make such overriding demarcations, the term cyberculture gains its utility from the idea that there are somewhat unique 'cultural constructions and reconstructions on which new technologies are based in which they, conversely, contribute to shaping' (Escobar 1994, p. 211). The complex social practices and formations that constitute online behaviours originate at least in part in the distinct traditions, constraints and trajectories of computer culture. As Laurel (1990, p. 93) noted, all online communities exist as 'villages of activity within the larger cultures of computing'. Throughout human society, computer technology and its related bank of practices and traditions are increasingly fusing with existing and new systems of meaning. This mingling can produce surprising and unique cultural formations; these new cultural fusions, specifically, would be cyberculture.

Anthropologist David Hakken (1999, p. 2) put it this way, 'the new computer-based ways of processing information seem to come with a new social formation; or, in traditional anthropological parlance, cyberspace is a distinct type of culture'. Canadian media scholar Pierre Lévy's (2001, p. xvi) definition of cyberculture as 'the set of technologies (material and intellectual), practices, attitudes, modes of thought, and values that developed along with the growth of cyberspace' is similarly comprehensive.

Jakub Macek (2005) usefully typologizes the various concepts of cyberculture into four categories: utopian; informational; anthropological; and epistemological.

The term cyberculture can be defined through a futuristic and technologically utopian perspective, as a symbolic code of the new information society, as a set of cultural practices and lifestyles related to the rise of networked computing technology, or as a term to reflect on the social changes brought about by access to the new media, respectively. These various definitions and demarcations of cyberculture, technologically utopian variants as well as dystopian and celebratory postmodern strains, are closely related to four core American ideologies of technology: the technologically utopian 'Techtopian'; the dystopian 'Green Luddite'; the pragmatic 'Work Machine'; and the celebratory 'Techspressive' (see Kozinets 2008).

The way that the term cyberculture will be used in this book – and it will be used rarely – is as follows. If we accept as a baseline definition that culture is learned and consists of systems of meaning, symbol systems of which language is primary, then we can ask about the particular features carried in specific technological contexts, such as in online communities or through computer-mediated communications. Are there symbol systems, rituals and norms, ways of behaving, identities, roles and, in particular languages, that help particular online social formations to organize and manage themselves? Are these linguistic systems, norms, actions, and identities distinctive to online groups, and online communications? Are they taught? Are they common to some groups and not to others? Are they common to some media and not to others?

If these meaning systems do exist in particular contexts that are either exclusively or mainly manifested and negotiated online (think emoticons or 'smiley faces' such as ;-) or :-(, acronyms like LOL or OMG, terms such as friending or flaming), then it seems sensible to use the term cyberculture to refer to them. My perspective is that, from a comparative perspective, there is not a lot that is particularly unique about much of what goes on in the online environment. Culture exists, and always has, in a continuous state of flux whose transformations have been driven by our inventions, which we simultaneously shape and drive. If we accept that Homo sapiens and Homo habilis are, by their nature, tool-makers and innovators, then perhaps it makes no more sense for us to talk about cyberculture as distinct from other forms of human culture as it does to talk about 'alphabet culture', 'wheel culture', or 'electricity culture'.[2]

Yet, because culture is unquestionably based within and founded on communication (Carey 1989), online communication media possess a certain ontological status for their participants. These communications act as media of cultural transaction – the exchange not only of information, but also of systems of meaning. Online communities form or manifest cultures, the 'learned beliefs, values, and customs that serve to order, guide, and direct the behaviour of a particular society or group' (Arnould and Wallendorf 1994, p. 485 f.2). To avoid the essentializing as well as the hyperbolization that runs rampant in so much Internet-related discourse, I prefer to talk about particular online cultures in their specific manifestations. Thus it may well make sense, depending upon our research focus, to talk about virtual world culture, the culture of the blogosphere, mobile phone culture, or online Bollywood fan culture. I tend to prefer the specificity of these latter terms over the generality of the term cyberculture, and would reserve the use of that term to references and discussions about the distinctive shared characteristics of these online or computer-mediated social formations.

Whether one chooses to adopt a terminology of cybercultural uniqueness, and whatever one chooses to call these social collectives, at least one thing seems assured. With global Internet access continuing to grow, and time online continuing to expand, we are going to see prodigious growth in the quantity, interests, and influence of these communities and their attendant cultures.

THE NATURE AND NUMBERS OF ONLINE COMMUNITIES AND CULTURES

Online connections and alignments are increasingly affecting our social behaviour as citizens, as consumers, as friends and family, and as social beings. In this section we will overview some important facts about online communities and cultures, in order to demonstrate their impact on the social world, and, consequently, on the conduct of relevant contemporary social research. As mentioned above, at least 100 million people around the globe regularly participate in online communities. In fact, both Facebook and MySpace social networking sites have over 100 million subscribers. It is likely that a significant majority of the 1.5 billion global Internet users 'participate' in one form or another in some form of online gathering and communication, even if that participation is merely reading messages, tagging, or offering the occasional short message.

Although studies of this new and dynamic reality are scarce, surveys point to the influence and pervasiveness of the online communal experience. In a research report in 2001, Pew's surveys explored the world online and concluded, even at that relatively early stage, that the online world constituted a vibrant social universe. Many Internet users enjoyed serious and satisfying contact with online communities (Pew Internet Report 2001). In that same survey, they reported that 84 per cent of all Internet users were reporting some sort of contact or activity with an online community, both new communities that they discovered online, or long-standing traditional groups such as professional or trade associations. The survey reported that people were using the Internet to become more involved with groups to which they already belonged, to deepen their ties to local communities, as well as to find new communities to join and partake in and to spur connections with 'strangers' and people whose racial, ethnic, generational or economic backgrounds were different from their own. In the 2001 survey, the people most interested in online community interaction were members of belief groups, ethnic groups, and particularly lifestyle-oriented groups.

It was already becoming apparent that online communities were becoming a part of people's daily experiences online. Further, the types of online communities covered a large range of human social and cultural interests, including: trade associations; professional groups; political groups and political discussion groups; hobby groups; fan groups of sports, music, television shows, and celebrities; community groups; lifestyle-oriented groups; medical support groups; personal or psychological issue groups; religious or spiritual organizations, or belief-oriented groups; labour unions; and ethnic or cultural groups. Examining this listing it is certainly difficult to think of very many communities or interests that were *not* the subject of online involvement.

More data on the prevalence and characteristics of online communities are provided by the Annenberg Digital Future Project at the University of Southern California. This research offers one of the most extensive recent surveys to date of Americans' life online. In their 2008 research results, they find that, of all Internet users surveyed, a full 15 per cent consider themselves to be members of an online community.[3] The survey results announced that the number of people claiming to be a member of an online community had nearly tripled, from 6 per cent in their 2005 survey to 15 per cent in 2007. The average longevity of membership sat at three years. These numbers kept increasing over the years, indicating that members of online communities were staying with their communities. Similar to the earlier Pew report, the most common online communities in which people reported membership were those related to the somewhat ambiguous category of 'hobbies'. Large percentages also reported that their online community involved their social lives, their professional lives, or were religious, spiritual, political or relationship-oriented.

Being in contact with an online community is increasingly a regular part of people's everyday social lives. A majority of online community members check in with their community at least once a day, 29 per cent of them several times a day – and, again recall that the survey *excluded* social networking sites from these figures. The Annenberg numbers harmonize quite well with the (2001) Pew Internet Report's finding that 79 per cent of those who were surveyed stayed in regular contact with at least one online community.

But are these online communities important to the people who participate in them? Resoundingly, the answer is yes. An almost-unanimous 98 per cent of the online community members responding to the Digital Futures Survey said that they considered their communities to be important to them. Over a third considered them 'extremely important', while more than a third considered them 'very important'. Similarly, 92 per cent of online community members said that they found benefit in their communities.

In this book, we will explore the popular dichotomy between 'online' and 'face-to-face' or 'real life' interactions and communities. Crumlish (2004, p. 7) talks about the way that Usenet groups traditionally scheduled in-person 'burgermunches' and the pioneering online service, the WELL, learned the value of parties where people got a chance to spend 'face time' with one another.

> Without embodied action, without face-to-face interaction, and without people meeting up together in place in time, the Internet might as well be a dream world. As the interconnectedness of the web reaches into the mundane details of ordinary reality and causes actual bodies to share space, real conversations to take place using lips and tongues, heard by ears and processed by auditory apparatus in brains – that's when the magic starts to happen. (2004, p. 7)

Once we are aware of the interconnectedness of social worlds, it becomes less surprising that a majority of people who belong to online communities meet other online community members face-to-face. Fifty-six per cent of online community members in the Annenberg study said that they met other members of their online community in person. This number is up from a figure of 52 per cent of online community members who met other members in 2006.

Again according to the Digital Future Report 2008, there is the keen relationship between participation in online communities and participation in social causes. A full 75 per cent of online community members said they used the Internet to participate in online communities that were related to social causes. A rather remarkable 94 per cent of online community members said that the Internet helped them to become more informed about social causes. Eighty-seven per cent of online community members who participated in social causes said that they got involved in causes that were new to them since they began participating in an online community. A full 31 per cent of online community members reported that they participated more in socially activist causes since they started participating as members of their online communities.

The most telling question in the 2008 Digital Future Project report may be the one in which online community members expressed how strong their sentiments were towards their online communities. A consequential majority, 55 per cent, said that they felt as strongly about their online communities as they did about their real-world communities, a significant increase from the year before. Consider that real-world communities would include affiliations to such groups as families, religions, neighbourhoods, nation states, or work or professional groups. The fact that online gatherings can rank alongside these core communities in people's hearts and minds speaks volumes about the meaningfulness of their connection.

These reports support the idea that what is happening in our society is not simply a quantitative change in the way that the Internet is used, but a qualitative shift. As more people use the Internet, they use it as a highly sophisticated communications device that enables and empowers the formation of communities. These communities, like the Internet itself, are being found by many to be indispensable. They are becoming 'places' of belonging, information, and emotional support that people cannot do without. Chatting and checking with one's fellow online community members before a purchase, a doctor's visit, a parenting decision, a political rally, or a television show is becoming second nature.

Online communities are not virtual. The people that we meet online are not virtual. They are real communities populated with real people, which is why so many end up meeting in the flesh. The topics that we talk about in online communities are important topics, which is why we often learn about and continue to care about the social and political causes that we hear about through our online communities. Online communities *are* communities; there is no room for debate about this topic anymore. They teach us about real languages, real meanings, real causes, real cultures. 'These social groups have a "real" existence for their participants, and thus have consequential effects on many aspects of behaviour' (Kozinets 1998, p. 366).

GLOBAL PATTERNS

As of the writing of this book, there are over 1.5 billion users of the Internet around the world accounting for 22 per cent of the world's population (see Table 1.1 for a regional breakdown). Conversely, this means that about 78 per cent of the world's

TABLE 1.1   GLOBAL INTERNET USAGE*

Global region	2008 population (estimated)	Internet users, latest data (June 30 2008)	Internet penetration (% of population)	Internet use as percentage of total global use	Growth in Internet usage, 2000–2008 (%)
Africa	955,206,348	51,065,630	5.3	3.5	1,031.2
Asia	3,776,181,949	578,538,257	15.3	39.5	406.1
Europe	800,401,065	384,633,765	48.1	26.3	266.0
Middle East	197,090,443	41,939,200	21.3	2.9	1,176.8
North America	337,167,248	248,241,969	73.6	17.0	129.6
Latin America/ Caribbean	576,091,673	139,009,209	24.1	9.5	669.3
Oceania/ Australia/NZ	33,981,562	20,204,331	59.5	1.4	165.1
GLOBAL TOTAL	6,676,120,288	1,463,632,361	21.9	100.0	305.5

Note: *Information from www.internetworldstats.com/; Internet usage information comes from data published by Nielsen//NetRatings, by the International Telecommunications Union, by local NIC, and other sources.

population, a vast majority, still have no Internet access. Penetration rates in some gigantic countries are still dismally small, such as India's rate in May 2007 of only 3 per cent. We still know very little about the qualitative differences in type of Internet use between countries, far less than we do about the easier-to-measure quantitative difference in Internet penetration rates.

Asian Internet users are well known for being more active and participative (Li and Bernoff 2008). In the Asian Pacific region, South Korea not only has the highest rate of Internet usage with over 65 per cent of its population using Internet, it also has a very advanced and sophisticated user base. They are an active online population using the Internet significantly more than other Asian populations, viewing far more of the 100 million websites available to global users. A generation of South Koreans has grown up shopping online and playing networked online games such as Lineage.

In South America, Internet penetration and usage rates have lagged behind many other continents. However, Brazil has over 50 million Internet users, more than twice as many as Mexico, the country with the second highest number of users. Brazilians are also sophisticated network users with experience in the application of ICT. Chile has the highest Internet penetration rates in the region (45 per cent of the population, as compared to Cuba's 2 per cent, or Nicaragua's 3 per cent). Chilean Internet use patterns appear to echo those of Western European countries in many respects.

Similarly, Western Europe exhibits considerable variety in the ways that online communities are manifested and articulated. Germany, Norway, and Austria are among some of the heaviest Internet users, as well as having some of the highest penetration rates, while countries like Spain, Italy, and Greece lag behind in both of these characteristics. Western European countries – in particular, Finland – and some Asian countries, like Japan, are excellent places to investigate online communities accessed using mobile devices such as mobile phones. North Americans and Japanese are advanced users of virtual worlds.

In all of these examples, we can see how certain countries, as well as certain regions within those countries, and particular demographic or cultural groups within the regions within those countries, could act as 'benchmarks' for us to study leading-edge online community, ICT, and Internet usage practices. If we want to study, for example, mobile online community use, or video blogging, it might make sense to go to the countries and the people within those countries who are in some senses demonstrating the most advanced or sophisticated uses of technology.

THE STRUCTURE OF THIS BOOK

Netnography: Doing Ethnographic Research Online is a methodological primer on a cultural approach to online research. The book seeks to thoroughly introduce, explain, and illustrate a particular approach to the conduct of ethnographies of online communities and cultures. Netnography differs from other qualitative Internet research techniques in that it offers, under the rubric of a single term, a rigorous set of guidelines for the conduct of computer-mediated ethnography and also, importantly, its integration with other forms of cultural research.

Because this book deals with a relatively new approach in a relatively new area, some overview material provided at the beginning of the book may be found useful. The introductory chapters to this book thus provide an overview of the field of Internet-based cultural and communal research, containing a number of summaries of noteworthy ethnographies of online cultures and communities in general, and discussing, organizing, and introducing some potentially useful theory. This overview covers a range of different types of research in the hope that it may inform those who are new to the field, refresh and perhaps broaden the knowledge of those who are familiar with it, and potentially trigger new ideas for exciting and innovative research in this area.

Much of the material in this book synthesizes existing methods, theories, approaches, and ideas, and attempts to place them together in a way that will be useful to both the interested student and the active researcher. The book helps researchers to consider the various options they have for investigating the cultural worlds of the Internet. The core of this book is procedural description. This also includes a considerable amount of introduction to methodological debates and decisions that need to be made in the course of conducting ethnographies of online cultures or communities. Much of the content of the book is therefore in the nature of a review or overview of related debates, concerns, procedures and approaches. What this book seeks to add to our extant knowledge is a coherent overview of the material, a framework for the conduct of cultural research on the Internet, discussions of issues and roadblocks to this sort of research, an updating of past approaches for current technological settings, and, particularly, an advocacy in favour of particular decisions.

This book is therefore structured as follows. It starts in Chapter 1 with a justification of the topic. *What*, exactly, are online culture and communities, and why are they an important topic for social scientists? *Why* should we study these phenomena? This chapter has sought to answer these questions, in the process explaining the significance, and defining the terminology surrounding online culture and community. It first demonstrated the pervasiveness of online communities and cyberculture in people's daily lives and asserted that social scientists need good tools to study these phenomena and their implications. The chapter then discussed the usefulness of general standards and having a distinct name for netnography, discussing the community and culture terminology as it applies to netnography, and offering a global perspective on online cultures and online community behaviours.

The book's second chapter, 'Understanding Culture Online', seeks to provide a general overview of extant research on online cultures and communities, giving a brief slice of some of the most important and influential research from the fields of sociology, anthropology, cultural studies, consumer research, and other fields. *What* do we know about online cultures and communities? This chapter will examine some of the research undertaken to understand and classify online cultures and communities, to describe the content of their communications and interactions, and to overview their cultural and ritual processes. Given the methodological focus of this book, this chapter will often emphasize not only what we know about the rich cultural worlds that this research has revealed, but will also foreshadow how these cultural understandings were achieved.

Chapter 3, 'Researching Online: Methods', will provide a more specific overview of the various methodologies that have been used in order to perform research on online communities. Moving into the domain of *how* we do our research, it will review some of the most popular ways that online culture and communities have been and can be studied: interviews (group and individual), surveys, social network analysis, observation, and ethnography. The chapter compares different online methodologies that use qualitative data to research online communities and offers some suggestions for their coordination with netnography. It also provides some guidelines for methodological adoption, offering determinations of research conditions under which particular methodologies may be preferable to others as well as a sense of where they can be effectively combined and hybridized.

With introductory matters covered, Chapter 4 proceeds with an introduction and more detailed explication of the method of netnography. It overviews the history and nature of the method, defines its terms, and offers an overview of how the method has already been used and adapted in particular contexts through a citation of various research studies that have used the method. Netnography adapts common participant-observation ethnographic procedures – such as making a cultural entrée, gathering data, carefully analysing and interpreting those data, writing a research report, and conducting ethical research – to the contingencies of online community manifesting through computer-mediated communications. Each of these elements is developed in turn over the next four chapters.

Chapter 5 begins the more detailed exploration of the netnographic approach by looking at planning, focus and entrée. The chapter offers specific guidelines to teach the online cultural researcher *how* to plan, focus, and begin a netnographic study. It discusses the steps that need to be followed preceding an entrée into the fieldsite and offers guidelines for a strategic entry into online fieldwork. The types of research questions and topics that are amenable to study with the method are discussed. The next decision concerns *where* and *how* to collect data. Given the wide range of choices of online communal forms, including newsgroups, boards, blogs, lists, wikis, playspaces, social networking sites, and virtual worlds, where should researchers spend their time? A logical research design process is outlined. Additionally, some protocols for deploying the resources of online search engines are provided, as well as suggestions about how to prepare for the formal data collection of a netnography.

Chapter 6, on data collection, discusses and illustrates particular approaches to the capture of online community and cultural data. This chapter emphasizes the cultural nature of these data. Because netnography is participant-observational research, netnographic data can take three or more forms: (a) data that the researcher directly (b) data that are generated through the capture and recording of online community events and interactions; and (c) data that the researcher inscribes. Each of these will be discussed and particular guidelines offered to enable the researcher to collect the appropriate type of netnographic data required for particular research projects.

This is followed by the chapter on data analysis and interpretation. Grounded theory and inductive coding procedures are overviewed, as well as the more interpretive and holistic 'hermeneutic circle' types of theory generation. Several software solutions will be overviewed. Some specific strategies will be discussed and illustrated to help researchers to understand the particularities of netnographic data analysis.

Research ethics may be one of the most important differences between traditional ethnography and netnography. Chapter 8 covers this issue in some detail. It offers moral, legal, and ethical stances to support guidelines and procedures that can be used to plan and undertake research and also to submit applications to overseeing bodies such as Institutional Review Boards and Human Subjects Research Ethics Committees. Ethical concerns over netnography turn on contentious concerns about whether online forums are to be considered a private or a public site, what constitutes informed consent, and what level of disclosure of research participants is appropriate. These issues and stances will be discussed in turn, and specific research procedures recommended.

Chapter 9 covers some of the big picture issues of research representation and the evaluation of netnographic research. In it, I discuss the representational choices facing the netnographic researcher. The nature of the online medium offers researchers more choices for reaching broad and diverse audiences than ever before and this chapter follows the discussion of representation with an elaborated set of evaluative standards.

The final chapter is devoted to a discussion of the changes and advances in the netnographic approach. It discusses the latest developments in the online environment of online community and culture, including blogging, microblogging ('Tweeting'), social networking sites, and virtual worlds. Extrapolating from the alterations of the method described throughout the book, this chapter will also provide some general guidelines for the adaptation of netnography to the particularities of these sites of online interaction and community. The book concludes with a look at the potential growth of online communities and the possibilities for the ongoing growth and adaptation of netnography by a new generation of scholars.

SUMMARY

Online communities and other Internet or ICT cultures are an increasingly important part of our contemporary social world. Researchers may benefit by adopting the approach of netnography, a form of ethnographic research adapted to the unique contingencies of various types of computer-mediated social interaction. Using a common understanding and a common set of standards for such studies will confer stability, consistency, and legitimacy. This first chapter has defined online communities and culture, and explained why they are a significant topic for social scientists today. This is a necessary step before exploring current theory about these topics in Chapter 2, and then explaining and demonstrating the method of netnography that studies these communities and cultures in the remainder of the book.

KEY READINGS

Garcia, Angela Cora, Alecea I. Standlee, Jennifer Bechkoff, and Yan Cui (2009) 'Ethnographic Approaches to the Internet and Computer-Mediated Communication', *Journal of Contemporary Ethnography*, 38 (1), February: 52–84.

Lévy, Pierre (2001) *Cyberculture*, translated by Robert Bononno. Minneapolis, MN: University of Minnesota Press.

Pew Internet Report (2001) 'Online Communities: Networks that Nurture Long-Distance Relationships and Local Ties', Pew Internet & American Life Project, available online at: www.pewinternet.org/report_display.asp?r=47/

Rheingold, Howard (1993) *The Virtual Community: Homesteading on the Electronic Frontier*, available online at: www.rheingold.com/vc/book/

2
UNDERSTANDING CULTURE ONLINE

ABSTRACT

Research and theory about online communities stretches back over three decades and involves all of the social sciences. The online social space of computer-mediated communications was once considered lean, cold, and egalitarian. But studies of actual online social groups instead emphasized the diversity and authentic cultural properties of online communities, and demonstrated the value of a participant-observational approach to the Internet.

Key Words: computer-mediated communications, ethnographies of online community, face-to-face communications, Internet research, Internet theory, lean media theory, online community, online identity, online participation, online social interaction theory, status equalization effects, technoculture

TECHNOLOGY AND CULTURE

Almost four decades ago, Canadian media theorist Marshall McLuhan predicted that the 'cool', participative and inclusive 'electric media' would 'retribalize' human society into clusters of affiliation (see, e.g., McLuhan 1970). As the decades passed, a number of other technological futurists, including Alvin Toffler, John Naisbitt, Peter Drucker, and George Gilder, located the important social changes and possibilities of an interlinked world.

Reading these past authors, it is easy to fall under the sway of a sense of technological determinism, an impression that technology is shaping our culture and changing our communities. Or we might assume instead a technocultural view of these changes. At an early stage of the Internet age, cultural theorists Constance Penley and Andrew Ross wrote that:

> Technologies are not repressively foisted upon passive populations, any more than the power to realize their repressive potential is in the hands of a conspiring few. They are developed at any one time and place in accord with a complex set of existing rules or rational procedures, institutional histories, technical possibilities, and, last, but not least, popular desires. (Penley and Ross 1991, p. xiv)

The insight that technology does not determine culture, but that they are co-determining, co-constructive forces, is a crucially important one. With our ideas and actions, we choose technologies, we adapt and shape them. To this realization it is also critical to add that our culture does not entirely control the technologies that we use, either. The way that technology and culture interact is a complex dance, an interweaving and intertwining. This element of technocultural change is present in our public spaces, our workplaces, our homes, our relationships, and our bodies – each institutional element intermixed with every other one. Technology constantly shapes and reshapes our bodies, our places, and our identities, and is shaped to our needs as well. Understanding of the way this transformation unfolds requires us to keep a keen eye on particular and general contexts – specific times and places, distinctive rules or rational procedures, institutional histories, technical possibilities, practical and popular uses, fears and dreams. A thorough understanding of these contexts requires ethnography.

As we move through our second decade of life in the Networked Age, the proliferation of computer-mediated communications (CMC) into everyday existence seems to be bringing some early predictions to life, and adding plenty of surprises along the way. Networked computers and the communication and coordination that they enable are driving major social changes and having a myriad of effects on people's everyday lives.

But these dramatic effects weren't always obvious to social scientists. Far from it, in fact. In recent years, we have only just begun to develop theories and sound analyses about the processes and practices surrounding these cultures and communities.

EARLY RESEARCH ON TECHNOLOGIES AND CULTURE

Initial Research on Online Interaction

Initial research into the burgeoning medium of online interaction was based on social psychological theory and experimental tests. This work suggested that the online medium provided a poor foundation for cultural and social activity. It asserted that social activity required the conveyance of rich social and emotional information, a sense of social presence, and the presence of social structure. Compared to face-to-face

('F2F' or 'f2f') exchanges, online communications were theorized to be 'lean' and equivocal (e.g., Daft and Lengel 1986). Communicators were presumed to suffer from a reduction in social cues. That is, there was uncertainty in the communication because of the online medium's reduced capacity to transmit nonverbal information relevant to social presence, such as voice inflection, accents, facial expressions, directions of gaze, gaze-meeting, posture, body language and movement, and touching (e.g., Dubrovsky et al. 1991; Short et al. 1976; Sproull and Kiesler 1986; Walther 1992, 1995). When tested in university laboratories with fresh sets of experimental subjects, these original assumptions were borne out.

Thus, from its beginnings, the online social environment was viewed with suspicion and cynicism, as a context that created task-oriented, 'impersonal', 'inflammatory', 'cold', and 'unsociable' interactions (Kiesler et al. 1984, 1985; Rice 1984; Rice and Love 1987; Sproull and Kiesler 1986; Walther 1992, pp. 58–9).

Another early stream of research suggested that the participants in online communities would be subject to a 'status equalization effect', a flattening of hierarchies where social status is equalized, social differences minimized, less rule-following occurs, and no leadership is possible. It was thought that the general lack of social context clues resulted in a reduction of social differences, an increase of communication across social barriers, less dominance, increases in self-absorption, and more excited and uninhibited communication (Dubrovsky et al. 1991; Sproull and Kiesler 1986). Many of these behaviours were already observable in online interactions, such as 'flaming', or insults, hostile language, and the use of profanities. These scientists thought that the technology behind online communities and online interactions undermined the social structure that was required for appropriate and hospitable social relations.

Testing Initial Assumptions about Online Sociality

However, it wasn't very long before further research began to question these initial suppositions and early findings. Analysis of the actual content of CMC started to reveal discrepancies. Social group members seemed to 'develop an ability to express missing nonverbal cues in written form' (Rice and Love 1987, p. 89). In CMC, putting cues of affection, affiliation and other communications-clarifying elements happens through new symbols, or electronic 'paralanguage' such the familiar 'emoticons' [or smiley faces, such as :-) or ;-)], intentional misspellings, absence and presence of corrections and capitalization, as well as visual ASCII art (Danet 2001; Sherblom 1988, p. 44; Walther 1992, 1995). Similar attempts to imbue textual messages with features intended to replicate a face-to-face communication are common among users of other media (Beninger 1987; Gumpert and Cathcart 1985). Interdisciplinary research into the online environment revealed that, rather than being socially-impoverished and 'lean', there were detailed and personally enriching social worlds being constructed by online groups.

Walther (1997) suggests that we can understand much of online community behaviour by referencing the 'anticipated future interaction' of participants. If participants believe that their interaction is going to be limited and will not result in future interactions, then their relations tend to be more task-oriented. If, however, a future interaction is anticipated, participants will act in a friendlier way, be more cooperative, self-disclose, and generally engage in socially positive communications. We can conclude from this that longer-term online gatherings, particularly those where individual identities are revealed, would have tighter and more positive social relations than groups that are shorter-term and more anonymous. Similarly, Olaniran (2004) asserted that in order to manage online groups with diverse members, there was greater need to focus on shared relations of trust and unity of common interests rather than on differences. Wellman (2001b) speculates about a type of 'networked individualism' in which online communities' lack of formal institutional structure means that communications will depend on the quality of the social ties that the individual forms with the group.

Further research, including some of the early ethnographic investigations, disputed the early assertions of status equalization by showing how online group members brought to bear various strategies of visibility and identity expression in order to compensate for the scarcity of traditional markers of status differentiation and to permit its re-establishment online (Meyer and Thomas 1990; Myers 1987; Reid 1996). 'Electronic communicators have developed a grammar for signaling hierarchical positions' (Walther 1992, p. 78). 'The newcomers to a computer conference or a MOO are immediately recognized as such and the same holds true of the leaders. Both acquire and use symbols that make them different one from the other' (Paccagnella 1997). Positions of dominance in an online group are achieved through the manipulation of various social cues, such as verbal floor-managing (Shimanoff 1988), and the presence or absence of signature files (Sherblom 1988). As communicators begin building longer-term relationships and start exchanging interpretive social cues, they also start to more actively manage their self-presentations in order to create more favourable social impressions and a greater level of intimacy or attraction (Walther 1997).

The participants in online communities

> communicate social information and create and codify group-specific meanings, socially negotiate group-specific identities, form relationships which span from the playfully antagonistic to the deeply romantic and which move between the network and face-to-face interaction, and create norms which serve to organize interaction and to maintain desirable social climates. (Clerc 1996 pp. 45–6).

Recent research at Forrester Research asserts that online communities running the gamut from forums and web-pages through to blogs and social networking sites enable personal expression, active participation, and the formation of relationships (Li and Bernoff 2008).

Walther (1992, p. 53) summarily notes of this early research that 'the characterizations of CMC born from experiments on groups seem contradictory to the findings of CMC in field studies'. Naturalistic investigations of content and culture enriched prior social psychology-based portrayals of online interaction by problematizing the reduced social cues and status equalization effects theories, theories whose evidence was largely based on short-term experimental studies of asynchronous 'zero history' or 'one-shot' groups. Examining what people actually did with CMC in their own social worlds, over the longer-term, as they wove webs of affiliation, turned out to be quite different from what people were doing in short-term situations with the technologies in laboratory situations. When information and communications technology is cast into the world, and moist life breathed into its brittle, dry circuitry, it turns out that it is used to manifest culture and build community.

DEVELOPING NUANCED UNDERSTANDINGS OF THE ONLINE SOCIAL WORLD

The development of the field of research about online cultures and communities is a story of multiple methods working to answer different research questions and reveal different facets of a new, highly complex, and rapidly evolving social phenomenon. Survey approaches inform us about the relative population, demographic constitution, and frequencies of behaviours of online community members. Social psychological and experimental approaches hypothesize about and test suggested causal relations between important individual and group level variables such as attitudes, memory, and beliefs. They enrich our understanding about the processes at work as participants engage in online communities. Netnography, the ethnography of online groups, studies complex cultural practices in action, drawing our attention to a multitude of grounded and abstract ideas, meanings, social practices, relationships, languages, and symbol systems. All of these disciplines offer complementary and necessary perspectives. Each of them is useful as we seek greater understanding of this new and ever-changing landscape of online communities and cultures.

Three decades of research have revealed that online gatherings follow many of the same basic rules as groups that gather in person. For example, the ways in which group norms develop and the importance of group identity are very similar in online and off-line groups. However, a range of research has concluded that the online community's unique characteristics – such as its anonymity and accessibility – create some unique opportunities for a distinctive style of interaction.

Most of the social psychological research conducted on computer-mediated communication and interaction in the 1990s was concerned with investigating whether the theories developed among other groups and in the earlier years of CMC research would still hold. There is also a considerable amount of information about early group and decision support systems, and virtual teams as applied in organizations. Researchers suggest that scholarly and relational bonds develop quite naturally through the use of virtual teams (Vroman and Kovacich 2002). This should be a reassuring finding given that scholarly and professional bonds were the founding reason behind the creation of the Internet in the first place.

McKenna and Seidman (2005) classify the emphasis of the earlier years of CMC research in social psychology as 'main effects' accounts, and conclude in their review that:

there are as few 'main effects' of communicating electronically as there are of communicating face-to-face. Online interactions can be and are as rich and as varied as traditional interactions; the processes that produce given outcomes can be as complex and multiply determined as those that occur in traditional interactions venues. [Social psychological] research is only beginning to demonstrate just how complex the 'online world' can be. (McKenna and Seidman 2005, pp. 192–3)

As we will see later in this chapter, some of the netnographic accounts offer portayals of exactly this sort of richness and complexity.

Initial concerns that Internet use might be corrosive to the existing patterns of group, family, and community life have been contradicted by later, and more thorough, investigation. They suggest that, in fact, the opposite may well be true. Analyses of national surveys suggest that Internet users are just as likely as those who do not use the Internet to call their friends on the telephone or to visit them in person, and actually conclude that Internet users have larger social networks than those who are not users (DiMaggio et al. 2001). A large, random-sample study relates that people believe the Internet enables them to keep in touch more effectively with their friends and family, and even to extend their social networks. This belief in the relational power of the Internet should come as no surprise to those familiar with social networking sites. In another, related, study, Howard et al. (2000, p. 399) conclude that their results 'suggest that online tools are more likely to extend social contact than detract from it'. A longitudinal study by Kraut et al. (2002) suggests that people who use the Internet more also engage in more face-to-face and telephone contact with their friends and family, and also that more Internet use is correlated with increased civic involvement.

Research that studies online communities that use e-mail and mailing lists to stay in contact has found these media to be useful for developing and maintaining networks with 'weak ties', that is, networks in which the participants do not have close relationships characterized by the exchange of lots of information or the presence of intimate personal friendships (Matei and Ball-Rokeach 2003). As we might expect of complex actual phenomena, online communities appear to have a number of different usages. They can intensify existing relationships as well as help to create and then maintain new relationships.

Meta-analyses of computer-mediated communication studies indicate that Internet users progress from initially asocial information gathering to increasingly affiliative social activities (Walther 1995). Kozinets (1999) theorized that there was a pattern of relational development as people who are interested in online communities became drawn into and acculturated by their contact with them. First, for a variety of reasons, an Internet user will become interested in an online community and its culture. The user often will have a particular goal that they want to accomplish, such as hearing others' political opinions, finding out about a car rental service, locating the best deals on wine, or learning how to properly install a new toilet. Doing so will lead them to search engines as they 'browse' information sources. There, they will often 'lurk', unobtrusively reading, but not writing about, their focal topic of interest.

Consider the theoretical example of 'Samantha', a dedicated and enthusiastic young backpacker, who is planning her vacation to Agra, India. Seeking 'hard' information, Samantha begins her quest by searching the city's name in Google, clicking on the link to Wikipedia, and then visiting the official Website of Agra. However, as she delves deeper and explores more of the online links from her Google searches and Wikipedia entries, she begins to notice and visit sites that have 'third party' information, information from other 'real people' like her, except that these people have actually been where she wants to go.

Samantha might seek out pictures of the Taj Mahal and, from the comments that she finds there, find out that there are communities and blogs dedicated to discussing travel stories. Eventually, she reads some of the posts written by members of these communities. Intrigued, she may make online contact with the people on a forum or on a blog. She reaches out to others who are planning similar trips. She might question a few blog authors individually, and then make a general post to an online community that gathers on a particular web-page's forum. One of her querying replies to an answer is found to be culturally-insensitive and offensive by one of the regular posters to the group (who happens to be Indian). That person insults Samantha's intelligence publicly on the forum. Another member, a leader in the group, gently defends her and suggests that she apologize. Samantha feels genuinely horrified at her faux pas. Despite her deep embarrassment, she apologizes. She thinks about never going back to the forum, but eventually, after ten days away, she returns. After posting several more questions to the community, she sees a question about Nicaragua, a place she has recently visited. At that point, Samantha feels obliged by norms of reciprocity – after all, with only a few exceptions, the community has been good to her – and she answers it in great depth and detail. After some time, she becomes an occasional participant in group discussions. When she actually does travel to India, she cannot help but think many times about what she has learned from the members of the online community; she even feels that somehow, she is carrying them along with her. After she returns from her travel to Agra, she posts a long contribution, with links to some amazing photographs. A few months go by in which she rarely visits the group, but then she starts to become a more intense participant in the group as she plans her next travel destination.

As depicted in Figure 2.1, the pattern of relationship development in an online community is one in which task-oriented and goal-directed informational knowledge is developed in concert with social and cultural knowledge and social relationships. As we saw from the example of Samantha, fact-based information is learned alongside knowledge of the online community's specialized language and sensitized concepts, norms, values, rituals, practices, preferences, and the identities of experts and other group members. As personal details and stories are shared, cultural cohesion ripens and empathy blooms. A group structure of power and status relationships is learned. What began primarily as a search for information transforms into a source of community and understanding (Kozinets 1999).

In the contemporary Internet realm, there are other pathways to community membership. Within a community format designed for social interaction, such as a social networking site or a virtual world, there initially might be no abstract or socially distant topics or information to exchange or share. In the social network, the exploration and building of that network might be the goal. In a virtual world or a

FIGURE 2.1   DEVELOPMENTAL PROGRESSION OF PARTICIPATION IN ONLINE
COMMUNITIES (ADAPTED FROM KOZINETS 1999)

gaming-based community, the learning of the social norms or game rules, or the
mastering of the online environment itself, might be the primary objective. In those
cases, topics about which people share information might be more personal in nature
or more about the characteristics of the social or constructed environment. From
there, the participant might follow a path to the learning of cultural norms, and the
broadening and spreading of social relations throughout the various extended arms
of the online community.

Regardless of the medium or exact pathway to participation, the theory suggests
that, over time and with increasingly frequent communications, the sharing of
personal identity information and clarification of power relations and new social
norms transpires in the online community – that social and cultural information
permeates every exchange, effecting a type of gravitational pull that causes every
exchange to become coloured with emotional, affiliative, and meaning-rich elements.

This emotional, affiliative element – its social psychological origins and its social
values – has been recognized repeatedly in research. Research using survey responses
and structural equation modelling by McKenna and Bargh (1998) revealed that many
respondents had, as a result of their online community participation, come out to
their families and friends about a stigmatized aspect of their identity for the first time
in their lives. Because of their online community experiences with others who
shared their own stigmatic status, they considered themselves less different, benefited
from the increase in self-acceptance, and felt less socially isolated.

Similarly, another study of online support groups for people with serious and often
stigmatized illnesses such as alcoholism, AIDS, and forms of cancer, established the
benefits of online communities (Davison et al. 2000). For those who sought out
similar others under conditions of great anxiety and uncertainty, the anonymity and
accessibility of these communities have been a virtual godsend. A range of studies also
suggest that online communities have considerable stress reduction, self-acceptance,
and informational value, even for people who have illnesses and conditions that are
not stigmatized, such as diabetes or hearing impairments (see, e.g., McKay et al. 2002).

Ethnographically studying the phenomenon in a subcultural context from a symbolic
interactionist frame, the findings of Williams and Copes also reinforce the utility of the
online communal forum for those who feel disenfranchised or marginalized. Using

'internet-based subcultural forums to combat the liminal feelings that are widespread in the face-to-face world … many individuals who feel marginalized in contemporary society search for others in emerging virtual spaces' (2005, p. 85).

As a result of their study of the impact of online communities on social capital and involvement in local communities, Kavanaugh and Patterson (2001, p. 507) suggested that 'the longer people are on the Internet, the more likely they are to use the Internet to engage in social-capital-building activities'. In their overview of this research, McKenna and Seidman (2005, p. 212) put forward that not only are people not substituting participation in online communities for involvement in physical activities and relationships, but 'if anything, Internet use appears to be bolstering real-world community involvement'. These and other results show us that not only do online communities have real social benefits, but also that they have powerful effects on people's sense of identity.

RESEARCH ON NEW PRACTICES AND SHIFTING SYSTEMS OF MEANING

Early ethnographic studies of online communities also underscored the dramatic impacts that the Internet and networked connectivity were having on self-identity and social relationships and then proceeded to detail the varied practices involved in achieving these effects. Two of the earliest and most influential works in the field of ethnographic online community studies are Rheingold (1993) and Turkle (1995).

Writer Howard Rheingold's (1993) *The Virtual Community: Homesteading on the Electronic Frontier*, is a trailblazing investigation into the early online community, the WELL. In this work, Rheingold offers a conceptual charting of online communities and the interactive potentialities they offer. Massachusetts Institute of Technology professor Sherry Turkle's (1995) book, *Life on the Screen: Identity in the Age of the Internet*, is a close examination of people's changing understanding of computers that also studies how they interact with the Internet, specifically with one another in multi-user domains (MUDs) (see also Cherny 1999).

Three other important early ethnographies of online communities are Baym (1999), Markham (1998) and Cherny (1999). One of the pioneers of online ethnography, University of Kansas media studies professor Nancy Baym (1999), conducts a detailed study of rec.arts.tv.soaps, a Usenet fan bulletin board devoted to soap operas. She theorizes that there are many similarities between audience communities and online communities (see also Jenkins 1995). Further, she suggests that online communities be viewed and studied as 'communities of practice', because 'a community's structures are instantiated and recreated in habitual and recurrent ways of acting or *practices*' (Baym 1999, p. 22). The book proceeds to explore and elaborate the various practices used in this online community, charting out the terrain of online communities. Baym describes a range of interpretive, informative, and social practices, such as evaluation, commiseration, criticism, and other strategies for the creation of a group identity. She details a number of ways that sociability and dissent are managed in the community, verbal strategies and rituals for accomplishing friendliness and managing the inevitable disagreements, and also notes the various formations – particularly the dyad – that online sociability within the greater community affords.

In *Life Online* – the result of her own intense experiences as a heavy Internet user – University of Wisconsin-Milwaukee professor Annette Markham (1998) also offers a detailed ethnographic account of linguistic practices and collective formations manifesting through CMC. The book is presented as the narrative of a journey from a naïve beginner to a knowledgeable insider and expert. It is a profoundly textual journey, and Markham emphasizes the textuality of life online by providing many excerpts that approximate for the reader how her computer screen appeared when she was encountering these various at-first alien cultures and communities. She also lists and explains various acronyms and computer commands she had to master in order to navigate this early online environment. Along the way, Markham theorizes about the practices, identities, consumption, and particularly the lived experience of online community membership, casting the online experience as simultaneously a tool, a place, and a way-of-being.

Markham's innovative (1998) book also self-reflexively considers issues of embodiment, and her auto-ethnographic accounts bring life and detail to her analysis:

> After a few hours of [online] work, my body is screaming with pain. My back constantly aches, no matter how I adjust my chair. If I do not chew gum, I clench my teeth; if I do not talk, my throat is raw and sore. My hands take the most punishment. (1998, p. 59)

She also offers many useful and honest reflections and suggestions about conducting ethnographic fieldwork in the online environment (see also Markham and Baym 2008).

The result of two years of research conducted in a 'multi-user dungeon' (MUD), user experience authority Lynn Cherny's (1999) *Conversation and Community* offers another ethnographic investigation into a close knit synchronous or 'real-time' chat-based community, its members' linguistic practices, their shared history, and their relationships with the members of other online communities. Cherny's book details necessary innovations and adaptations made by community members to address the limitations of the textual medium. Speech routines, vocabulary and abbreviations, syntax and semantics, and turn-taking strategies distinguish the online community's 'register' – its variety of speech that has adapted to a particular recurrent communication situation. Her study demonstrates and also explains the ability of people interacting online to use language in order to create a genuine sense of online community, analyses the impact of power structures and hierarchy (revealing a technocracy in which the technically empowered are the most influential actors), and also considers the role of elites, gossip, and conflict in the formation and maintenance of an active, thriving community.

Brenda Danet, in her (2001) book *Cyberpl@y*, collected a decade's worth of discourse analyses to examine the variety of online forms of play. Her account provides a detailed historical, literary, sociolinguistic, aesthetic, folkloric, and theoretical unpacking of five particular forms of linguistic online performance, as they manifest in various online communities. Danet examines the convergence of playfulness, art and communications through five case studies which elaborate and interpret the language of e-mail, playful performances on Internet Relay Chat, the construction of elaborate multi-coloured ASCII images, text-based art and communication on a chat channel called 'rainbow', and community members' enthusiastic play with, and collection of, digital fonts. Her rich visual examples, results, and discussion theoretically illuminate the interplay of technology, play, art, and community in the online environment. Each of these valuable books is noteworthy for its thorough breakdowns and descriptions of the developing systems of meanings and practices that we can observe as online community members build and share their cultures.

TYPOLOGIES AND CLASSIFICATIONS OF ONLINE COMMUNITIES AND ONLINE PARTICIPATION

In an early study demonstrating the genuineness of the online communal experience, Correll (1995) conducted an ethnography of 'The Lesbian Café', an electronic bar. Her ethnography suggests that the online community experience is mediated by impressions of real-world locations as well as by the unique contingencies of computer-mediated communications. Based on her observations in this site, she offers a typology of four styles of online community membership and participation: regulars, newbies, lurkers, and bashers. There is an apparent developmental progression from lurker to newbie to regular, and an oppositional status displayed by the bashers who come from outside of the community in order to harass members. Correll's early descriptions here of online community and the progression from one membership stage to another have been influential.

Another idea is that the members of online communities have two main elements bringing them together, which can interrelate in many ways. We may be able to better understand membership identification and participation by studying these two non-independent factors. The first considers the relationship between the person and the central consumption activity that they are engaging in, with, and through the online community. The term consumption is intended to be interpreted with considerable flexibility. In an online community devoted to the videogame 'Spore', for example, the central activity would be gaming. In a beer brewing community the central 'consumption' activity might not be consumption per se, but the production of a homemade brew, maybe a nice mead mélange fermented with an ancient Egyptian yeast strain and Manuka honey (of course, its consumption would also play a role). In a virtual world such as Second Life, the central activity might be 'consuming' new friends in a general sense or having interesting and exciting new online experiences.

The guiding notion underlying this dimension is that the more central is this activity to a person's sense of identity, and the more that they believe the pursuit and development of the skill or activity is central to their self-image and core self-concept, then the more likely this person is to pursue and value membership in a community, be it online or otherwise. Because the activity is so important to them, any connection to it, to others who share it, or to pathways to knowledge about it and social discourse surrounding it, is going to be held in great esteem, coveted, and cherished. Conversely, if this consumption activity is not particularly important to them, their relationship to the online community is going to be more distanced.

This category of consumption interest centrality is correlated and interrelated with consumption proficiency. Thus, the greater the centrality of the consumption interest to the person, the higher the interest level and concomitant level of activity knowledge and skill. This is a measure not only of self-identification, but of identity and interest combined with expertise.

The second factor concerns the actual social relationships of this particular online community itself. How deep, long-lasting, meaningful, and intense are those relationships? Are these people considered to be merely somewhat-interesting strangers, or are they long-term friends who are as close to the participant as anyone else in their life? Obviously, some forms of online community are more likely to promote this sort of affiliation than others. Social networking sites operate under the assumption that affiliations are already pre-existing, and use technological connection to intensify them. Virtual worlds like Second Life are structured so that social intercourse is the primary pursuit and objective. Blogs can be a bit more impersonal in their communal forms, with one or several major authority figures relating with a more traditional 'audience' form, but this perspective cloaks the often close relationships between related groups of bloggers (Rettberg 2008). There is not an online communal form that we will deal with or mention in this book where deep and meaningful personal relationships cannot be built.

It is also important to note that these two factors will often be interrelated. For example, imagine a young woman who is extremely devoted to collecting Hello Kitty items and who lives in a rural community in Korea. If she has broadband Internet access, and has no one in her face-to-face community who understands – let alone shares – her passion for Hello Kitty, then she is more likely to seek out and build social bonds with the members of one of the many Hello Kitty online communities. In addition, particular online forms such as social networking sites, virtual worlds, and many gaming sites (such as, say, a poker site that encourages chat while the players play) already have social dimensions 'baked in' to their formats. In that case, the central consumption activity is already social, and the question of actually knowing and having relationships with the members of this online community is almost repetitive.

TYPES OF ONLINE COMMUNITY PARTICIPATION

We need alternatives to the rather essentializing clustering of all members of online communities into a single category of membership or non-membership. Netnographer and consumer researcher Kristine de Valck (2005, p. 133) suggests

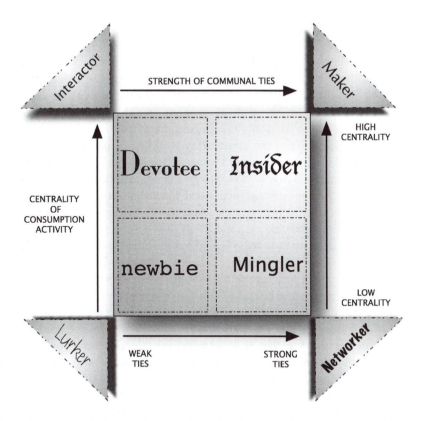

FIGURE 2.2   TYPES OF ONLINE COMMUNITY PARTICIPATION (ADAPTED AND DEVELOPED FROM KOZINETS 1999)

in her detailed study of SmulWeb, a Dutch online community dedicated to food, that there have been many converging typologies of online community members types. This, she argues, is strong evidence that the dichotomizations of online community members as either lurkers or contributors is too simple to be theoretically useful.

In its basic form, the two factors described above – the centrality of the identification and expertise with the core activity of the community, and relations with other online community members – are distinct enough that they can guide our understanding of the four idealized member 'types' shown in Figure 2.2. *Newbies* are the first of the four types. Newbies lack strong social ties to the group, and maintain only a superficial or passing interest in the consumption activity itself and have relatively weak abilities and skills. *Minglers* come next. They are the fraternizers of these communities, socializers who maintain strong personal ties with many members of the community but who are only superficially interested or drawn to the central consumption activity. *Devotees* reverse this emphasis: they have relatively shallow social ties with the members of the community, but maintain a focal interest in and enthusiasm for the consumption activity in the community, as well as refined skill and knowledge sets. Finally, *Insiders* are those who have strong social ties to the online community as well as deep identification with, aptitude in, and understanding of the core consumption activity.

The diagonal dimension indicates various relationships, and proposes four additional 'types' of relationship and interrelationship with a given online community. At the lower left diagonal is the much-recognized category of the *Lurker*, the active observer who learns about a site through initially watching and reading. The lurker has the potential, over time, to become a newbie, a neo or neophyte, a new member who is using the community to learn about the core consumption activity or to reach out and build social relationships. Lurkers feed into the community. We cannot actively observe their participation, but we can learn about them through other means, such as the electronic shadow trails they leave in cyberspace, and the retrospective reflections that people have of their own time as lurkers (see Schlosser 2005).

At the other extreme are those who have developed their social and consumption-focused skills and connections to such a high level that they become central to the community, or even form new communities of their own. This diagonal stretches out from the top-right corner, reaching out from the category of the insider into the category of the *Maker*. Makers are active builders of online communities and their related social spaces, such as the person who has been involved in the online Ferrari culture for so long that they eventually begin their own online forum devoted to a particular model of Ferrari, and excluding other models that are not, in their not-so-humble opinion, 'classic' Ferraris.

The other two diagonals reflect interrelationships with other kinds of communities, both online and off. The top-left diagonal depicts the *interactor* reaching into the community from other communities that are highly engaged with the consumption activity, usually from in-person venues, or those that are primarily in-person with only peripheral use of CMC to keep members connected (such as a football or book club that uses a mailing list to keep members in contact with one another). So, as an example, consider *Star Trek* fans that have local in-person fan clubs connecting to a few *Star Trek*-related online communities by offering consumption activity-related news, how-tos, or information to devotees, or engaging in devotee-like behaviours, in particular online communities.

The final diagonal is at the bottom-right of the diagram. Here, members of other communities, which the model terms *Networkers*, will reach into a particular online community in order to build social ties and interact with the members of that other community. This contact might come from another community that is totally unrelated in terms of content, but which is connected by particular members' weak or strong social ties. Or it could come from a related community that seeks to link up and exchange ideas with, or even steal members from, that community. The point of the networker is to build ties between different online communities.

Generally speaking, a lurker has the potential to progress from newbie status to becoming an insider as she gains social capital with the group and cultural capital with the core consumption activities in which it engages. Another, related, model considers the general trending and movement through these relational modes. Participation can move from a factual and informational type of exchange to one

INTENSITY OF COMMUNAL RELATIONSHIPS

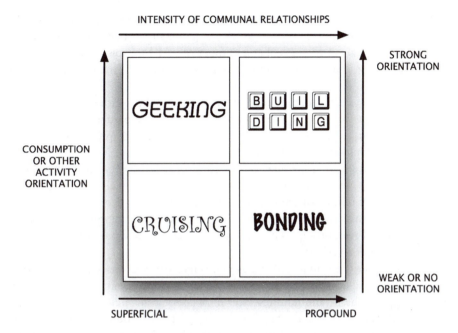

FIGURE 2.3   TYPES OF ONLINE COMMUNITY INTERACTION

that effortlessly mixes factual information and social, or relational, information (see Kozinets 1999).

TYPES OF ONLINE COMMUNITY

These types of membership and participation might also help us to understand some of the different forms of online communities, as represented in Figure 2.3. As we have already noted, the nature of relationships in online communities can vary from intensely personal and deeply meaningful to those that are quite superficial, short-lasting, and relatively insignificant. They can also vary from those that are oriented strictly around a particular activity, such as wood-carving or discussing America's Next Top Model, to those in which a unifying activity or interest is irrelevant. Online gatherings that are known for their weaker social relationships and the low centrality of any particular kind of consumption activity might be known as *Cruising communities*. Particular virtual worlds, chat-rooms, and certain gamespaces would fit well into this cruising classification. They would satisfy the 'relational' and 'recreational' needs that draw people to online communities (Kozinets 1999).

Online locations that are known to have and create very strong social ties between members, resulting in deep and long-lasting relationships, but whose members are not particularly focused on a shared or unifying consumption behaviour, might be termed *Bonding communities*. Social networking sites, many virtual worlds and particular places in virtual worlds, as well as a number of social forums would fit into this category. Bonding online communities would primarily fulfil their members' relational needs.

A third type of online community would be the online gatherings where the sharing of information, news, stories, and techniques about a particular activity is the community's raison d'être – again, it could be consumption or production, or even 'prosumption' (Tapscott and Williams 2007). With all due respect – and I do mean this sincerely, since I am a member of this club – I call these *Geeking communities*. Many newsgroups, website forums, social content sites and services, and blogs would be Geeking communities, offering their member and readers deeply detailed information about a particular set of activities, but not deeply engaging most of them in meaningful social relationships. The modes of interaction on these communities are predominantly informational.

Finally, we have the online gatherings that offer both a strong sense of community as well as detailed information and intelligence about a central, unifying interest and activity. These communities I term *Building communities*. Although blogs, wikis, Social networking sites (SNS) interest groups, and other forms of online gatherings could certainly be Building communities, I have seen more of these online communities grow from website forums, devoted websites, and virtual worlds. A good example of a Building community would be the Niketalk forum devoted to in-depth discussions, evaluations, and even design of sports shoes and basketball sneakers (see Füller et al. 2007). Another is the open source software community, in all of its various manifestations, such as slashdot (Hemetsberger and Reinhardt 2006). The mode of interaction in these types of communities is informational as well as relational. These categories mingle and for many participants become recreational and even, for some, transformational. Transformation is most often actively pursued by insiders, whose social and active skills empower their online experience. However, these transformational activities, which can include resistance and activism, will also be followed by devotees whose interests and skills inspire them to take leadership positions in seeking to enact positive change.

DEVELOPING STUDIES OF ONLINE CULTURE AND COMMUNITIES

As more researchers conduct creative ethnographies on the online communities that continue to burgeon, mutate, and spread, we learn just how much online communities are changing society. Ethnographies of online communities and cultures are informing us about how these online formations affect notions of self, how they express the postmodern condition, and how they simultaneously liberate and constrain. They reveal the enormous diversity of online groups, from skinheads to economically privileged new mothers, from youth subcultures to the elderly. They reveal how our human relationships, our work relationships and our structures of power are changing. They reveal tensions between commercial orientations and power structures online and the communal forms that they promote. They tell us about the promotion of cultural transformation, and the creation of change agents.

Many of these ethnographic investigations, particularly the earliest ones, have been undertaken by scholars working from within the discipline of cultural studies. It is somewhat surprising that more anthropologists have not conducted online ethnographies. In one anthropological investigation, Lysloff (2003) is cautiously optimistic about the online community's expressionistic impacts on human culture. She relates cyberculture to the postmodern notion of the fragmented, multiple self as well as to a Situationist sense of voice:

> When we go online, the computer extends our identity into a virtual world of disembodied presence, and at the same time, it also incites us to take on other identities. We lurk in, or engage with, on-line lists and usenet groups that enable different versions of ourselves to emerge dialogically. The computer, in this way, allows for a new kind of performativity, an actualization of multiple and perhaps idealized selves through text and image. (2003, p. 255)

Demonstrating the ability of online ethnographies to reveal cultural nuance, Campbell (2006) studies skinhead culture online, arguing that skinhead identity as expressed online is remarkably heterogeneous. He further elaborates that there is a surprisingly complex and dynamic relationship between skinhead culture online and notions of race and racism. Studies such as this one underscore the utility – perhaps even necessity – of studies of online gatherings to help reveal additional nuances to our understanding of existing cultures and communities, and to demonstrate how these communities are inflecting, hybridizing, and transformed by the unique abilities conferred by Internet connectivity.

In their study of an edgy, post-punk, quasi-neoconservative 'straightedge' online community, Williams and Copes (2005, p. 86) also suggest that there are links between 'the postmodern condition', the 'fragmentation of identity', 'the weakening of commitment to anything but oneself', and the 'liminal quality' of the Internet communal experience. They see online communities functioning 'as a communication interlock' between the mass media and face-to-face subcultural interaction, facilitating 'subcultural diffusion via nomadic Internet users who share subcultural values and feel a part of a virtual community but who do not feel the need to self-identify as subcultural members' (Williams and Copes 2005, p. 86).

Online communities are widespread phenomena, and their norms and rituals are shaped by the practices of cyberculture and those of the general cultural groups using them. Studying the role of the Internet in the lives of a group of technologically proficient, socially advantaged, white, heterosexual, new mothers, Madge and O'Connor (2006), sought to explore in what sense online communities might fulfil their vaunted potential for empowerment and feminist activism. They asserted that online community contact definitely provided a sense of social support and alternative sources of information that increased the women's sense of being empowered in the crucial transition to motherhood. However, they also suggest that traditional stereotypes of mothering and gender roles persist in online communities devoted to it. They describe a paradox in which the Internet is both liberating and constraining in the lives of those partaking in this particular community of practice. Demonstrating that the use and importance of online communities are not limited to the young or middle-aged, Kanayama (2003) asserts that elderly Japanese people beneficially partake in online community interactions with one another in a variety of ways and use diverse linguistic formats such as emoticons and haiku.

In her study of relationships and friendships online, Carter (2005) advances the argument that some people are investing as much time and effort in online relationships as they are in their other relationships. Her study, focused on an online ethnographic site called Cybercity, provides evidence that 'many of the friendships formed in Cybercity are routinely being moved offline', and, as a result of this, 'individuals are extending their webs of personal relationships to include cyberspace. In this respect cyberspace is no longer distinct and separate from the real world. It is part of everyday life, as these relationships are becoming embedded in everyday life' (2005, p. 164). However, the nature of relationships and friendships may be changing because of the different forms and freedoms available to us through computer-mediated communications. Because of online communities and ICT, social relationships, she concludes, are currently in a state of transformation.

A similar conclusion could be reached from Whitty's (2003) study of 'cyber-flirting'. However, Whitty also explores the widely reputed aspect of disembodiment online. She suggests that, rather than there being an absence of the body in online community interactions, the body is reconstructed or re-embodied online in different ways. She also recounts the interesting combination of realistic and fantastic elements that allow for rich and playful online communication to arise.

Online communities even appear to be changing the nature of work and work relationships. Gossett and Kilker (2006) undertook a study of counter institutional websites, in the context of a close examination of RadioShackSucks.com. They assert that these sites enable and empower individuals to publicly and anonymously voice their work-based frustrations. They do this in an anonymous and supportive environment that offers them a reduced fear of retribution or termination from their jobs. There are a number of important theoretical and practical implications to the fact that participants can use these sites to engage in voice and resistance efforts outside of the formal boundaries of various types of organizations such as human resource departments or labour unions. 'It is clear', they state, 'that the Internet is increasingly becoming a place for workers to come together, share information, and engage in collective action outside the boundaries of the organization' (Gossett and Kilker 2006, p. 83).

Another important theme is that of the interrelationship between commercial and marketing institutions and the communities that they foster, maintain, and propose to serve through ICT. Kozinets (2001) identified several core tensions between the stigmatized *Star Trek* and media fan communities, their utopian and inclusive ideologies, and the large corporate enterprises that gathered them together for commercial purposes in venues both physical and online. Kozinets and Sherry (2005) also studied these tensions between communities and the commercial organizations of wider society in the setting of the Burning Man festival and its all-year-round online community.

A precautionary note is sounded by Campbell (2005) in his examination of lesbian, gay, bisexual and transsexual (LGBT) online communities. He depicts gay Internet portals openly courting the gay community online with promises of inclusion and an authentic communal experience. However, they also simultaneously reposition gays and lesbians in a commercial panopticon that places them under corporate surveillance. He wonders if 'all commercial portals purporting to serve politically marginalized groups beg the question of whether there can be a harmonious balance between the interests of community and the drives of commerce' (2005, p. 678; see also Campbell 2004; Campbell and Carlson 2002).

Germane to this discussion of commercial empowerment are emerging research streams suggesting that increasing ICT and online community participation around the world is removing power 'from nations and their regulatory agencies in terms of surveillance, monitoring, and administrative and cultural management policies' (Olaniran 2008, p. 52). It is also the case that online community participation seems to weaken the influence of existing local cultures and their embedded practices. Online community members' easy access and exposure to the different values of diverse national and regional cultures can have dramatic impacts on how individuals view their own local lifeways. Along these lines, Robert McDougal (1999) suggests, in a study of the introduction of e-mail among the Mohawk tribe, that members of this group considered that the technology altered what they held to be important ways of relating to the world and even to their own traditional way of life.

A salient point is raised by Olaniran (2008). He notes that:

> a factor mediating interaction experiences in e-tribes is the fact that members are set apart from the general population of the country of origin. This factor creates, or at a minimum establishes, the need to conform and adopt group norms in e-tribes. The communication implication is that members must develop a new set of norms that is unique to their particular group. (Olaniran 2008, pp. 44–5)

As the new sites and forms of community become institutionalized – a process whose alacrity cannot help but impress anyone watching YouTube or Facebook's meteoric rise – local communities may find their own norms and standards taking a backseat to those of these new institutions. The longer-term implications of this delocalizing trend for local communities and traditional ways of life are far from clear.

Finally, online communities change the way that people seek to change their world. An early study concludes that environmental organizations became more politically active because of the Internet and online communities (Zelwietro 1998), and suggests that online communities have a transformational effect on their participants, allowing them to organize more effectively and to focus on the specific tasks needed for longer-term realization of their objectives. Bolanle Olaniran (2004, p. 161) asserts that online community participants can and will serve as social agents for cultural transformation in their other various cultures and communities. He suggests that, in online communities, 'group interests [can] inspire devotees to demand and seek positive change inside and outside the group' (2008, p. 47).

SUMMARY

Interdisciplinary research demonstrates how authentic, beneficial, and diverse communal qualities transfer to the online environment. Ethnographic investigations teach us about the varieties of strategies and practices used to create a communal sense and also teach us about the varieties and substance of online community participation, members, participation styles, and forms. Recent developments in ethnographic online research reveal how much online communities are changing notions of the self, systems of social support, personal and work relationships, institutional power, and social activism. The following chapter overviews and compares various research methods used to understand the social world of online communities and cultures. This will help you evaluate these approaches before we proceed to the chapters that introduce, explain, and demonstrate the netnographic approach.

KEY READINGS

Baym, Nancy K. (1999) *Tune In, Log On: Soaps, Fandom, and Online Community*. Thousand Oaks, CA: Sage.

Kozinets, Robert V. (1999) 'E-Tribalized Marketing? The Strategic Implications of Virtual Communities of Consumption', *European Management Journal*, 17(3): 252–64.

Markham, Annette N. (1998) *Life Online: Researching Real Experience in Virtual Space*. Walnut Creek, CA: Altamira.

McKenna, Katelyn and Gwendolyn Seidman (2005) 'You, Me, and We: Interpersonal Processes in Electronic Groups,' in Yair Amichai-Hamburger (ed.), *The Social Net: Human Behavior in Cyberspace*. Oxford: Oxford University Press.

Walther, Joseph B. (1992) 'Interpersonal Effects in Mediated Interaction: A Relational Perspective', *Communication Research*, 19: 52–90.

3
RESEARCHING ONLINE:
Methods

ABSTRACT

This chapter provides a general review of some of the methods used to examine different aspects of online communities and cultures: surveys, interviews, journals, focus groups, structural network analysis, and ethnography. The focus and research domain of each method is compared. Question-centered guidelines help the researcher integrate these approaches with one another and with netnography.

Key Words: ethnographies of online communities and cultures, ethnography, Internet research, online focus groups, online interviews, online journals, online research methods, online surveys, structural network analysis

CONSIDERING THE CHOICE OF METHOD

One of the fundamental choices that any researcher can face concerns what method to use. In contemporary academia, researchers can become wedded to particular techniques when they decide to enter particular scholarly fields, work with particular dissertation chairs or supervisors, or publish in particular journals. This is unfortunate. However, the depth of knowledge and skill required for many of these highly specialized fields necessitates that students and professionals focus their knowledge and attention.

One of the first major choices faced by the researcher is whether to use a quantitative approach, a qualitative approach, or an approach that uses mixed methods. Creswell (2009) complicates the neat division between qualitative and quantitative research. Consider that the conversational data flowing through the Internet are composed of various numerical bits riding wires between various distant servers, and that coding the nouns and verbs in this data relatively easily transfers qualitative words back into their machine-readable form, a form that is easily quantified and analysed as quantitative data. Creswell (2009, p. 4) offers that the key difference between these approaches is that qualitative research is useful for exploring and understanding meanings, whereas quantitative research is used for testing theories by examining the relationships between measurable variables. However, Sudweeks and Simoff (1999, p. 32) question 'this neat qualitative and quantitative dichotomy', arguing that 'each methodology has its own set of costs and benefits, particularly when applied to Internet research, and that it is possible to tease out and match the strengths of each with particular variables of interest'. It is this matching process between approaches and questions that should interest netnographic researchers, and with which this chapter will mainly concern itself.

The guiding advice here is that your research method should be directly related to provide data and analysis capable of answering the research question that you want to investigate. The method you choose to do your research should depend upon the nature and scope of your question. In a new or constantly changing field such as Internet studies, qualitative techniques can help to draw (or re-draw) the map of a new or rapidly-changing terrain. These techniques can also help to tell other researchers who will come later what are the most interesting constructs and relationships. As thinking becomes more developed about some of these topics, quantitative and more confirmatory analyses are generally employed to refine knowledge of the way that small sets of constructs interrelate with one another. Yet, at any point in this process, qualitative research can 'stir things up' by questioning definitions, re-operationalizing constructs, or by introducing new and overlooked constructs and relationships.

My general advice to scholars is to read in an area of scholarship that interests you, and become familiar with the constructs and theories in use. Simultaneously, stay attuned to a particular real-world phenomenon as much as you can. Ask yourself: which theories or constructs fit or do not fit into this actual social world that I see and experience? From there, you will have some direction about the kinds of research questions that interest you. The explanations that follow, along with other methodological texts, will help you to discern the appropriate type of data that you need. Collecting and analysing those data, and then turning them into an answer to your research question, will require that you adopt a rigorous, legitimate research methodology.

Many methods are complementary with netnography. Netnography, like its older sibling, ethnography, is promiscuous. It attaches itself to and incorporates a vast variety of different research techniques and approaches. Thus, comparison and contrast are not necessarily a sign of competition. Despite what anyone might tell you, one research method cannot be inherently superior to another research method. It can only be better at studying a particular phenomenon or at answering particular types of research questions.

BOX 3.1   WHAT SHOULD DETERMINE THE ONLINE RESEARCH METHOD THAT YOU USE?

- Methods should always be driven by research focus and research questions.
- Match the type of data you need to the type of question you are trying to answer.
- Use the methodological approach best fitted to the level of analysis, constructs, and type of data.

SURVEYS

Surveys can be used to inform a range of important questions about online communities and cultures. Surveys have been useful for providing an initial overview of the area of online communities, from which we have been able to discern large-scale patterns. Once researchers have determined adequate categorizations and classifications, surveys can assist in understanding how popular and even how valid these categorizations might be. Similarly, surveys can tell us much about people's activities in online communities, and also about the way that their online community and online culture activities influence other aspects of their daily lives. Surveys can also be used after online interviews in order to confirm or verify particular kinds of local understanding.

How many people read blogs? How many use online communities to learn about a hobby? How often do people check with their online communities? All of these questions require survey research.

The application of surveys using web-pages or other online formats is called the online survey method. Online survey methods have grown rapidly in the last decade (Andrews et al. 2003; Lazar and Preece 1999). From practically a standing start, online surveys have become the major method for investigating a wide variety of social questions. Online surveys are an excellent way to gain a particular kind of understanding about online communities and culture. There are two kinds of online surveys salient to this discussion. The first are surveys that deal with online community topics, and reveal to us aspects of online community and culture. The second are surveys that deal with other topics not directly related to online communities or cultures, but which study topics using or among members of an online community.

Let us talk about the latter, more general, type of online survey first. Whereas the traditional mail or telephone survey excluded a lot of potential researchers from large-scale data collection (Couper 2000), online surveys are far more accessible and easy-to-use. For example, the online service SurveyMonkey.com is simple to set up and use and includes a ready group of participants. The service is also currently free to use for students or others doing small-scale samples. It has been very popular with students in my courses. Other popular online surveys systems and companies include Surveywiz, SurveyPro, SurveySaid, Zoomerang, and WebSurveyor, and there are many others.

Online survey research can be quite inexpensive when compared with mail surveys (Weible and Wallace 1998). Research by Watt (1999) even demonstrates that the cost per respondent can decrease dramatically as the online sample size increases, something that does not happen with any other form of survey. In terms of accuracy, research thus far indicates that the results of online surveys seem not to differ significantly from the results of postal surveys, but offer strong advantages in distribution and turnaround time (Andrews et al. 2003; Yun and Trumbo 2000).

Online surveys are unique. They have distinct characteristics – such as their technological features, the particular demographic characteristics of the groups they survey on the Internet, and the particular patterns of respondent responses. These unique characteristics alter the way that survey designers must write their questions, when the surveys can be used, how to involve traditional non-responders or Internet 'lurkers', and how to analyse the survey results accordingly (Andrews et al. 2003; Sohn 2001).

The Pew Internet Reports (2001) are valuable sets of data that help us to understand the rapidly changing world of online activity. They are the results of survey research. Many researchers interested in the overall complexion of the Internet and its online cultures and communities employ these data. They use them in order to understand the frequency, popularity, and changes in the activities of people as they interact and communicate online, use blogs, and utilize social technology tools. These survey-based studies also illuminate interesting patterns of usage by different demographic groups, such as men and women, different ethnic groups and races, and different ages and generational cohorts. Similarly, repeat surveys of online panels such as The Digital Futures Project (2008) are useful as tracking studies enabling us to discern changing general patterns in online community usage. Forrester Research also use survey information to form its 'Social Technographics Profile'. This profile helps us understand the 'people-to-people activities' transpiring in the multitude of available online communities (Li and Bernoff 2008, p. 41). For example, they find that the largest group of people involved with online communities are 'Spectators', who lurk, read, and use online community postings. The Spectator category encompasses 48 per cent of online adult Americans, two-thirds of Japanese online adults and those in large Chinese cities, and 37 per cent of online adult Europeans (Li and Bernoff 2008, p. 45). They also find that there are a considerable number of 'Creators' who publish a blog or an article online at least once a month, edit their own web-page, or upload videos, podcasts, or audio files to sites like YouTube. According to Forrester Research, 18 per cent of the adult online population in the United States, 10 per cent of European adults online, and an amazing 38 per cent of South Koreans online are Creators, the backbones of many online communities (Li and Bernoff 2008, pp. 41–42). These survey-derived global statistics reinforce the widespread nature of online community participation.

Surveys about the world of online culture and communities provide answers to questions about adoption, usage patterns, usage preferences, and demographics. In order to get a 'big picture' view of the phenomenon, to compare a community behaviour to that of other communities, to talk about demographic constituencies, to provide numerical estimates of population or influence or provide other comparative information, a netnographer may need to incorporate survey-related data and analysis. Online surveys are therefore good for research on online cultures and communities in which you want to:

- draw conclusions about online community usage that are representative of a particular population
- draw conclusions about changing patterns in online community usage
- understand expressed attitudes about online community
- gain a sense of the correlations between various factors, such as demographics, attitudes, and online community usage
- gain retrospective accounts regarding what online community members recall about their actions
- gain a sense of people's attitudes and opinions about online communities
- learn about people's self-reported representations of what they do, or intend to do, in regards to their online community and cultural activity.

Online and other surveys can help answer research questions about online cultures and communities such as:

- How many people around the world participate in online communities?
- Do men participate in online communities more than women?
- What are the most popular online community activities?
- How many people in Finland log on to a virtual world daily?
- How much time do teenagers spend using e-mail versus social networking sites?
- How many people plan to meet someone they met through an online community in the next year?

Surveys are not particularly appropriate for research that must:

- explore a new online culture or community topic about which little previously was known
- explore an online community or culture whose characteristics you do not understand, and in which you do not know the relevant questions to ask
- understand what people actually did or said in the past
- gain unvarnished disclosures (for example ComScore (2001) reports that online survey respondents consistently and drastically over-estimate how much they purchase online)
- precisely specify relationships or community structure
- gain a deep understanding of another person's point of view
- learn the unique way that language and practices are used to manifest culture
- exhibit a complex, nuanced understanding of a phenomenon, culture, or community.

INTERVIEWS AND JOURNAL METHODS

At its most basic, an interview is a conversation, a set of questions and answers between two people who agree that one will assume the role of the questioner, and the other the role of the answerer. The only difference between an online interview and a face-to-face interview is that the online interview occurs through the mediation of some technological apparatus. That, however, is a big difference.

In the physical world, the topic of interviewing is so intertwined with the conduct of ethnography that the two are virtually inseparable. So it is with netnography and online interviewing. The online interview has become a staple of online ethnographic research, present as part of the method from the very beginnings of work in this field (e.g., Baym 1995, 1999; Correll 1995; Kozinets 1997b, 1998; Markham 1998). In this chapter, I will overview the conduct of online depth interviews. Although, as we will see in the next few chapters, it is possible to conduct a purely observational netnography, the recommended participant-observational stance very often dictates an interview component (online or off). Bruckman (2006, p. 87) opines that 'online interviews are of limited value' and asserts that face-to-face or phone interviews offer far greater insight. Although I agree that synchronous, text-based, chat interviews tend to offer a very thin and often rather rushed and superficial interaction, I believe that other online means such as e-mail, and of course online audio and audio visual connections, are extremely valuable (see Kivits 2005). Chapter 6, which examines netnographic data collection methods, will feature a detailed discussion and set of guidelines to help plan and conduct interviews.

Online interviews have traditionally been hindered by the lack of individual identifiers and body language. Who, exactly, am I speaking to? Barring some way to contextualize the social and cultural data beyond the self-evident fact of the online encounter, the data can be difficult to interpret. This interpretive challenge can mean that the data's utility for understanding other social and cultural contexts is in question. In Chapters 6 and 7, we will discuss these issues and provide some strategies for dealing with them.

Conducting an interview through your computer means that your communications are going to be shaped by the medium you use. Studies seeking to understand the subjective impact of Internet connectivity can also collect documents from research participants. These documents often take the form of diaries or journals in which participants record day-to-day or even hour-by-hour events, reflections, or impressions of experiences. For example, Andrusyszyn and Davie (1997) describe the interactive journal-writing study they undertook online. The online format of journal writing or diary keeping has several inherent advantages. Participants can be reminded or prompted automatically for their entries. Entries can be automatically saved. As well, participants can enter their journals in a form that is easier to read than handwriting, and in computer-readable text form. Many of the advantages of online interviewing can also pertain to the data arising from online diaries or journals.

Depending on your research focus, you may or may not need the sort of detailed, open-ended, descriptive, reflexive personal understanding that can be gained from journals or depth interviews. As with in-person ethnography, a simple in situ conversation, or a quick exchange of information, might suffice to inform your research question. As with research in general, the recommended type of interview is going to be determined by the type of data that are required. For the type of nuanced cultural understandings of online social groups that are usually sought in a netnography, depth interviewing is usually the method of choice. Most online ethnographers in cultural studies, anthropology, and sociology have employed depth interview techniques.

Depth interviews allow netnographic researchers to broaden their understanding of what they observe online. For example, in a depth interview, one can try to understand the social situation of the culture member – their age, gender, nationality, ethnic orientation, sexual orientation, and so on – and how it influences their online community participation, and is also influenced by it. Depth interviews also allow netnographers to question the relationship between online community activities and other social activities in the community member's life. In this way, a fuller portrait of the role of online community membership in the person's entire life – online and away from the computer – can be drawn.

Online depth interviews are appropriate for research on online cultures and communities in which you must:

- bring in a detailed subjective understanding of the lived experience of online community participants (what is called a 'phenomenological' understanding)
- deepen the understanding of the relationship between a person's own unique socio-cultural situation and their online culture or community activities or behaviours
- gain a detailed, grounded, subjective sense of an online community member's perspective and sense of meaning
- hear people's recollections and interpretations of events.

Online interviews can help answer research questions about online cultures and communities such as:

- How do people relate to and apply the information they learn from online communities in their daily lives?
- What are the most common metaphors that people in Norway use to understand online culture?
- How do family members experience their loved ones' behaviour in online communities?
- How do people use their online connections to moderate their emotional states throughout the day?
- How are narratives about online relationships related to important health care topics in people's lives?
- What impact do the stories that people hear in online communities have on the way that they connect with their spouse?

Interviews are not necessarily useful when you want to:

- draw conclusions that are representative of a particular population
- draw conclusions that are generalizable to other populations
- understand what actually happened in particular places
- understand the causal relations between events
- quantify relationships.

FOCUS GROUPS

When an interview is conducted in a group format, it is often called a focus group. Focus groups are a popular form of qualitative research used to gather opinions and perspectives rapidly as an input for industrial or governmental decision-making. The dynamic group interactions of a focus group create challenges for moderators as well as interesting research findings, and can also create heightened, artificial attention for a particular research topic.

Online focus group interviews have become popular in the last five years. The reason can be discerned in Mann and Stewart's (2000, p. 125) capsule summary of the method: 'the online focus group is an efficient and highly-cost-effective mechanism for gathering detailed data, in large quantities'. The online medium also offers the focus group moderator new flexibility. The online focus group session can be staggered in time, mixed culturally, dispersed geographically, or organized using any combination of these factors. Members of the focus group might see each other, or not. The group could be moderated in order to prevent one or two people from dominating the session (as often happens in the face-to-face settings), or not. In an early exposition, Gaiser (1977) considered some of the opportunities for methodological innovation with online focus groups. Software is now readily available for online focus group interviews. The focus group conducted through teleconferencing software has been heralded as one of the major trends in focus group development (Greenbaum 1998) and the procedures for conducting them have been honed by a number of commercial marketing research companies.

A majority of research studies using focus group techniques have used asynchronous methods, such as bulletin boards, rather than synchronous (real-time) methods (Fox et al. 2007). It may be at this point that these methods begin to shade subtly one into the other. An asynchronous posting of a set of questions to a group is also a common technique in netnography. In addition it could be quite similar to a series of personal depth interviews conducted in sequential or even parallel fashion. The ability to conduct question-and-answer sessions in asynchronous fashion with the group is, in fact, one of the hallmarks of many forms of online community.

Krueger (1994) suggests several interesting focus group archetypes such as 'the Expert, the Dominant Talker, the Shy Participant, and the Rambler'. Contrasting their work online with Krueger's (1994) face-to-face focus group guidelines, Hughes and Lang (2004) offer a range of useful methodological guidelines for online focus groups, and note that textual communications tend to form into particular patterns, such as monologuing, dittoing, one-liners, writing essays and challenging. These patterns are quite familiar, and converge with the descriptions of newsgroups and forums by others (see, e.g., Baym 1999, Cherny 1999, Jenkins 1995, Kozinets 1997a).

Other important conclusions about synchronous focus group interviews are that: (1) chat-room fatigue tends to set in after about one hour; (2) the online forum is more appropriate for online rather than physical topics, for example, to gain responses to a new website, rather than to a new mobile phone; (3) it may be harder to enforce full participation online than in person; (4) online groups cannot be as large as a face-to-face group, because even five people can be difficult to manage;

and (5) the method requires technologically literate and keyboard-skilled participants who may not always be available or appropriate (Hughes and Lang 2004; Mann and Stewart 2000).

Unlike online depth interviews, which would be commonly used, there would likely be fewer occasions when online focus group interviews would fit into a netnographic approach. Netnography tends to be more concerned with the naturally occurring interactions of online groups rather than those of artificial groups that are assembled by researchers for the purpose of some particular investigation. However, online focus groups do have their roles. As mentioned above, online focus groups can present corporate or public managers with a way to cost-effectively gain a timely understanding of a particular topic using an established budget. This understanding would be based upon significant quantities of qualitative data gathered from a focus group comprised of specific, often identifiable, recruited individuals.

In a netnography, focus groups of existing community participants might be valuable for two main reasons. First, online community and culture members can be group interviewed – just as individuals can be interviewed singly. They can be used to learn about the norms, conventions, histories, and roles of online community members as they interact online. This data collection can happen quickly, and the data can often be provided in significant detail. Secondly, they can be interviewed to understand how online and offline activities are related. Questions to the focus group can extend and broaden our understanding of the interrelation of the online community with people's other social groups and activities, and the impact of other social groups and activities on what we observe in the online community and culture. Because they are managed and 'moderated', the group processes of meaning negotiation cannot replace observational data, but they can certainly be a useful adjunct.

SOCIAL NETWORK ANALYSIS

An Overview

Social network analysis is an analytical method that focuses on the structures and patterns of relationships between and among social actors in a network (Berkowitz 1982; Wellman 1988). In social network analysis there are two main units of analysis: 'nodes' (social actors) and 'ties' (the relations between them). A network is composed of a set of actors connected by a set of relational ties. The actors, or 'nodes', can be persons, teams, organizations, ideas, messages, or other concepts. The term 'tie' or 'relation' can be used interchangeably to describe the link between actors. Examples of ties would include sharing information, an economic transaction, transfer of resources, shared associations or affiliations, sexual relations, physical connections, sharing ideas or values, and so on (Wasserman and Faust 1994). A group of people who are connected by particular social relationships, such as family kinship, friendship, working together, a shared hobby or common interest, or exchanging any sort of information, can be considered to be a social network.

Social network analysis has its foundations in sociology, sociometrics and graph theory, and in the structural-functionalist line of 'Manchester anthropologists, who built on both of these strands to investigate the structure of 'community' relations in tribal and village societies' (Scott 1991, p. 7). Social network analysis thus deals in relational data and, although it is possible to quantify and statistically analyse these relations, network analysis also 'consists of a body of qualitative measures of network structure' (Scott 1991, p. 3). There is, thus, a very natural relationship between a structural approach to ethnography, or netnography, and the approach of social network analysis.

Over the last 30 years, the social network analysis approach to research has grown rapidly in sociology and communication studies, and has spread to a range of other fields.

> Social networking analysts seek to describe networks of relations as fully as possible, tease out the prominent patterns in such networks, trace the flow of information (and other resources) through them, and discover what effects these relations and networks have on people and organizations. (Garton et al. 1999, p. 75)

University of Toronto sociologist Barry Wellman (2001a, p. 2031) convincingly argued that 'computer networks are inherently social networks' and that, as computer networks proliferated, we were finding ourselves in a network society that was 'loosely bounded and sparsely knit'. Wellman has been one of the key figures, but certainly not the only one, pioneering the application of social network analysis approaches to the online communities and cultures that populate the Internet (see, e.g., Wellman et al. 1996). Examining a computer network that connects people together as a social network, social networking approaches are widely applied to help understand the interaction between computer networks, computer-mediated communications, and social networks.

Social network analysis is structural. Its unit of analysis is the relationship, and what it finds interesting in relationships are their patterns. There is, therefore, considerable overlap with certain kinds of netnography, which can be focused upon culture and its patterns of meanings and relationships.[4] Social network analysts consider the various resources that are communicated between people in online communities and cultures – these can be textual, graphical, animated, audio, photographic, or audio-visual, and can include sharing information, discussing work-related rumours, sharing advice, giving emotional support, or providing companionship (Haythornthwaite et al. 1995). Netnographers also consider those resources, viewing them as sources of meaning and bearers of culture.

Netnographers need not adopt social network analysis techniques in their studies. However, netnographers would be wise to familiarize themselves, at least on a basic level, with social network analysis techniques, procedures, and general research findings. There are many opportunities for synergies between the structural analysis of social networks and the more meaning-centered analysis of netnography. The following offers a necessarily brief overview to the adaptation and integration of social networking techniques into netnography. The interested researcher should, of course, consult source texts and perhaps other researchers familiar with these approaches before proceeding further.

Netnographers should first realize that the relationships and ties studied by social network analysis result, in general, in different descriptive approaches. The first looks at these relationships from the 'personal' or 'ego-centered' perspective of people who are the centre of their network. 'In an ego-centered network study, a set of people (selected on the basis of some sampling criteria) are asked questions to generate a list of people (alters) who are the members of their personal social network' (Garton et al. 1999, p. 88). For example, in a questionnaire or an interview, people may be queried about who they would ask a personal question, and who they might ask a leisure or hobby related question. These questions can be limited to certain groups, or be unrestricted. Unrestricted studies can reveal the different communities and cultural groups from which particular people draw particular cultural and informational resources.

It is certainly possible for software to collect the data about everyone that a person contacts online, however there are 'coding and privacy invasion questions' about doing so (Garton et al. 1999, p. 89). Although incomplete, some of these data are publicly available online. Public profiles of individuals – or their pseudonyms, or their service provider data – and their postings on groups such as Google groups can be qualitatively and quantitatively analysed to show the different types of social groups that people relate to online, the interrelationship of their postings, and the overall nature of the personal or ego-centric network that collects around everyone who participates in online culture.

The second descriptive approach, often called the whole network approach, considers an entire social network based on some particular research definition of the boundaries of that network. In a netnography, the boundary of a social network might be the online site where the cultural activity was found, or where the community defined itself, such as the alt.coffee or rec.arts.startrek.current newsgroups. Alternatively, the boundaries of the social network might be focused around a particular activity, interest, or goal. So, for example, the coffee connoisseur community could be studied across many venues including web-pages, newsgroups, mailing lists, coffee shops and stores, coffee tasting groups, magazine subscription lists and call-in cable television show viewers. We could also conceivably study the online coffee connoisseur community as one whole network, and the community as it exists in physical locations as another whole network. Because the consideration of group boundaries is so critical, netnographic analysis can be extremely useful for comprehending the nature of the various communities and cultures under investigation prior to measuring the social network.

In studies of whole networks, we are interested in the identification of the different connections between the members of particular groups. One approach is to survey either an entire group, or a sample of people in a group, about their connections to specific other people in a given group. These questions can also be automated, through an online survey administered to community members, or through various coding or web-crawling techniques that capture 'who-to-whom on-line contact data within a group' (Garton et al. 1999, p. 89). This provides a representation of the overall structure of relations, which reveals social connections as well as disconnections. The whole network approach also helps researchers to identify the relative positions that members occupy within a network as well as suggesting the very important partitioning of subgroups or 'cliques' within the group.

Each tie belongs, at its most basic level, to the 'dyad' formed between two actors. Relations refer to the resources that are exchanged, and these relations can be characterized by their content, their direction, and their strength. Online community members' ties can include sharing a picture, sharing a blog link, exchanging stories, linking up as friends on a social networking site, telling one another about an interesting show or news story, offering criticism, and so on. Strong ties appear to include 'combinations of intimacy, self-disclosure, provision of reciprocal services, frequent contact, and kinship, as between close friends or colleagues' (Garton et al. 1999, p. 79). Often, ties will be referred to as either weak or strong. In general, because definitions of weak or strong will vary by context, a weak tie is one that is sporadic or irregular, and has little emotional connection. An example might be people who are regular visitors to the same blog, but who have never communicated or commented on each other's comments. The strength of ties can be operationalized depending on the type of community. Peers may communicate more or less frequently; they may exchange large or small amounts of information or goods; the information that they share might be important or trivial. It is worth noting that these judgements tend to depend upon the cultural situation of social actors – whether information is important or trivial is a cultural determination of value.

There is a range of interesting units of analysis used in social network analysis. To understand the relationships created by these ties, social network analysis focuses on the properties of the relationship. Two actors could have a tie based on a single relationship – such as belonging to the same *American Idol*-discussing mailing list. This pair could also have a multiplex relationship based within a number of different relationships, such as working for the same company, living in the same part of New Delhi, belonging to the same Hindu temple, and being a member of the same karaoke-devoted MySpace group. Multiplex ties are more supportive, long-lasting, voluntary, and intimate and are also maintained through more different forums or media. Multiplexity is one of the properties of social ties, as are directionality, reciprocity and symmetry, strength, and homophily.

The 'dyadic' level is only one possible level of analysis. Analysing 'triads' and even larger networks, such as those that comprise online communities, involves consideration of the structural properties of those networks as well as the structural properties of individuals within those networks. One important measure to netnography is centrality, a measure that reveals the actors that may be the most important, prominent, or influential ones in a network. There are several different kinds of centrality. Degree centrality looks at the most popular active actors in a network. It focuses on measuring how many other actors a particular actor is in direct contact with. Eigenvector centrality measures how much a node is connected to other nodes that are also tightly connected to one another. Eigenvector centrality is more concerned with power and influence than popularity. Betweenness centrality measures an actor's sphere of influence. A central actor in this context is truly in the middle of things. The more influence an actor has over the flow of information, the more power and control that actor can potentially wield (Wasserman and Faust 1994). Finally, closeness centrality looks at 'reach and reachability' instead of power or popularity (Van den Bulte and Wuyts 2007).

Social network analysis helps us learn about how social networks manifest through computer network connectivity. Haythornthwaite (2005, p. 140) notes how technological change is merging with what she calls 'social mechanisms'. Online communities appear to be able to help tip latent ties into weak ones. Online communities and community networks can also help weak ties grow into strong ties, as people in these peer-to-peer networks add new types of connections, such as meeting face-to-face, meeting synchronously online, and adding private e-mail to their public discussions (Haythornthwaite 2005, p. 141). A practical use is to 'build strong enough ties between strangers so that they will engage in online commerce' (Haythornthwaite 2005, p. 140). Developing trust through reputation systems such as the one that eBay uses to provide members with feedback on successful transactions is one example. Trusting relationships, linked to strong ties, are also relevant to understanding and planning the online provision of many types of public information. Other uses include managing social activism and grassroots campaigns, such as the political campaign for Howard Dean and the even more successful one for President Barack Obama.

Collecting Data for Social Network Analysis

Information about social networks has traditionally been 'gathered by questionnaires, interviews, diaries [and] observations' (Garton et al. 1999, p. 90). Increasingly, it has also been gathered by computer monitoring and various methods – such as 'data mining' for capturing publicly accessible computer network data. Most network researchers seem to agree that the best approaches use a combination of data collection methods. The automated capture of data can raise concerns about data management, about their interpretation, as well as concerns regarding privacy. Although it is a relatively simple matter to routinely collect information on whole networks or subsamples of networks, these concerns arise in social network analysis, just as they do in netnography. Many of the suggestions in this book about matters such as data collection and analysis and Internet research ethics therefore apply equally to netnography as well as to social network analysis of this kind.

Netnography can inform and interrelate with social network analysis in several important ways. With its expansive, situated, rich descriptions, netnography can help to position a network study within the boundaries of its analysis. Netnography can identify appropriate nodes – whether they are individuals, activities, messages, groups, or some other social 'actor'. Netnography can be used to identify appropriate relationship types to examine further. Netnography can also help to inform whether egocentric or whole network analyses are appropriate. Netnography can investigate the meanings behind relationships and ties. It can also help to provide 'why' explanations for a range of structural characteristics such as power and influence relationships, various types of social ties, and the clusterings of subgroups and cliques. Similarly, social network analysis and its rich visualization techniques can illuminate, broaden, and provide additional ideas and evidence to help reveal the properties and relationships that constitute the complex world of online communities and cultures.

There is a vast amount of social network analysis software currently available to assist the social network analyst. Some programs that are commonly used for academic research purposes would include UCINet, KrackPlot, Pajek, ORA, and GUESS. There are many other software programs for business and marketing purposes. These software packages can be used to mine relational data from the Internet, to extract these from databases of various formats, or to generate these from surveys and questionnaires. They are also very useful in analysing relational data and providing visualizations of different arrangements of social networks. Welser et al. (2007), for example, used analysis and visualization techniques to distinguish 'answer people' – who predominantly answer others' posted questions – from 'discussion people' in online communities, and to clearly represent the way that their behaviours were enacted in social networks. Fournier and Lee (2009) use social network type diagrams to suggest that there are different, yet complementary, structures to interest- or consumption-based 'brand communities'. Visualization techniques have even been used to study extremely large and diffuse communities, networks, or conversations – even the Internet itself (see Sack 2002). In netnographies, this software can be employed to map out the relationships between individuals, topics, message threads, constructs or ideas, values, groups, or communities. It can be used to provide additional information, and visual representations, of the social structures operating in online communities and cultures.

In summary, social network analysis is often a useful complement to netnography and can even be blended into a netnographic study. Social network analysis is suitable for research on online cultures and communities in which you want to:

- learn about the structure of a community's communications
- discuss patterns of social relations or 'ties'
- describe different types of social relations and exchanges between members of an online community
- study actual patterns and actual content of online community communications
- study flows of communication and connection between different online communities
- study flows of communication and connection between different forms of online community
- compare community structures and communication flows between online and face-to-face communities.

Social network analysis will allow you to answer research questions such as:

- What is the structure of the communications in this online community? Who is communicating with whom? Who communicates the most?
- Who are the most influential communicators in this online community network?
- Is there a core group and a peripheral group in this particular community?
- What are the various subgroups in this community or culture?
- How does information flow through this particular online community?
- How does communication in a virtual world differ from face-to-face communications in terms of who uses it, and what is communicated?
- What are the overall patterns in information spread between these particular two online communities?

Social network analysis, by itself, is not particularly appropriate for research that seeks to:

- gain a detailed, nuanced understanding of the lived experience of online community or culture members
- understand the social practices and related systems of meaning of online communities or cultures
- convey and compare the unique ways that language is used to manifest culture through online social formations.

ETHNOGRAPHY AND NETNOGRAPHY

As we will detail in the next chapter, netnography complements and extends these other research approaches. In this short section, we will briefly overview and contrast ethnography with netnography. As it was in the previous sections, this contrast is rather artificial because many netnographies will be conducted as part of a research project that combines several techniques. This chapter has been about highlighting the contrasts between these different methods. But the student and researcher should be aware that what is far more important is that other techniques and approaches complement and extend netnography. This is particularly true of in-person, or face-to-face, ethnography.

In-person ethnographies are extremely valuable in industrial and in academic research, finding wide application across virtually every literature and domain of knowledge application, from medicine and nursing to economics, from architecture to computer science and design, organizational behaviour and accounting, and of course in cultural studies, sociology, and anthropology. Ethnographic research enables the researcher to gain a detailed and nuanced understanding of a social phenomenon, and then to capture and convey its cultural qualities. It provides a sense of the lived experience of culture members, as well as a grounded analysis of the structure of their group, how it functions, and how it compares to other groups. Social practices are carefully attended to and systems of meaning delicately unpacked. In 'interpretive ethnography', a single phrase or event can be analysed in minute detail, events can be captured through a cinematic 'voyeur's gaze', placed into a poem, or woven into a rich tapestry of related pictures, graphic images, and texts (Denzin 1997). Contemporary ethnography offers many rich opportunities not only to 'write culture' as Clifford and Marcus (1986) would have it, but also to represent it.

Full-length, 'classic', immersive, in-person ethnographies are certainly not easy to conduct. They are time and resource intensive. Because they involve in-person participant-observation on the part of the researcher, they are unavoidably intrusive. When we compare in-person ethnography with face-to-face focus groups and personal interviews, there is no doubt that focus groups and interviews are less time-consuming, as well as simpler and easier to conduct. In industrial settings, focus groups are considerably less expensive than professionally undertaken ethnographies. This is very likely why they are the more popular techniques. However, focus groups and interviews – as well as surveys – are obtrusive. The questions that they ask are preconceived and the situations in which they put participants are artefacts of the researcher's design. The data they produce, then, must be seen as somewhat artificial and decontextualized when compared with ethnographic data. The rich insight they provide may be why professional ethnography is increasingly valued in the world of marketing management, new product innovation, and design (Sunderland and Denny 2007).

One of the major advantages of netnography is the fact that, like the ethnography it is so closely related to, it is a naturalistic technique. In many cases, netnography uses the information publicly available in online forums. However, there are differences that can lead to some useful efficiencies. In terms of expending time making choices about fieldsites, arranging personal introductions, travelling to and from sites, transcribing interview and handwritten fieldnote data, and so on, netnography is far less time consuming and resource intensive. Netnography also has the potential to be conducted in a manner that is entirely unobtrusive, although, as we will discuss in the next chapter, this is an option that raises some distinct limitations on engagement. Nevertheless, when employed in a rigorous fashion, netnography can provide the researcher with a window into naturally occurring behaviours, such as communal discussions, and then enhance that understanding with more intrusive options such as communal participation and member interviews. In-person ethnographers do not have the option of invisible lurking, or the ability to flawlessly track communal conversations back in time.

The analysis of existing online community conversations and other Internet discourse combines options that are both naturalistic and unobtrusive – a powerful combination that sets netnography apart from focus groups, depth interviews, surveys, experiments and in-person ethnographies. Social network analysis also has this important benefit. Its techniques are not able to provide a richly textured, cultural understanding, however, but offer instead a structural one.

It is apparent that many of these techniques can easily work in concert with one another. Results from one type of study can simply and usefully inform the research questions of any other type of study. For example, a netnographic charting of the contours and classifications of new online cultures and communities will inform the survey work done to confirm and to quantify these classifications of different types. Similarly, netnographically-derived assertions about the relationship between different types of online community participation and different attitudes or demographics can be studied with further survey work. Causal, individual-level reasons drawn from the rich history and constructs of social psychology can be marshalled to explain some of the observed elements of online community relationships. These hypotheses can be analysed in online experiments. And the social structures underlying these divergent networks can also be analysed using social network analysis. In conjunction with one another, a fuller portrait can be painted of the mulitifaceted nature of online phenomena.

SUMMARY

The previous chapter reviewed many interesting new theories about online cultures and communities. This chapter outlined and overviewed several of the methods used to produce those theories: surveys, interviews, journals, focus groups, structural network analysis, and ethnography. There are opportunities to integrate one or more methods into studies that examine multiple facets of online community phenomena. The general methodological guidelines and comparisons found in this chapter set the stage for the detailed introduction of netnography in the next chapter.

KEY READINGS

Garton, Laura, Caroline Haythornthwaite and Barry Wellman (1997) 'Studying On-Line Social Networks', *Journal of Computer-Mediated Communications*, 3 (June), available online at: http://jcmc.indiana.edu/vol3/issue1/garton.html/

Mann, Chris and Fiona Stewart (2000) *Internet Communication and Qualitative Research: A Handbook for Researching Online*. London: Sage Publications.

Welser, Howard T., Eric Gleave, Danyel Fisher and Marc Smith (2007) 'Visualizing the Signatures of Social Roles in Online Discussion Groups', *Journal of Social Structure*, 8, available online at: http://www.cmu.edu/joss/content/articles/volume8/Welser/

4
THE METHOD OF NETNOGRAPHY

ABSTRACT

Netnography adapts common participant-observation ethnographic procedures to the unique contingencies of computer-mediated social interaction: alteration, accessibility, anonymity, and archiving. The procedures include planning, entrée, gathering data, interpretation, and adhering to ethical standards. This chapter explains the nature and role of netnography, comparing it with related online and offline techniques and explaining when and how ethnographic and netnographic approaches should be combined.

Key Words: anonymity, bricolage, computer-mediated communications, ethnography, Internet research methods, netnography, online community research

THE PROCESS OF ETHNOGRAPHY AND NETNOGRAPHY

Ethnography and netnography should work in concert to illuminate new issues in the social sciences. However, the manner in which this coordination should take place has, thus far, been unclear and confusing. This chapter seeks to delve into the relation between ethnography and netnography, and then to provide a simple, yet flexible, guide to the coordination of ethnography and netnography.

What is ethnography, exactly? Ethnography is an anthropological approach that has gained popularity in sociology, cultural studies, marketing and consumer research, and many other fields in the social sciences. The term refers both to the act of doing ethnographic fieldwork and to the representations based on such a study. Dick Hobbs provides a cogent definition of ethnography, defining it as:

> a cocktail of methodologies that share the assumption that personal engagement with the subject is the key to understanding a particular culture or social setting. Participant observation is the most common component of this cocktail, but interviews, conversational and discourse analysis, documentary analysis, film and photography all have their place in the ethnographer's repertoire. Description resides at the core of ethnography, and however this description is constructed it is the intense meaning of social life from the everyday perspective of group members that is sought. (2006, p. 101)

Ethnography's popularity probably flows from its open-ended quality as well as the rich content of its findings. Ethnography's flexibility has allowed it to be used for over a century to represent and understand the behaviours of people belonging to almost every race, nationality, religion, culture and age group. Wonderful ethnographies have even been conducted of the local ways of life of non-human 'tribes' of gorillas, chimpanzee, dolphins, and wolves. Ethnographers in the last two decades have also become increasingly concerned with the acknowledgment and inflection of their own reflexivity as researchers. This is because ethnography relies very heavily on what consumer anthropologist John Sherry (1991, p. 572) calls 'the acuity of the researcher-as-instrument'. Good ethnographies are the creations of good ethnographers. The nature of the ethnographic enterprise, its techniques and approaches as well as its requirement for subtle, metaphorical, and hermeneutic interpretation, rapidly renders transparent the rhetorical skill level of the researcher. Although ethnography is closely related to the case study and, like case studies, ethnographies build into a body of knowledge that is comprehensive and comparable, individual ethnographies tend not to be used to offer universal generalizations. Ethnography is grounded in context; it is infused with, and imbues, local knowledges of the particular and specific.

Ethnography is thus an inherently assimilative practice. It is interlinked with multiple other methods. We give these other methods that it is linked to other names: interviews, discourse analysis, literary analysis, semiotics, videography. They have other names because they are sufficiently different from the overall practice of ethnography that they require unique new designations. They require special, new training. Although they relate to participation in, and observation of, communities and cultures, they do so in particular ways, capturing data in specific ways, dictated by specific, agreed-upon standards.

Any given ethnography, therefore, already combines multiple methods – many of them named separately, such as creative interviewing, discourse analysis, visual analysis, and observations – under one term. Sirsi et al. (1996) followed their ethnography of a natural food market with a series of social psychological experiments, which they fed into a causal equation model. Howard (2002) offered a 'network ethnography' that pragmatically combined social network analysis with ethnography. Because it is attuned to the subtleties of context, no two ethnographies employ exactly the same approach. Ethnography is based on adaptation or *bricolage*; its approach is continually being refashioned to suit particular fields of scholarship, research questions, research sites, times, researcher preferences, skill sets, methodological innovations, and cultural groups.

Netnography is participant-observational research based in online fieldwork. It uses computer-mediated communications as a source of data to arrive at the ethnographic understanding and representation of a cultural or communal phenomenon. Therefore, just as practically every ethnography will extend almost naturally and organically from a basis in participant-observation to include other elements such as interviews, descriptive statistics, archival data collection, extended historical case analysis, videography, projective techniques such as collages, semiotic analysis, and a range of other techniques, so too will it now extend to include netnography.

It would be right, then, to see in a method section of an ethnography a line stating that the method included participant-observation as well as interviews, videography, and netnography. The use of the term netnography in that case would represent the researcher's attempt to acknowledge the importance of computer-mediated communications in the lives of culture members, to include in their data collection strategies the triangulation between various online and offline sources of cultural understanding, and to acknowledge that, like interviews or semiotics, netnography has its own uniquely adapted set of practices and procedures that set it apart from the conduct of face-to-face ethnography. As we will detail later in this chapter, research need not be conducted exclusively either as an ethnography or netnography. The use of the term and approach of netnography in the overall project would signal not only the presence but the gravity of the online component. It would mean that significant time was spent interacting within and becoming a part of an online community or culture.

Referring to netnography as a particular practice beyond ethnography is significant. What it signals to various constituents of the research – those who approve its ethics, those who sponsor and finance it, those who consent to it, those who participate in it, those who audience it, those who review it, and those who read it – is that this particular research follows in a specified, distinct, common set of methodological procedures and protocols that have been agreed upon by a community of scholars. Like ethnography itself, it has inherent and necessary flexibility. Also like ethnography, however, it aims at legitimacy and seeks the trust of its constituents by a careful attention to shared, detailed, rigorous research practices.

Given all of this differentiation, variety, and *bricolage*, one might be led to ask what ethnographies have in common with one another? The combination of participative and observational approaches lies at the centre of the ethnographic initiative. To do an ethnography means to undertake an immersive, prolonged engagement with the members of a culture or community, followed by an attempt to understand and convey their reality through 'thick', detailed, nuanced, historically-curious and culturally-grounded interpretation and deep description of a social world that is familiar to its participants but strange to outsiders.

In order to engage in this undertaking, ethnographers have developed a set of general protocols and procedures to help regulate, but never completely determine, their approach. Ethnographers entering and working in a cultural or communal

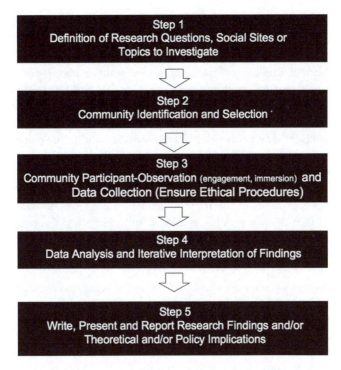

FIGURE 4.1   SIMPLIFIED FLOW OF A NETNOGRAPHIC RESEARCH PROJECT

field confront similar issues.[5] First, they must plan the research and plan for the fieldwork. They must reach out, find, and enter the field of a culture or community – the part of the ethnography called entrée. While situated in the field, they must gather data about the culture and community. These data require consistent analysis and interpretation. Throughout the approach and the fieldwork, the ethnographer will need to adhere to strict ethical research standards and procedures. Finally, the ethnographer will need to present the end-product of finished research to the scientific (or other) community, and in so doing represent the research work as well as the community or culture itself.

Netnography therefore follows in these six steps of ethnography: research planning, entrée, data collection, interpretation, ensuring ethical standards, and research representation. Figure 4.1 offers a diagrammatic flowchart. The figure obviously offers a much neater-and-cleaner representation of the netnographic research process than ever actually occurs in reality. Before we can proceed to describe these procedures, however, we need to cover two important areas. First, we need to understand when and how to combine ethnography – which uses data gathered through in-person or face-to-face cultural interactions – with netnography – which uses data gathered through online interactions. Second, we need to understand the differences of the online social environment, in order to appropriately and consistently guide the adaptation of ethnographic techniques. These matters are the topic of the following two sections.

VIEWS OF NETNOGRAPHY AS AN INCOMPLETE ETHNOGRAPHY

There have been a number of excellent books written about the ethnographic approach, guiding researchers through its complex and fluid procedures (see, e.g., Atkinson et al. 2001; Denzin and Lincoln 2005; Fetterman 1998). For quite some time, however, there were no guidelines at all for the conduct of online fieldwork. As works regarding online fieldwork and representations of online cultures and communities began to reach publication, many of them contained some fundamental confusion about the role and nature of netnography.

Virtual Ethnography by Christine Hine is one of the most extensive single-authored methodological treatments of the topic of online ethnography to date. Comparing the online and face-to-face variants of ethnography, Hine (2000, pp. 63–6) suggests that online ethnography is deficient in some important ways. She offers a somewhat sceptical view of what she calls 'virtual ethnography', stating that:

> virtual ethnography is not only virtual in the sense of being disembodied. Virtuality also carries a connotation of 'not quite', adequate for practical purposes even if not strictly the real thing … Virtual ethnography is adequate for the practical purpose of exploring the relations of mediated interaction, even if not quite the real thing in methodologically purist terms. It is an adaptive ethnography which sets out to suit itself to the conditions in which it finds itself. (Hine 2000, p. 65)

The idea of adaptation of ethnography to new conditions is one of the key elements explaining ethnography's success as a method. But consider Hine's (2000, p. 10) suggestion that an ethnographic narrative is presented as authentic when it contains 'Face-to-face interaction and the rhetoric of having travelled to a remote field site'. Clearly, by definition, an online ethnography cannot have these qualities. The location question is especially vexing because 'the concept of the field site is brought into question. If culture and community are not self-evidently located in place, then neither is ethnography' (Hine 2000, p. 64). As a result, 'virtual ethnography is necessarily partial. A holistic description of any informant, location or culture is impossible to achieve' (Hine 2000, p. 65). Online ethnographies, to Hine are therefore always 'wholeheartedly partial'. They are 'almost but not quite like the real thing' (2000, p. 10).

All constructions of 'reality' and 'authenticity', practicality, and even 'adequacy' and 'holism' are, however, in ethnography and elsewhere, socially constructed, contextually determined, and contingent upon standards that we deem or do not deem to accept. There is no *really real* ethnography, no *de facto* perfect ethnography that would satisfy every methodological purist. Nor does there need to be. There is, in fact, a delectable variety of different types of ethnography, from realist narratives to fantastic travelogue adventures, from reflective auto-ethnographies to polyvocal polylogues, from impressionistic tales to starkly statistical large-scale portraits and even vivid videographies (see, e.g., Van Maanen 1988).

As we understand various new social phenomena, we construct the meanings of methodological terms anew. Anthropology is a very diverse field, with a range of standards, and ethnography has spread far beyond it, changing fields and being changed by them in the process. Under these circumstances, what is 'the real thing', that is, a genuine, authentic, faithful, reliable ethnography, is a piece of ethnographic work that satisfies some particular group or groups' particular standards for what is needed at a particular time. Hine (2000) is absolutely correct that many anthropologists have looked down, from their high cultural capital perch, on ethnographies of online communities and, perhaps, many other types of not-invented-here (low culture?) cultural studies ethnographies. Writing from within the field of anthropology to fellow anthropologists, Lysloff (2003) says as much. But this certainly does not imply that their critiques are true or should be accepted at face value, particularly by those of us using and developing ethnography from outside of the field of anthropology. Or even, certainly, by that unruly and ever-questioning bunch of scholars practising from within it.

Under some conditions, netnographies are necessarily 'partial'. What we need to discern is what those conditions might be. Where is a netnography, based solely upon online data, insufficient? And, conversely, where is it sufficient? Its sufficiency or partiality would depend entirely upon the research focus and questions the ethnographer was attempting to investigate. Is the ethnographer studying some phenomenon directly related to online communities and online culture? Or is the ethnographer interested in studying a general social phenomenon that has some related Internet group aspect? How important, or not, is the physical component that is always attached to human social behaviour?

This leads to an important distinction that helps to guide the coordination of netnography and ethnography. This distinction and its implications help to illuminate the nature of netnography as an approach that is sometimes used as a stand-alone technique and, at other times, used as a part of a larger study that includes in-person interviews, fieldwork, and perhaps other methods. In the next section, we distinguish between research on 'online communities' and research on 'communities online' and then provide guidelines relating to this distinction.

DIFFERENTIATING RESEARCH ON ONLINE COMMUNITIES FROM RESEARCH ON COMMUNITIES ONLINE

Research on 'Online Communities'

To simplify this argument, we will draw a dichotomy. Research on 'online communities' studies some phenomenon directly relating to online communities and online culture itself, a particular manifestation of them, or one of their elements. For example, research that is interested in the social processes that govern the behaviour of newbies entering online hobbie-based communities would, by this definition, be research on 'online communities'. Investigations that consider the different types of roles manifesting among a variety of different online cultures relating to political discussion would be uniquely concerned with a CMC-related phenomenon. Research into the changing language, graphics, and symbol use by online communities would be, again, research on 'online communities'.

Nancy Baym's (1999) ethnographic study of the online soap opera newsgroup rec.arts.tv.soaps was a study of one particular online community, as was Shelley Correll's (1995) study of the Lesbian Café online. In a more general sense, Annette Markham's (1998) study of what it meant to be living in online spaces and interacting in online communities was also clearly a study concerning online communities and cultures. A study of a particular newsgroup, of a particular virtual world, of a type of behaviour in a social networking site, of a linguistic pattern in a microblog, of a particular kind of linking pattern on blogs: these are all examples of research concerned with online communities. These studies are notable because online communities, online identity, online sociolinguistic patterns, cyberculture(s), relationships that emerge through CMC, and various other online human social interactive elements *will be central, core constructs that the research tries to explain.*

Research into 'Communities Online'

On the other hand, we have research into 'communities online'. These studies examine some extant general social phenomena whose social existence extends well beyond the Internet and online interactions, even though those interactions may play an important role with the group's membership. Studies of communities online take a particular social or communal phenomenon as their focal area of interest and then extend this, arguing or assuming that, through the study of the online community, something significant can be learned about the wider focal community or culture, and then generalized to the whole.

In many cases, the researcher is interested in this study of the community online because that group's communications inform and relate to the wider social phenomenon, behaviour, its participants, their values or beliefs. Kozinets (2001) looked at the wider phenomenon of *Star Trek* culture and community, and more generally, how fan cultures and communities created and distributed alternative meanings and social structures relating to commercially produced products. This was a study of a 'community online'. Although Internet-based participants' perspectives were extremely valuable, the online community of *Star Trek* fans and their various cyber-cultural pursuits was not this article's focal area of interest. Similarly, Campbell (2006) studied an online skinhead group in order to understand the meaning that the group associated with the 'white race'. Campbell's results were used to inform our understanding of skinhead cultures' alleged racism in general, not simply as it pertains to the skinhead culture expressed online. Studies of teenagers and the effect of technology on their lives, Indonesian immigrants in China, or the way that *Twilight* fans are affected by the television show might involve these groups' use of the Internet and online communities. But this component is not likely to be of central importance to the study. Regarding research into communities online, the key question to ask is whether the online component is *considerably less important* to the investigation's theoretical orientation than other aspects of the research. Do the online information and access instead sharpen our understanding of some wider, focal construct, theory, or set of concerns?

This dichotomy is a convenience, and overlaps between these categories will of course occur. Like almost all the dichotomies in this book, this one should be read as more like a continuum. Studies can shade over from a general focus on a social topic to a more specific focus on various elements of the online site that informs our understanding of that topic. However, as a general rule, I would like to suggest that *research on online communities should tend to have a primarily netnographic focus. For research on a community online, netnography should play more of a supporting or secondary role.*

BLENDING ETHNOGRAPHY AND NETNOGRAPHY

The following characteristics can further help to clarify the relative use of netnography in a project and also the blending of a netnography. Let us think of a 'pure' netnography as one that is conducted purely using data generated from online or other CMC or ICT-related interactions – be they online interview, online participation, or online observation and download. A 'pure' ethnography would be conducted using data generated via face-to-face interactions and their transcription in field-notes, with no data from online interactions. A 'blended' ethnography/netnography would be a combination of approaches, including data gathered in face-to-face as well as online interaction. Blended ethnographies/netnographies could take many forms, using many particular methods and favouring different ratios of online to face-to-face interaction, data, and analysis.

We must ask ourselves, first, whether we are studying an online community, or conducting other research focusing on online cultural or communal phenomena, or their elements. If we are, then we can usefully employ netnography as a stand-alone method. We can justifiably conduct a 'pure' netnography. A netnography in this case is entirely appropriate, exhaustive, and complete within itself.

Alternatively, where the focal construct extends beyond the online community context into the larger social world, it would be wrong to assume that we could gain a complete picture through a pure netnography. If we were studying the experiences of Turkish migrant workers in Denmark, and we found a small bulletin board dedicated to this topic, our netnography of this bulletin board should not be cast as a general understanding of the experiences of Scandinavian Turkish migrant workers. In order to make the more general claims suitable to such an ethnography, we would need to supplement the netnographic work with various other kinds of investigation such as in-person participant-observation and face-to-face interviews. Depending on the kind of access that is provided and the insights and disclosure of its participants, the netnography of the bulletin board might be a very helpful component of a broader investigation that blended netnography with ethnography. But alone, the pure netnography would be partial and incomplete.

The researcher will want to carefully consider the following aspects of the research question and its focal concerns before deciding whether to conduct a pure netnography, pure ethnography, or blended ethnography/netnography.

- *Integration vs. Separation of Social Worlds.* How closely related are the behaviours online and in face-to-face social situations? Is there a direct relation, or are they different, separate behaviours? For example, if we are studying teenagers' use of social networking sites, do we need to watch them typing at their keyboards to know that they are performing this task? The social worlds of usage are interlinked at the level of online/off-line. On the other hand, if we are theorizing about how teenagers playing linked computer games in the same room interact with one another, it is probably insufficient to study only what is transmitted and manifested on the computer screen. These social worlds will be different.
- *Observation vs. Verbalization of Relevant Data.* How important is the repeated observation of physically manifest rather than verbally articulated behaviours? Is it likely that there is useful new information that will or will not be communicated online? Are there rich online representations of the behaviour, perhaps including photographs or audiovisual recordings? For example, although people may talk about the way they interact with their dogs, actual observation may reveal interesting tacit elements of the behaviour that they cannot, do not, or are unwilling to communicate.
- *Identification vs. Performance of Members.* How important is the further identification of the individual culture member, i.e., their linkage to demographic characteristics such as age, race, gender, and so on? Or are the performances of the actions captured and recorded in the online community or culture entirely sufficient for the generation of theory? For example, if the researcher is studying a particular group of people, say, young unwed fathers, then confirmation and verification of the identities of message posters may be warranted and useful. If anonymity does not affect findings, as would be the case if one were studying the persuasive strategies of for-profit bloggers spreading word-of-mouth messages on their blogs, then identification may not be necessary.

Figure 4.2 provides a visual representation of the weighting of online and off-line fieldwork leading to blended or pure netnographies and ethnographies. In practice, these judgements are delicate. Nonetheless, research that is more like a study of an online community would have a much more prominent and central netnographic component, whereas netnography would play more of a supporting role in studies focusing on communities online.

How prevalent are these distinctions? Or, to put it another way, are the days of the pure ethnography limited?

They may be. Garcia et al. (2009) begin their appraisal of ethnographic approaches to the Internet by stating that the distinction between online and off-line worlds is becoming increasingly useless. The reason? These categories have become hopelessly intermeshed in our contemporary society. They note that 'most ethnographers still conduct studies firmly situated in the "offline" social world' (Garcia et al. 2009, p. 53). However, we are quickly reaching the point, if we are not already there, at which we

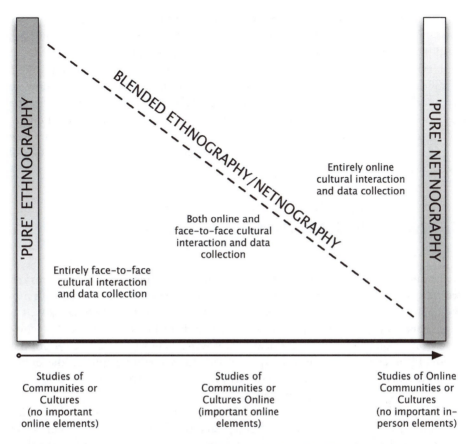

FIGURE 4.2   COORDINATING ONLINE AND FACE-TO-FACE INTERACTION AND DATA COLLECTION

need to reference, study, and understand the data in online communities and cultures in order to effectively and meaningfully study some of the 'main and enduring concerns of ethnographic research' in anthropology, sociology, and cultural studies (Garcia et al. 2009, p. 53). These would include topics such as: the nature, configuration, and hybridization of subcultures and microcultures; the processes and elements of identity construction; the values and worldviews prompting contemporary human action and social life; the influence of technologies and media; and the roots and transformations of social movements and social activism. The authors go so far as to advise that practically all ethnographies of contemporary society 'should include technologically mediated communication, behaviour, or artifacts (e.g., Web-sites) in the definition of the field or setting for the research' (Garcia et al. 2009, p. 57).

If we believe this argument then the value of 'blended' netnographic accounts is only going to magnify in the future, as online communities and cultures increasingly permeate global society. What the argument suggests is that online community and technological mediation is no longer a new form of communication and community, but has passed – or very shortly will pass – into the realm of the status quo, the way that our society simply is. If this is true, then researchers who ignore this reality will find their work increasingly passed by, rendered and judged irrelevant.

Having made these important differentiations, and carefully considered these justifications, we can now move into a more specific discussion about how to approach this netnographic work. The next and final task of this chapter is to develop a framework about how the computer-mediated environment faced by ethnographers is different from the face-to-face environment faced by ethnographers. Once this understanding is in place, we will have a guiding structure for the adaptation of these techniques.

THE CONTEXT OF COMPUTER-MEDIATED FIELDWORK

Rice and Rogers (1984, p. 82) stated that the new online environment provides contexts that 'may limit how a faithfully traditional research design and methods may be applied ... the nature of the media themselves may create limitations, as well as new opportunities'. The adaptation of ethnographic techniques to the online environment is not, therefore, straightforward. If it were, there would be no need for this book. In order to adapt the techniques of face-to-face ethnography to the online context, a necessary initial step is to specify the differences between face-to-face and computer-mediated social interactions.

Fortunately, we have over a decade of ethnographic and related social scientific literature about computer-mediated communications and online communities to guide our adaptation. A close reading of this literature reveals that we can meaningfully parse out four critical differences. First, and perhaps most obvious, is *alteration*. Alteration simply means that the nature of the interaction is altered – both constrained and liberated – by the specific nature and rules of the technological medium in which it is carried. Next is *anonymity*, that widely-analysed difference, particularly relevant in the early years of online interaction, but still meaningful today. The wide *accessibility* of many online forums to participation by anyone is the third crucial difference that our revised techniques must accommodate. Finally, there is the automatic *archiving* of conversations and data facilitated by the online medium. We will repeatedly return to these differences in order to develop and justify our differentiated netnographic approach. Thus, our understanding will benefit from a discussion of these four differences.

Alteration

Much has been made of the so-called 'technological mediation' of online interaction. There is, of course, nothing inherently 'unnatural' about technologically-mediated social interaction. Historians, archaeologists, and other artefactual cultural analysts have had to deal with the fact that much of their data come in the form of 'mediated' communications: letters, public documents, epithets on gravestones, hieroglyphs on papyrus scrolls, scratches on clay tablets, and so on. The radical textualization of Internet communications is, in this light, not such a new thing. Consider also that telephone interviews are technologically mediated communications and television shows are a form of ICT. Some letters and telephone calls suffer from the same dubious anonymity and lack of embodiment as textual communications and interactions online.

History teaches us that the new ages heralded by the introduction of new technologies are not always as revolutionary as they at first may seem. As Schivelbusch (1986, p. 36) noted, after the introduction of the railway it was widely believed that 'the railroad annihilated space and time … [however] what was experienced being annihilated was the traditional space–time continuum which characterized the old transport technology'. But just as the railways altered peoples' subjective perception of what was possible in terms of covering a certain distance in a certain amount of time, so too did networked computing radically transform people's ideas about who they could communicate with, when, how, how often, and even why. It is this subjective understanding that is in many ways so significant to a cultural understanding of the Internet, because with it comes reflexivity, awareness, perceptions of constraint, and discourses of emancipation.

Because they seem at first and upon introduction so unnatural, communications online open up multiple possibilities. They also deprive. Bandwidth and technological limitations can create the characteristic of time lag, evident in synchronous communication media such as chat windows, especially when there are several people chatting together. Time lag can also be evident in virtual worlds or games, which can require sets of keystrokes in order to subtly convey body language through an avatar. Interactions through these media tend not only to be more elongated than face-to-face communications, but more fragmented. Messages suffer interruptions, false starts, lapses and sporadic frequency (Baym 1995; Cherny 1999).

In asynchronous ('time delayed') CMC media such as bulletin boards, newsgroups, forums, and blogs, the textualizing and lengthening of communications are pronounced. The result is an altered symbolic and temporal topography to the social interaction – presenting its participants with a more artificial form of communication, more opportunities to engage in strategic control over information and self-presentation than face-to-face exchanges, and requiring investments of time in order to gain the information and comfort level necessary for culture sharing and communal intimacy.

It seems relatively clear that once a person is online, particularly during their early online experiences, technical aspects of the communicative medium create a distinctly new and, at first, obtrusive cultural experience – this awkward and inadequate feeling, mixed with a sense of possibility and wonder, is often their introduction to cyberculture (see, e.g., Cherny 1999; Holeton 1998; Jones 1995; Markham 1998). Online interaction forces the learning of additional codes and norms, abbreviations, emoticons, sets of keystrokes and other technical skills in order to transfer the emotional information vital to social relations.

After some time, however, the linguistic and technical conventions start to become second nature, as acculturated languages tend to do. The elements of this second nature are often highly informative to the netnographer. The technological alteration of online participation is a key reason that face-to-face ethnographic procedures must be altered for the cultural worlds of online interaction.

Anonymity

Without resorting to the simplistic causality of technological determinism, computer-mediated interactions can be considered to provide distinct new opportunities for liberating behaviours not as easily afforded by face-to-face interactions. One of the key factors precipitating this sense of liberation is the anonymity often optionally afforded by the online medium. This anonymity confers online actors a new sense of identity flexibility. In the world of text and controlled images, self-presentation has much wider degrees of freedom, and online social life provides many more opportunities for identity experimentation. Or as Peter Steiner put it in a much-quoted cartoon published in the *New Yorker* in 1993 (July 5) – and I paraphrase here – 'On the Net, no one is cognizant of the fact that you are actually a small canine creature using a computer and keyboard, pretending to be a human being'.

Sherry Turkle (1995, p. 190) describes a young male who simultaneously opened several windows on his computer, acting as a 'flowery and romantic' male in one online forum, a 'quiet' and 'self-confident' male in another, and a 'flirtatious' and sexually open female in another. Jones (1995) suggests that role- and game-play online provides multiple opportunities for a type of 'ungendered' being, and the inhabiting of 'imaginative nonhuman bodies'. Anonymity combines with imagination in ways that allow the exhibition of characteristics and desires that might be difficult, socially unacceptable, or illegal to express under other contexts, as the massive success of cybersex chat-rooms, online pornography, erotic web-cams, subversive diatribes, and ultra-violent games demonstrate. Online expressions of identity can thus in some ways be more revelatory of consumers' 'true', or hidden, selves and intentions than a prosaic observation of everyday life and consumption might divulge (Jones 1995; Turkle 1995).

Nonetheless, this anonymity can also confound and trouble researchers seeking to fix a particular demographic onto textual and other productions posted online. Who *is* one communicating with in an online cultural interaction or through an online interview? The medium makes it difficult to see the messenger. Anonymity and its close cousin, pseudonymity (the use of pseudonyms instead of names), make the netnographic approach necessarily different from the approach of face-to-face ethnography.

Accessibility

Once someone clears the financial and technical hurdles required for aptitude at computer-mediated searching and communication, an extremely wide array of social interactions is made accessible to them. The participatory, egalitarian ethic of the Internet apparently originated from its contact with academic and hacker communities whose ethos was 'information should be free'. Online social interactions manifest this ethos through the general democracy and inclusiveness of many, if not most, online social groups. Many newsgroups, forums and boards offer open membership, and also provide informational FAQs ('frequently asked questions') to introduce neophytes to the cultural vagaries of the group and guide them rapidly to the status of participating members. Blogs are generally inclusive, and virtual worlds, gaming clans, and social networks have their own sets of rules governing membership, often based on the expansion of networks and the enrichment of existing communities by the frequent addition of 'new blood'.

Although gaining acceptance and status in online communities is still knowledge- and norm-dependent, and certainly not independent of one's social standing and cultural capital in other social worlds, a participative and democratic ethos is widespread. Moreover, the online world offers a heretofore unheard of global accessibility. Social gathering of geographically-dispersed participants have almost instantaneous access to one another. Global accessibility leads to the potential for mass membership, but other factors lead to fragmentation. Foremost among these must be linguistic differences. Mandarin speakers tend to remain with Mandarin speakers, and only very rarely partake in conversations with Hungarian and Portuguese speakers, however global the group or its topic might be.

Prior studies suggest that large online groups are less communal, social, and friendly than small groups (e.g., Baym 1995, Clerc 1996). The smallest of groupings is the most intimate, as with the chat-room pick-up line, '[Do you want to go] 1 on 1?' Smaller online communities and the sub-groups within them provide a more communal feel, hybridizing and transcending the traditional boundary markers of 'community' – geography, politics, gender, genealogy, ethnicity, occupation, religion. Whether we are talking about a blog's audience, a social network, or a computer constructed 'race' in a virtual world, the participants in these groups often self-segment by arranging themselves into online groupings sorted by interests, tastes, or pre-existing commitments.

Online social interaction is a unique public–private hybrid that offers participants the allure of stepping into the global spotlight before an 'audience' from the ostensibly secure confines of their own home. Opportunities abound not only to broadcast one's own private information, but also to publicly partake in the private information of others. This new level of voyeurism and exhibitionism is substantially unlike anything a face-to-face ethnographer would encounter. Accessibility is therefore another key difference to which the netnographic approach must be tuned.

Archiving

There is something else distinctive about online connections and communications. The term persistent world has been coined to refer to the persistence of virtual worlds online, and changes made to them by users, even after a user has exited the site or software program. This persistent quality applies equally well to many aspects of the Internet. Newhagen and Rafaeli (1997, n.p.) note that 'communication on the

Net leaves tracks to an extent unmatched by that in any other context – the content is easily observable, recorded, and copied. Participant demography behaviours of consumption, choice, attention, reaction, learning and so forth, are widely captured and logged'.

Newsgroups, forums, and other bulletin boards, blogs, mailing lists, and most other asynchronous media are automatically archived. The Wayback Machine or Internet Archive captures snapshots of the Internet at certain points in time and saves them for future reference. Efficient search engines make accessible every interaction or every posting on a given topic to a specific newsgroup, or every posting by a given individual to any newsgroup. The physical analogy would be to have access to recordings of every public social contact in a given culture, or every public social contact of a specified individual. Synchronous media may not be automatically archived in a publicly accessible format. However, the recording of synchronous conversations and interactions does not present much of a technical challenge. In either case, having a near complete record of online social interactions is far easier than the surreptitiously recorded fieldnotes and fragmented recollections of the in-person ethnographer.

> Thanks to the hardware and software, we have the artifactual textual traces of inter-action created instantaneously, at the moment of utterance. For scholars with an interest in discourse analysis, literary criticism, rhetorical studies, textual analysis, and the like, the Internet is a research setting par excellence, practically irresistible in its availability. (Jones 1999, p. 13)

It is no wonder, then, that content analytic techniques are enjoying a renaissance in their application to the analysis of online conversations. The instant archiving of social communications present in the Internet sphere makes this a very different context for doing ethnographic research than the context of face-to-face social interaction.

SUMMARY

Netnography is an approach to participant-observational online research that follows a distinct set of procedures and protocols. Netnography is appropriate for the study of both online communities and communities and cultures that manifest important social interactions online. Considerations guiding the use and coordination of netnographic and ethnographic field-work include: the extent of integration of focal online and face-to-face social behaviours, the relative importance of embodied observation rather than verbal or other self-representation, and the necessity of individual identification. This chapter identities four key differences between online and face-to-face social interaction: *adaptation* to various technological media; participation under optional conditions of *anonymity*; vastly enhanced cultural *accessibility*; and automatic *archiving* of exchanges. Ethnography is calibrated to these unique contingencies in the remainder of the book. We begin the first of the following five procedural chapters with a discussion and set of specific guidelines for planning ethnographic fieldwork and making an entrée into the netnographic field.

KEY READINGS

Hine, Christine (2000) *Virtual Ethnography*. London: Sage.

Kozinets, Robert V. (2002a) 'The Field Behind the Screen: Using Netnography for Marketing Research in Online Communities', *Journal of Marketing Research*, 39 (February): 61–72.

Markham, Annette N. and Nancy K. Baym (2008) *Internet Inquiry: Conversations about Method*. Thousand Oaks, CA: Sage.

5
PLANNING AND ENTRÉE

ABSTRACT

This chapter shows you how to plan, focus, and begin your netnographic study. You will learn about the research questions and topics that are appropriate for netnographic study. You will learn about the resources you need, including search engines, to investigate, refine, and begin your research, and also about the many forms of online interaction. Finally, you will learn about proper and improper ways to enter and begin to research an online community as a netnographic researcher.

Key Words: blogs, entrée, fieldwork, Internet forums, Internet research resources, newsgroups, participation, participant-observation, research design, research planning, research questions, search engines, social content, social networking sites, virtual worlds, Web 2.0 research, wikis

A FEW WORDS ABOUT PARTICIPATION

The core of netnography – what differentiates it from a gathering and coding of qualitative online data – is that it is *a participative approach* to the study of online culture and communities. When asked to contribute an entry to the *Sage Dictionary of Social Research Methods*, my definition carefully emphasized that netnography is an adaptation of 'participant-observational ethnographic procedures' (Kozinets 2006b, p. 135).

Some scholars have indirectly disputed the value of researcher participation in netnography (Langer and Beckman 2005), asserting that 'covert studies' of online communities are sometimes desirable. Others have coined a specialized language to refer to their adaptation of netnography, such as specifying that they are performing a purely 'observational' or 'passive' netnography (e.g., Beaven and Laws 2007; Brown et al. 2003; Brownlie and Hewer 2007; Füller et al. 2007; Maulana and Eckhardt 2007). The observational approach might even imply that the interactive, conversational data from online communities should be treated as qualitative data to be 'content analysed.'

There is a spectrum of participation and observation that ethnographers regularly negotiate in their fieldwork. However, removing the participative role of ethnographer from netnography also removes the opportunity to experience embedded cultural understanding. Without this profound knowledge and experience of the cultural context, the interpretation is impaired. The netnographer is forced to engage in guesswork about cultural meanings she does not fully understand. Because the researcher is not a participant in the community, she has no one in that community to turn to in order to validate, dispute, or expand upon her interpretation. Or, even worse, the netnographer might then ignore those meanings and offer up a superficial, purely descriptive analysis that codes and classifies the words and other content she finds online.

When we are seeking the simpatico, tribal-dance-joining, phenomenological, eureka-yielding gestalt for which ethnography is famous, then counting mentions of a particular word, or noting how many times it is modified by terms like 'good' or 'great', will simply not achieve our objective. Without ethnographic insight, netnography becomes primarily a coding exercise. The netnographic report also becomes flat and two-dimensional. It is far easier in many ways to code cultural data than to live, probe, be frustrated and shamed by, and profoundly ruminate over these. But if we want to write netnographies that can stand up to the standards of quality ethnography, filled with deep understanding and thick description, then lurking, downloading data, and analysing while sitting on the sidelines are simply not options.

READY? SET?...

So now you are completely ready to participate in the online world? Great. So just sit down with that nice mug of coffee, point your magic search engine in the right direction, click a couple of times, and start up that free-flowing online conversation about the woes of graduate students and how they relate to global warming. Whoah, hold on there ... maybe you are *not* ready.

Before you take action, enter that online culture, and begin your participation, there are just a few important things you need to get straight. You need to decide exactly what it is that you are going to be studying. How you are going to study it. How you are going to represent yourself. How you are going to handle this project ethically. And just how much of a disruption you are going to create in the communities or cultures you are studying.

We can usefully start this discussion with an illustrative example of a netnographic entrée gone wrong. A brand new – and perhaps overly eager – adjunct professor seeking to do a research project on online boycotts posts a message that says something like this:

Hello Everyone:

I am a professor at [University X] in [location]. A colleague and I have begun to research boycotts from the consumer's point of view. We are very interested in finding out more about individual's [sic] involvement in boycotts and we are currently using the Internet to try to gather some information.

The information we are trying to gather we believe will help everyone who has a stake in helping to understand how boycotts are perceived and understood by the people who are persuaded (or not persuaded) by them. This would include anyone who organizes or supports boycotts, and might contribute to helping make future efforts maximally effective. We would be happy to share our findings with you on an individual basis, if you are interested in becoming involved in this very important research area.

All responses will be totally confidential. If quoted, you will be given a 'pseudonym' so that you always remain anonymous. *If* you have ever been involved in a boycott, we would greatly appreciate it if you would take a few minutes to e-mail me [at eager-adjunct@email.com] with your answers to these THREE, fairly short, sets of questions: [3 questions here].

Thank you very much for your participation in this 'cyber-interview'. Again, please send the answers to [email] (or, if you like, you can post them publicly on this news-group). We will respond to everyone who answers our request for help.

Sincerely,

[eageradjunct, name anonymized]

P.S.: If you have any questions about this research, please feel free to post them on the group or send them to me.

The approach taken here seems, at first sight, reasonable as well as eager. Eager adjunct professor introduces himself, gives his affiliation, accurately conveys the research focus, and offers some questions. He seems polite. He talks about participant anonymity and the use of pseudonyms in the final research report. The researcher even tries to suggest that there will be some benefit to those interested in the topic of boycotts from participation in the research.

So what is the response from this posting? Mixed. And instructive.

The first response, written by 'Josphh' (a pseudonym) is a detailed and useful set of answers to the questions, posted to the entire newsgroup. The next response, from 'Father Wintersod' (another pseudonym), a regular poster on this community bulletin board, is not as positive.

Father Wintersod states that he is completely convinced that research like this is part of an overall system of mind control. He suggests that the research is under the control of the government, large corporations, and other institutions. Research like this helps them to learn how to psychologically manipulate the public. He suggests, in no uncertain terms, that this researcher is looking for useful intelligence to use against good people. This influential respondent then advises the other members of the community to 'boycott this research on boycotts'. He claims that this is important and he says that he is 'deadly serious'. In large capital letters, he writes 'BOY-COTT ALL RESEARCH', then analyses the negative intentions of the original questions and the harmful uses to which they might be put, terms the research a 'cyber-interrogation' rather than a cyber-interview, and finishes with a large, banner-like posting of three lines in capital letters, surrounded by rows of asterisks, urging fellow newsgroup members to 'BOYCOTT THIS RESEARCH'.

I can tell you that this response completely caught that new netnographic researcher off guard. I know, because that eager young adjunct professor – who had just gotten a black eye and bloody nose – was me.

The information intentionally left out of my description was that I was posting to a newsgroup called alt.gathering.rainbow. Alt.gathering.rainbow had shown up among my search engines results as a group with some interesting boycott and consumer activism related posts. In 1997, they were one of several newsgroups that contained messages and conversations discussing boycotts. However, I had not performed a deeper investigation into this online community. Alt.gathering.rainbow is an online community for members of the annual radical underground environmentalist gathering/happening group The Rainbow Family. Because I knew little if anything about the community, my entrée was entirely inappropriate. Knowing the background of this illicit, anti-establishment group would have directed me to other online communities, or else at least suggested that I invest the time to educate myself about their idiosyncratic beliefs and unorthodox values before I attempted to communicate with them.

Scan the Internet and you may find that these sorts of missteps by online researchers are very common. Consider another example recently found posted on a popular shopping newsgroup. A student researcher 'Alexandra34567' (an assigned pseudonym) posted a message that opened with a research question asking newsgroup members about 'the influence of family and peers' on their levels of trust of 'a brand online'. Alexandra34567 explained that she was a student from a certain University involved in research about brand trust online, and that she would be using what she called 'a rather new research method called netnography'.

'Lloyd' replied. He informed Alexandra34567 that 'we have already heard this before'. It turns out that this newsgroup has been receiving postings like this, using the same basic question, for five years. This might not be Alexandra34567's fault; it could be that her instructor has given this assignment to her class every year. She may have suggested that her students proceed directly to this newgroup or its related website. That does not seem to sway Lloyd. He critiques her question, which is the same one he has seen, year after year, posted and reposted to the community (see Bruckman 2006 for invaluable insights about student projects using netnography).

One of Lloyd's major critiques seems to be in Alexandra34567's approach to research. Lloyd calls it 'spamming' newsgroups. What is the implication of this term? I have learned, partly from my education in the alt.gathering.rainbow and other communities, that the members of newsgroups and other online communities generally believe that they have better things to do than to answer some anonymous someone's research question dropped onto their forum. Most of them resent the intrusions and interruptions of online researchers. This resentment obviously grows when the intrusions are repeated or not particularly mindful of the community and its norms.

It is a testament to the good nature of many online community members that many questions such as this one still end up netting great answers. Culture members have even rewritten students' research questions for them and then offered lengthy, detailed answers. Alas, those golden days are ending. Increasingly common encroachments mean that online community members are cautious and often unabashedly negative about being contacted by researchers (see Bruckman 2002 for an example). This is a shame. But it is also the reality that all netnographers are faced with today.

There is much you can learn from these powerful examples. Whether we were aware of it or not, Alexandra34567 and I adopted an approach or entrée strategy that could be labelled 'distant'. I had no knowledge of the values and history of the Rainbow Family group that I was approaching. After I received the digital tarring-and-feathering, I did some investigation, and then offered a careful, rational reply to Father Wintersod's critique of my research and its intentions, telling them a bit about my background and motivations for doing this research. A few members of the news-group posted some supportive comments. 'Reg', invited me to attend a Rainbow Family Gathering. 'Paulie', suggested that I consider how inescapable 'the system' is and how guilefully it is able to use broad-minded people such as him, or me, to achieve its own ends.

In Alexandra34567's case, she uses some advanced vocabulary and offers up her academic credentials. These rhetorical moves could be read as class-laden signals that she is an outsider who knows, and wants to know, little about the community or its interests. They could suggest that she has little interest in the community beyond their use as a 'resource' to help her complete her assignment. His annoyance seems to motivate Lloyd into offering his own corrective translation of several of the terms in the posting that he found particularly objectionable.

One of the specialized academic terms that Alexandra34567 used in her post was, ironically enough, netnography. Lloyd's response to her use of the term is also instructive. As scholars, students, academics, and other researchers, we cannot assume that we know more than the community members we are approaching. In fact, it might be useful to assume the opposite attitude in your own research. Genuinely try to approach community members with humility, knowing that they know much more about their own culture (and very likely many other things) than you do. So when Alexandra34567 mentions that netnography is 'rather new', Lloyd is quick to correct her that it is six years old (actually, the technique celebrated its 12th birthday in 2007), and he attributes the methodology to me. Remember in your own research that anyone with web access can search the term netnography, or any specialized professional or academic term, and discover what it means and who has written about it. Or perhaps Lloyd is a professor, or a marketing researcher. We do not know. And cannot assume.

Consider, for a moment, if Alexandra34567 is actually conducting a netnography in the sense in which it is explained in this book. Would the posting of a single question to a selection of different newsgroups be netnography? Is there participation? What sort of observation is there? Is this an interview?

Lloyd finishes by telling Alexandra34567 that the answer to her question is [AN ALL-CAPS-SHOUTING]: 'NO', which is not really very helpful as an answer. It is helpful, however, to realize that a yes-or-no question is not going to yield very good data about many topics, including this one – brand trust and online recommendations. Indirect observation might reveal some interesting patterns, but probably not in this newsgroup. Lloyd ends his feedback with a statement that she is studying 'the wrong group'. This newsgroup's messages and its FAQ indicate it to be a frugal group devoted to bargain hunting. Although the members of this group probably appreciate a quality brand as much as the next person, Lloyd is almost certainly right that this probably is not the best online community location to be looking for brand appreciation.

How can we use these two rather painful illustrations to consider what you need to think about before you make your initial posting? What will you need to do to prepare for your netnography?

- You need to know your research focus and research question.
- You need to find and read related research studies and if possible connect with other researchers in your topical domain.
- You need to find appropriate online places in which to investigate your question.

  o This means avoiding sites that have been 'tapped out' by other researchers recently, or sites than have been 'turned off' by poor research in the past.
  o This investigation process should already be the topic of your fieldnotes.

- You need to think about whether you are going to use Computer-Assisted Qualitative Data Analysis software programs (abbreviated as CAQDAS; see Chapter 7).

  o The use of CAQDAS is not essential, but it is very helpful in organizing and managing projects with large amounts of data (many netnographies will fit into this category).
  o If you are going to use CAQDAS, you should purchase and begin familiarizing yourself with the software program as early as possible, before you begin collecting data.

- You need to familiarize yourself with several online communities that you are considering studying, their members, their language, interests, and practices.

  o This can also include familiarizing yourself with related communities, particularly if your study is research of a community online (see Chapter 4).
  o This familiarization process also belongs in your fieldnotes.

- You must gain ethical approval for your research project (if this is academic research), and ensure that you are meeting or exceeding all ethical, professional, and legal standards that apply to your research project (for all researchers; see Chapter 8).
- You need to hone and re-hone the way you will approach this community.

- You need to craft, review, and refine the question or questions you will pose to them.
- You should consider using several different strategies for data collection, and plan them carefully.
- You should have a clear, written set of guidelines representing decisions you have made that will structure and supervise your on-going observation and participation in this community or set of communities.
- You need to have already started keeping fieldnotes, and be ready to add to them every time you contact, think about, or do something else related to your online social group.

Then, and only then, *might* you be ready to start your netnographic research.

RESEARCH FOCUS AND RESEARCH QUESTION

In this section, we will learn how to construct and focus research questions appropriate for netnography. In his volume on the principles of research design, John Creswell (2009, p. 129–30) advises qualitative researchers to choose broad questions that ask for 'an exploration of the central phenomenon or concept in a study'. He asserts that the intent of qualitative researchers should be to explore a complex set of factors surrounding a central phenomenon and then to present the varied perspectives or meanings held by the participants experiencing this phenomenon.

This perspective fits with a netnographic approach. It implicitly suggests a more open exploratory approach that suits the novel context of Internet cultures and communities. However, netnographies are appropriate for gathering more than personal perspectives or meanings. They are also useful for analyses of many of the cultural aspects of online social phenomena. For instance, a netnography can reveal a wide variety of social processes, such as how informational and social communications and connections are made. It can reveal hierarchical or 'flat' cultural arrangements and styles, and discuss how they are perpetuated and how they change. It can analyse how systems of meaning alter, are shared between different communities and cultures, are borne by participants, and are enacted through rituals and other behaviours.

Netnographies do not necessarily have to start with a brand-new phenomenon, providing a *tabula rasa* or open slate approach to theory development. They can also hone in, narrow, and focus on particular relationships or previously identified constructs, in order to provide us with a deeper or more detailed understanding of them. It can be useful to start with one set of research questions that evolve during the process of the investigation. By the time the final research product is complete, that original set of research questions may have changed quite dramatically, with new ones emerging in the process of investigation and analysis.

Cresswell (2009, pp. 129–31) also offers some useful general guidelines for writing broad research questions to guide qualitative inquiries:

- Ask one or two central questions followed by no more than seven related sub-questions.
- Relate the central question to the specific qualitative strategy of inquiry.
- Begin the research questions with the words 'what' or 'how' to convey an open-ended and emergent research design.
- Focus on a single phenomenon or concept.
- Use exploratory verbs such as 'discover', 'understand', 'explore', 'describe', or 'report'.
- Use open-ended questions.
- Specify the participants and the research site for the study.

Consider the way that Michelle Nelson and Cele Otnes represent their research question in their netnographic article in the *Journal of Business Research*:

> We explore the ways virtual communities help brides-to-be manage cross-cultural ambivalence as they plan their weddings. We address the following two research questions: (1) What roles do wedding message boards play for brides as they plan cross-cultural weddings? (2) How do brides use these Internet communities to cope with the cross-cultural ambivalence they experience? (2005, p. 90)

Comparing these questions with the guidelines, it seems apparent that two central questions focused the entire investigation. The questions are intimately related to the focal investigation of the role of online communities in managing the cross-cultural ambivalence of brides, focusing upon two main concepts: online communities and their roles, and the cross-cultural ambivalence of brides-to-be. The questions begin with the words 'what' and 'how'. The questions are open-ended, they easily suggest who the participants for the research study should be, and they help the researchers narrow down the almost infinite number of possible sites for netnographic fieldwork into just a few relevant areas. In their case, it is the three wedding-related websites theknot.com, ultimatewedding.com, and weddingchannel.com. When they report their conclusions, Nelson and Otnes (2005, p. 94) use positioning terms such as: 'this research examined', 'an analysis of messages posted across three wedding websites demonstrated', and 'we identify'. These are all appropriate exploratory verbs.

In general, Creswell's (2009) seven suggestions constitute good advice for narrowing your research approach and deciding upon your research questions. However, prescriptions such as these are not to be slavishly followed. In particular, caution should be used in regard to Creswell's (2009, p. 131) contingent advice for qualitative researchers to 'use open-ended questions without reference to the theory or literature'. This advice should not be read as suggesting that researchers disregard the written works of others in their areas. The idea of approaching fieldwork with a fresh set of eyes is a good one, but we can never fully achieve it. We should not step into our fieldsite with 'theory goggles' that allow us little latitude to do anything but confirm or validate existing theories. But we should possess as much knowledge about what others have done and thought in related areas as we can, at every single stage of our research investigation.

In particular, you should try to obsessively scour all written works, particularly scholarly academic works (but certainly not exclusively so) for demarcations, delineations, conceptualizations, and theorizations that are related to your netnography's focal topics of interest – regardless of whether the exact same terms or framing have been used by prior scholars. So, for instance, if you are interested in 'media-related fantasy worlds' but others are writing about related ideas as 'spectacle' or 'hyperreality', then you would also want to include the related ideas, perhaps organizing, comparing and contrasting them with one another, and show your readers how this literature is a budding, growing, vital field, rather than one in which you, alone, have the single, correct term.

Remember that the future value of your new netnographically-derived idea or theory will lie in how broadly and deeply others are able to deploy it in their own thinking and writing. By connecting your work with a larger frame of reference of scholarly – and even not-so-scholarly – thought, you will not only be building bridges with related literature in this area, you will also be increasing the chances that your research will impact how other thinkers understand the world.

In order to evaluate and extend your theoretical reach, scholars of online cultures and communities will find it very useful to consult past works in related areas and to network with scholars working in these areas. As noted by Silver (2006, p. 2), scholars of online communities and cultures, or the broader field of 'Internet studies to which it belongs', now have the benefit of drawing upon 'a community of scholars; conferences and symposia; journals, journal articles, anthologies, monographs, and textbooks; university courses, common curriculum, and majors; theses and dissertations; theories and methodologies; and academic centers'. Hoping that these links are not outdated by the time you read this, this chapter conveys as much of this information as possible in Boxes 5.1, 5.2, and 5.3. You may want to consult these resources carefully prior to undertaking your netnography.

The value of a single precise journal article in your area that clarifies your thinking and leads you to dozens of rich new references, or a single helpful scholarly contact, can never be overrated. Whatever effort you put into reaching out to other scholars and delving into related theoretical works will very likely be copiously rewarded.

BOX 5.1   COMMUNITIES OF SCHOLARS INTERESTED IN SOCIAL, POLITICAL AND CULTURAL ELEMENTS OF THE INTERNET, NEW MEDIA, AND GAME STUDIES

- The Association of Internet Researchers (AIR) (www.aoir.org/)
- The Institute of Network Cultures (www.networkcultures.org/)
- The German Society for Online Research (www.dgof.de)
- Ciberpunk (www.ciberpunk.net) (in Spanish)

- The Digital Games Research Association (www.digra.org/)
- Second Life Research Listserv (http://list.academ-x.com/listinfo.cgi/slrl-academ-x.com)
- Digital Ethnography at Kansas State University (http://groups.diigo.com/groups/ksudigg), and see blog at http:// mediatedcultures. net/
- Synthetic Worlds Initiative at Indiana University (http://swi.indiana.edu/)
- TerraNova (http://terranova.blogs.com)
- Facebook Netnography group www.facebook.com/home.php#/group.php?gid=40383234118
- LinkedIn Netnography group www.linkedin.com/e/gis/1602247
- LinkedIn Cyber & Web anthropology www.linkedin.com/groups?gid=146486

BOX 5.2 RELEVANT JOURNALS

- *Convergence: the Journal of Research into New Media Technologies* (http://convergence.beds.ac.uk/)
- *Ctheory* (www.ctheory.net/)
- Ebr-electronic book review (http://www.electronicbookreview.com)
- *First Monday* (www.firstmonday.org/)
- *Game Studies* (www.gamestudies.org/)
- *Information, Communication & Society* (www.tandf.co.uk/journals/titles/1369118X.html
- *The Information Society* (www.indiana.edu/~tisj
- *Journal of Computer-mediated Communication* (http://jcmc.indiana.edu)
- *M/C: Media & Culture* (www.media-culture.org.au/)
- *New Media & Society* (http://nms.sagepub.com)
- *Surveillance & Society* (www.surveillance-and-society.org/ojs/index.php/journal)
- *Teknokultura* (http://teknokultura.rrp.upr.edu/)
- *Journal of Web-based Communities* (www.inderscience.com/)
- *Journal of Virtual Worlds Research* (http://jvwresearch.org/)
- *Games & Culture: A Journal of Interactive Media* (www.gamesandculture.com)
- *CyberPsychology & Behaviour* (www.liebertpub.com)
- *Cyberpsychology: Journal of Psychological Research on Cyberspace* (www.cyberpsychology.eu/index.php)

Note: Always search Google Scholar (http://scholar.google.com) or another good general purpose academic search engine for relevant articles across multiple fields, check through the citations in these articles, and then search for those who have cited the articles you find to be relevant.

BOX 5.3   ACADEMIC CENTRES FOR CYBERCULTURE STUDIES

- Europe

  o International Center for New Media (Austria; www.icnm.net/)
  o Center for Computer Games Research (Denmark; http://game.itu.dk)
  o Oxford Internet Institute (Great Britain; www.oii.ox.ac.uk/)
  o Institute of Network Cultures (Netherlands; http://networkcultures.org/wpmu/portal/)
  o govcom.org (Netherlands; www.govcom.org)
  o e-Society (www.york.ac.uk/res/e-society)

- Asia and Oceania

  o fibreculture (Australia; www.fibreculture.org/)
  o Singapore Internet Research Center (www3.ntu.edu.sg/sci/SIRC)

- USA

  o Berglund Center for Internet Studies (Pacific University, USA; http://bcis. pacificu. edu)
  o Center for Digital Discourse and Culture (Virginia Tech; http://www.cddc. vt.edu)
  o Center for Women and Information Technology (University of Maryland, Baltimore County, USA; http://www.umbc.edu/cwit)
  o Internet Studies Center (University of Minnesota, USA; http://yorktown.cbe. wwu.edu/ISC)
  o Institute for New Media Studies (www.inms.umn.edu)
  o Resource Center for Cyberculture Studies (University of Washington, USA; http://rccs.usfca.edu)

FINDING YOUR SITE: LOCATING AN APPROPRIATE ONLINE FIELD

The Varieties of Online Social Experience

The next stage of planning for your netnographic investigation is to identify particular online forums that might help to inform you about the research topics you have identified and answer the research questions you have posed.

Early writings about netnography suggested that, at the time, there were five main outlets or 'locations' for online connections, 'places' to be used as netnographic field-sites where two or more people communicated, bearing and sharing culture, expressing and building community. These five forums were: chat-rooms, bulletin boards, playspace dungeons, lists, and rings of interlinked web-pages (Kozinets 1997a, 1998, 1999). There was then, and still is, considerable diversity in the form and structure of the social interaction experienced in these places. They vary in the types of conversations that they carry (playful and game-related, social, informational), in their user interface (textual, graphical, audio, audiovisual), their temporal orientations (synchronous/real-time, asynchronous/time-delayed), and their interpersonal modalities and implicit communications hierarchies (individual broadcast, one-on-one, group). In addition, these forums can be a part of a corporate website run as part of a profit-making or public relations effort, such as are many online forums. Or, they could be grassroots efforts owned and managed by individuals out of their own interest. These categories tend to fuse into one another. Actual sites rarely map neatly onto these characteristics. The qualities are often agglomerated together into single sites and media, and considerable overlap between them exists.

A very general and updated introduction and description of some of these sites of online culture and community follows:

- *Bulletin boards* or *forums* are one of the oldest and richest online community forms. They are text-based exchanges often organized around particular shared orientations or interests. Participants post textual messages (these could also include graphics or photos, and often contain hyperlinks), others reply and over time these messages form an asynchronous, conversational 'thread'. Bulletin boards tend to originate with interested individuals, while forums tend to be part of corporate or professional websites.
- *Chat-rooms* are a form of online communications in which two or more people share text, usually for social objectives, interacting synchronously – in real time – and usually without any fantasy role-playing (but often with a complex symbol set of acronyms, shortcuts, and emoticons).
- *Playspaces* are communications forums where one or more people socially interact through the structured format of role- and game-playing. The term playspace is used here as a general designation to indicate several different types of ludic online communication. Contemporary playspaces, such as online networked video gaming, or MMOGS (massively multiplayer online games; also MMORPGS, or massively multiplayer online role-playing games), as well as Alternate Reality Games (ARGs) are synchronous and intensely graphical, and can include textual or audio communications between players, offering multiple modes of communication. Dungeons (whose name, Multi-User Dungeon, or MUD, also MOO, derives from Dungeons & Dragons, the original text-based game environment) are online locations where participants engage in text-based, synchronous ludic – and often highly social – online communications. All currently exist simultaneously, although older forms are, understandably, less popular than they once were. World of Warcraft, Runescape, The Sims Online, and Guild Wars are all popular MMOGs boasting millions of active users.
- *Virtual worlds* are a type of playspace that combines the synchronous, graphically-intense environment of the online game with the more open and grassroots social processes of many of the original dungeons, MUDs, or MOOs. Second Life is one of the best-known virtual worlds, although Habbo Hotel, Club Penguin, BarbieGirls, Gaia Online, and Webkinz are other popular sites.

- *Lists* are groups of participants who collectively produce and share regular e-mails about a particular named topic or subject of mutual interest; the communications, like bulletin boards, are asynchronous and largely textual; unlike bulletin boards, these conversations are often considered to be private rather than public.
- *Rings* are organizations of related web-pages that are linked together and structured by interest; the interconnection between pages was considered to be a type of (rather weak) communication.

As you can tell from these descriptions, much has changed in a decade. Dungeons have evolved and changed. Web-rings are far less common and have largely been replaced by blogs and the interconnections of blogrolls. To these forums of online community interaction, we must add the following:

- *Blogs* are a special type of web-page that is, in the ideal, frequently updated. It consists of dated entries arranged in reverse chronological order, so that what appears first is the most recent entry (Walker 2008). The community aspect to blogs occurs through comments on the blog where interaction takes place between the blog author and blog readers, between the blog author and other blog authors, as well as between different blog readers, who can potentially form communal relationships (see Walker 2008, pp. 21–2). Blogs are an asynchronous type of communication in which text still predominates, although many blogs use graphics and photographs quite extensively, and some (vlogs, or video blogs) use audio-visual media. Microblogs, such as Twitter, are a recent extension of the blog utilizing small amounts of frequently updated text, distributed selectively and often across multiple platforms including mobile.
- *Wikis* are a specialized, collaborative form of the web-page in which the page is designed so that it is open to contributions or modifications of its content. Communities can form on wikis through the asynchronous, generally textual, interactional comments that contributors make to one another, as well as in optional forums or bulletin boards, or other interactional media, attached or linked to the central wiki. The free online encyclopedia Wikipedia is the best-known wiki, renowned for its large, active community.
- *Audio/visual sites* are online locations where participants asynchronously share and comment upon one another's graphical, photographical, audio, or audiovisual productions. Interactions occur through the content of the shared product itself, as well as through ratings and asynchronous, textual comments. Productions shared can include artwork as well as photographs, music as well as podcasts and videos. Well-known sites of this type include Flickr, iTune's distribution of various interest-related podcasts, and YouTube.
- *Social content aggregators* are sites and services designed to help people communally discover and share Internet content, vote on it, and comment upon it. Three popular social content aggregators are Digg, del.icio.us, and StumbleUpon.
- *Social networking sites* (or services; both abbreviated to SNS) are a hybrid communications format that offers devoted individual pages, various interaction media, interest and activity groups, and communities made available to users through selective linkages. Online interaction on SNS occurs through various media, including web-page-like posting of identification and messages (which can also

include graphics and photos as well as links to audiovisual material), email-like message exchanges between members, microblog-like status updates and comments thereupon, forum-like comments between sites users, bulletin board-like fan and interest groups (all asynchronous), and chat room-like instant messages (synchronous and textual). The two most popular social networking sites in North America are MySpace and Facebook. Other sites popular around the world are Bebo, Orkut, 51.com, and Vkontakte.ru.

Undoubtedly, other forms and hybridizations where online communication occurs and where online communities grow have been missed in this introductory accounting. In the amount of time it takes for a book to make its way through the publication process, I would expect at least one new form of online communication to spawn and gain prominence.

Although these forms (and the others) still exist as separate types, one of the trends in the Internet and online interaction in general is that these are increasingly blurring one into the other. Social networking sites are an excellent example of a hybrid form combining web-page, private e-mail, (micro)blog, forums, and chat-room access. Therefore, making research choices of one type of interactional form over another seems forced and unnatural. What is important in your netnographic investigation is for you to experience online social interaction in the way that your participants are experiencing it. This often means following many different types, forms, and structures of online communication — perhaps moving in the same day from following a newsgroup or forum attached to a web-page to reading and commenting on a blog, to becoming a fan of a related group on a social networking site, to joining in an online chat discussion with the other members of that group.

Much past research has considered bulletin boards to be very useful (e.g., Baym 1995, 1999; Correll 1995; Jenkins 1995; Langer and Beckman 2005; Markham 1998; Muñiz and Schau 2005; Schouten and McAlexander 1995).[6] But given the changing nature of the Internet, its expanding universe of forms and influences and the fluid migration of people between these forms, bulletin boards should not enjoy a privileged status in our researching of online communities. The netnographic field-site or fieldsites should match your research focus and the questions you want to investigate. A researcher interested in how elderly people play games online to stave off loneliness might be drawn to Internet portals that attract large numbers of online game players. A researcher interested in how business consultants use technology to stay in contact with clients might be drawn to the microblog Twitter, and the social networking site LinkedIn.

Using Search Engines to Locate Specific Communities

Now that we have a common understanding of the names and descriptions of some online sites of interaction, we need to learn where to locate online communities of interest. Recall from the last chapter that archiving and accessibility were two of the major differences between online fieldwork and its traditional face-to-face variant. These two differences make finding a relevant community very different in netnography. In fact, whereas the traditional ethnographer might travel great distances in order to study a particular culture, or a sociological or cultural studies ethnographer might rely on an influential personal introduction to a particular local community or subculture, the nascent netnographer's best friend is the judicious deployment of a good search engine.

As the Internet has grown and changed, so too have search engines been transformed. Major search engines like Google.com, Yahoo!, and MSN currently have group search options that allow one to search newsgroup and blog archives, as well as their current postings. These major, exhaustive search engines are often the best source of community information. Google.com is the best of the lot, but researchers should also check Yahoo! because results from the two major search engines will vary. Doing a thorough 'community sweep' of the Internet using Google is a fairly straightforward affair:

(1) Enter search terms related to your research area, focus, and questions into the main Google search window. For example, if you are studying online communities devoted to green activism, then consider entering variations on 'green', 'environmental', 'activist', 'recycling', 'conservation', and 'community'. This will give you listings of websites, many of them corporate. However some of those corporate websites may contain interesting links as well as communal forums of their own.

(2) From the descriptions, you can decide which websites to investigate. Take your time. This is an important step.

(3) You will notice that on the top left corner of the main Google search page you are provided with a number of options for additional types of search. If you click on the option titled 'more', you will be presented with a number of other options. Two highly relevant searches to run are 'Groups' and 'Blogs'.

(4) Search 'Groups'. Groups is an archive of many newsgroups combined with a web-based reader and interface. The Google Groups site is actually an updated version of the old DejaNews, or deja.com newsgroup reader.

(5) Search 'Blogs'. This will direct you to noteworthy blogs related to your topic.

You can do the same sort of search for Yahoo! with Yahoo!groups (http://groups.yahoo.com/). There are also a number of high-quality blog search engines available designed specifically for the blogosphere, including bloglines, blogscope, and Technorati. Some other good general purpose search engines for searching for community-related information are:

- Wikiasearch, from the Wikipedia group (http://search.wikia.com/)
- Twitter search, which allows a search of the active microblog Twitter (http://search.twitter.com/)
- Ning.com, a site devoted to online communities that enables and collects over 100,000 online groups (http://www.ning.com/)
- A nice compilation of different kinds of search engines is provided on Wikipedia at: (http://en.wikipedia.org/wiki/List_of_search_engines/)

In addition, consider entering search terms on some of the other popular sites on the Internet for specific groups that might relate to your topic. These popular sites would include YouTube, Flickr, Digg, Wikipedia, MySpace and Facebook (particularly the groups and fans of sections of these sites). Use a variety of keywords and search terms. You will need to continue to refine and develop these search terms as you get results related to your initial search words.

In general, you want to keep combining general search engines (like Yahoo!) with community search engines (such as groups.google.com) and searches on specific social sites. It is also important to note that a broad and thorough computerized search may be required, as the topic of interest may be categorized at varying levels of abstraction. For example, if you were trying to study breakfast cereal consumer communities, these communities could exist at the brand level (Lucky Charms), product category (sweet cereal), demographic level (children's food), media level (fictional cartoon characters) or activity type level (eating breakfast). The more that you search and the longer you devote to it, the better will be your chances that you have adequately covered relevant communal terrain, and discovered the requisite group or groups that will best serve your investigative needs.

GUIDELINES FOR SITE CHOICE AND ENTRÉE

In this section, we will learn how to choose sites for netnographic fieldwork. Let us assume that you have settled upon your research question and have identified a number of communities and sites that seem relevant to your research topic. How do you judge those sites and decide which ones to focus on? In general, unless there are good reasons why you would want it otherwise, you should look for online communities that are:

(1) *relevant*, they relate to your research focus and question(s)
(2) *active*, they have recent and regular communications
(3) *interactive*, they have a flow of communications between participants
(4) *substantial*, they have a critical mass of communicators and an energetic feel
(5) *heterogeneous*, they have a number of different participants
(6) *data-rich*, offering more detailed or descriptively rich data.

It might make good sense to trade off one or more of these criteria. For example, you might choose to investigate a small and thus less substantial online community that nonetheless has many data-rich postings, rather than one that is larger and more active, but contains mostly short, perfunctory postings or re-postings of information from other sources. You will probably find that larger groups are less communal, containing less elaborate messages with less personal disclosure, than smaller groups. Alternately, you might find smaller groups to be more homogeneous. All of the search procedures listed in this chapter can potentially yield access to appropriate groups of people self-segmented into categories, but you may need to explore a number of options before you find the site or sites that best suit your research purposes.

As you begin reading through these options, but before initiating contact or formal data collection, you should pay careful attention to the characteristics of the online community. Remember my example above of carelessly entering the Rainbow Family newsgroup. Read the FAQ first, if there is one. This will answer a number of your introductory questions. Then, start reading through archives. The archive function is incredibly valuable to netnographers. At this point, you are still anonymous; you have not yet entered the online community because you have not yet made your decision to study it.

As you narrow your choices, continue with your study of the online community or communities. Who are the most active participants? Who seem to be the leaders? What are some of the most popular topics? What is the history of the group? Have there been major conflicts in its past? What other groups are its members connected to? What can you tell about the characteristics (demographics, interests, opinions, values) of the message posters and commenters? What are some of the concepts and precepts that they hold dear? What sort of specialized language, if any, is the community using? Do they have any particular rituals or activities? What are some of their common practices? If you are studying a community online (see Chapter 4), then you should also be familiar with some of the practices, terminology, values, personnel, and icons of the overall community linked to this online manifestation. You do not need a detailed, dissertation-like understanding of all of these matters, but a pragmatic working understanding that will help you to choose your fieldsite and, when it comes time, to enter it in a culturally appropriate manner.

By the time you make first contact, much about this online community should be very familiar to you: its members, its topics, its language, how it works. If you find that an online community has been visited by a researcher in the recent past, you might consider leaving it alone and finding another one. Its members may be 'tapped out' by the recent research effort. They may have been researched in a way that was intrusive or inconsiderate, for instance by a researcher who portrayed one person unfavourably, or who wrote about the community in a way that community members felt was disrespectful. These communities are likely to be unreceptive to further research overtures. In that case, leaving the community alone is even more advisable, rather than trying to convince them that you are going to do a better/nicer/more rigorous/more respectful netnography than the last researcher did.

SETTING YOUR INITIAL STRATEGIES FOR DATA COLLECTION

This section offers some summary recommendations regarding how to manage the initial approach to a netnographic fieldsite. We are going to detail in the next chapter exactly how to interact in a participative way in your chosen online community or communities and capture data in that fieldsite. These guidelines will set the stage for your approach.

Ethics

If you are an academic you will need to gain the approval of an Institutional Review Board or Human Subjects Research Ethics Committee in order to be able to start your netnography. Chapter 8 of this book deals with these ethical issues and offers specific recommendations about how to plan and conduct your research ethically. You will benefit from reading this chapter before beginning any netnographic research, and building its suggestions into your research plan.

Written Guidelines

As you begin your research, stay organized and focused. Use this book as a manual, but also keep a binder with your guidelines and other relevant documents.[7] The guidelines should represent research decisions you have made, are making, or will need to make. Have your research focus and research questions written on it. Work those more general questions into the specific questions that you will pose to participants. Write out a paragraph detailing how you will be approaching this community, and the participation style you intend to engage in. Write about the forums and communities you have examined, and about why you chose to follow certain ones and not others. Keep a section on research ethics. In that section, keep your IRB or Human Subjects Research documentation. Keep any forms you have or permissions you may need. Use your written guidelines to structure and supervise your netnographic research as it proceeds from entrée through to engagement and immersion.

Preparing for Data and Analysis – and Choosing Data Analysis Software

In netnography, the boundaries marking the inside and outside of a culture or community are much less clear than they are in a traditional, face-to-face ethnography. There is thus no general rule about when to start keeping fieldnotes. I recommend jotting notes about initial sites visited as you begin your investigation. As you return to particular sites and find that they hold potential value for you and meet relevant criteria, you should develop your jottings into more structured fieldnotes and continue to add detail to them.

Even at this early stage of the process, you should be preparing yourself to collect data. In fact, you should be collecting related documents as soon as you begin planning a project. Lyn Richards (2005) advises that you should choose a qualitative data analysis package and learn it before you begin collecting data, not once you are becoming overwhelmed by data. We will be discussing some of these packages in the next chapter. If you are using qualitative data analysis software, you will want to store these initial fieldnotes and forays into online communities somewhere, in order to keep your project organized.

> Start in your software – storing literature reviews, early designs, memos to the supervisor, research diaries. Good qualitative software is not merely about managing data records, but about integrating all aspects of a project – design, reading, field data, analyses and reports. By the time the project data records are being created, you will be skilled in that software. (Richards 2005, p. 27)

You may also want to save correspondences with co-authors, e-mails, scans or downloads of related articles, new stories, or videos. Save anything that might relate to your research project in any way.

If you do this, there will not be much of a start-up to your data collection procedure. By the time you make your formal entrée, you will already have several documents that chart its progression, you will also already have initial data from early forays into the field, you will have correspondence and some theoretical and literature-related ideas, and you will have memos on your data and fieldnotes about your initial fieldwork. In addition, you will already be in the habit of adding to this pool of data every time you contact, think about, or do something else related to your online social group or your research on it. And you will have some good familiarity with your qualitative data analysis software package, and will already be organizing, memoing and perhaps even coding your data.

Interaction

You also have a number of choices about how you will interact with your online community. Are you going to interact in a fairly limited way, such as informing people of your research study and then asking a few clarifying questions over a period of time? Or are you going to interact as a full participant in the local culture and community, perhaps even becoming a valued member and contributing your knowledge or skills to the betterment of the community? In the next chapter, I will discuss how my involvement in some online communities changed and deepened over the course of my netnographic inquiry.

For many academics, their initial approach to an online community may resemble the following posted message:

Hi Everyone:

My name is [your name] and I am a [position] at [University or company]. I have been studying [culture X or topic] for the last six weeks, and I have been finding [online community's name or description] really helpful. I have a few questions that I would like to ask and I am hoping that I can get in contact with some of you.

Thank you,

Your Name Here

This is actually very similar to a posting I made to the alt.coffee newsgroup in 2000, where I said that:

> I've been lurking here for a while, studying online coffee culture on alt.coffee, learning a lot, and enjoying it very much … I just wanted to pop out of lurker status to let you know I am here … I will be wanting to quote some of the great posts that have appeared here, and I will contact the individuals by personal e-mail who posted them to ask their permission to quote them. I also will be making the document on coffee culture available to any interested members of the newsgroup for their perusal and comments – to make sure I get things right.

Then, I gave them my credentials so that they could see for themselves who I was and how I had represented other communities in the past. Thanks followed, along with an offer that community members should 'feel free to contact me with any questions or comments at all', providing my full name, title, and mailing address.

Although this sort of an entrée is not bad, it may not be the best strategy. A better one has the researcher start, from the beginning of their contact with the community, to act like a new member, while also clearly stating that they are undertaking a research project. Why not post a link to a news article? Or enter a thread with an interesting, timely, and well thought-out comment? Offering some new piece of knowledge or new perspective, perhaps from the academic or scientific arena? As you emerge from dark lurking anonymity into the light of an online communal day, you want to have something to say besides, 'I am a student/professor at the University of ABC, and I want to study you.' Be creative. Be mindful and exacting about crafting your entrance. Make it good.

In September, 1996, I posted a message to a few *Star Trek* newsgroups titled 'Is *Star Trek* like a Religion?' I cited some academic research that had been published indicating that *Star Trek* fans were like religious devotees, and then asked fans to comment on it. I also told them who I was, and invited them to learn more about my research. The somewhat controversial message worked well. Community members commented, had some fun with it, and got involved in the research. Unlike my Rainbow Family example, I had taken the time to understand the online community where I was posting my message. I took the time to fit my research questions and approach appropriately to the community. Probably assisted by my in-person fieldwork, I was acting like a genuine cultural participant.

Be aware as you begin your project that archiving and accessibility cut both ways. The Internet is forever. Everything you post online is accessible to everyone, very likely for a long time to come. So, in a few years, as I am researching examples of excellent and embarrassing netnographic research for my next book, remember that I may come across *your* netnographic research entrée. So, before you think about incorporating the cultural interaction of online community members into your research, consider what your netnographic incursion might look like as a part of *my* research.

SUMMARY

The netnographer has a number of important decisions that need to be made prior to first contact with an online community. Decisions about research questions and topics must be made. Appropriate forms of social interaction and communities must be investigated using search engines and other means. In general, communities should be favoured that are relevant, active, interactive, substantial, heterogeneous, and data-rich. An appropriate stance towards the netnographic research, its participative options and its ethical protocols, must also be devised. In the next chapter, we will discuss exactly how to collect data during your fieldwork.

KEY READINGS

Creswell, John W. (2009) *Research Design: Qualitative, Quantitative, and Mixed Methods Approaches*, 3rd edition. Thousand Oaks, CA: Sage Publications.

Kozinets, Robert V. (1998) 'On Netnography: Initial Reflections on Consumer Research Investigations of Cyberculture', in Joseph Alba and Wesley Hutchinson (eds), *Advances in Consumer Research*, Volume 25. Provo, UT: Association for Consumer Research, pp. 366–71.

Nelson, Michelle R. and Cele C. Otnes (2005) 'Exploring Cross-Cultural Ambivalence: A Netnography of Intercultural Wedding Message Boards', *Journal of Business Research*, 58: 89–95.

Silver, David (2006) 'Introduction: Where is Internet Studies?', David Silver and Adrienne Massanari (eds), in *Critical Cyberculture Studies*. New York and London: New York University Press, pp. 1–14.

6
DATA COLLECTION

ABSTRACT

This chapter teaches you how to create and capture the three different kinds of netnographic data: archival data, elicited data, and fieldnote data. This approach to data collection is specifically attuned to saving netnographic data as computer files that can be coded, printed, or recognized by human researchers and data analysis software programs.

> **Key Words:** cyber-interviews, data collection, fieldnotes, online interviews, screen capture software, spam, visual data

THE ESSENTIALS OF NETNOGRAPHIC DATA COLLECTION

The terms data and collection used in relation to netnography are actually unfortunate and not very helpful. They seem to imply that these things, 'data', are scattered about, like leaves on the ground or documents on a table, and that your job is simply to gather them up and 'collect' them. This is obviously very tempting in netnography. But to do this would be analysis of online 'content' rather than netnographic participant-observational fieldwork 'in' an online community. Data collection in netnography means communicating with members of a culture or community. That communication can take many forms. But whichever form it takes, it entails relevant involvement, engagement, contact, interaction, communion, relation, collaboration and connection with community members – not with a website, server, or a keyboard, but with the people on the other end.

In netnography, data collection does not happen in isolation from data analysis. Although I will treat them separately in different chapters in this book, they are intertwined. Even if the data are of archival interactions, during data collection it is incumbent upon the netnographer to struggle to understand the people represented in these interactions from within the online communal and cultural context in which they are embedded, rather than to collect this information in a way that would strip out context and present culture members or their practices in a general, unspecified, universalized manner. The very act of participating in a community changes the nature of later data analysis. This is what makes ethnography and netnography so thoroughly different from techniques such as content analysis or social network analysis. A content analyst would scan the archives of online communities, but she or he would not be reading them deeply for their cultural information, pondering them and seeking to learn from them how to live in this community and to identify as a community member. This is the task of the netnographer.

Data collection is also interconnected with netnographic participation. It thus may be useful prior to beginning to collect data to learn and consider the nature of netnographic participation. For example, you might wonder if reading messages regularly and clicking on posted hyperlinks, but not posting a message, is appropriate netnographic participation. Does participation have to involve posting a message or making an online comment? Does it need to involve some form of communication or interaction with members on the part of the researcher? Is simply registering and joining a group sufficient?

In general, participation will be active and visible to other community members. Preferably, it will contribute to the community and its members. Not every netnographic researcher needs to be involved in *every* type of community activity. But every netnographic researcher needs to be involved in *some* types of community activity. A netnographer probably doesn't want to be leading the community, but she should not be invisible, either.

There is a spectrum of engagement and involvement in online and related off-line communities that ranges from reading messages regularly and in real time (as opposed to downloading them en masse to be searched and automatically coded), following links, rating, replying to other members via e-mail or other one-on-one communications, offering short comments, offering long comments, joining in and contributing to community activities, to becoming an organizer, expert, or recognized voice of the community. Figure 6.1 demonstrates this increasing participative involvement in the activities of an online community. This level of increasing involvement can indicate some of the stages of netnographic participation and, consequently, suggest the different types of data that will be collected.

Consider the participative stance adopted by Al Muñiz and Hope Schau (2005) in their excellent article about online communities that are devoted to the defunct Apple PDA, the Newton. As well as monitoring websites and bulletin boards frequented by community members, these researchers bought a used Newton and began using it. The effort to make this old technological dog do new tricks was not insubstantial. Their acquisition of the device put them 'in the shoes' of fellow community members and gave them common ground, as well as providing reasons for accumulating an enhanced understanding of the community.

Content analytic approaches take the observational stance of netnography to an extreme, offering unobtrusive downloads without any social contact. This approach

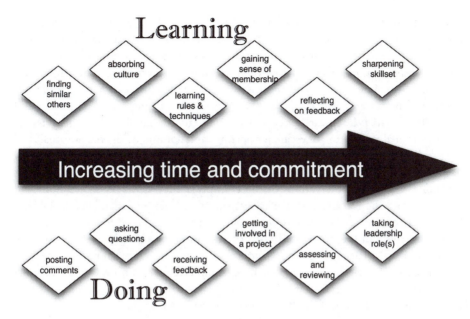

FIGURE 6.1 POTENTIAL FORMS OF NETNOGRAPHIC PARTICIPATION IN AN ONLINE COMMUNITY (ADAPTED FROM KOZINETS ET AL. 2008, FIGURE 1, P. 342)

puts the researcher at risk of gaining only a shallow and cursory cultural understanding. In a methodological book chapter about netnography I suggest that it can sometimes be useful to take the participative element to a similar extreme (Kozinets 2006a). We can speculate about the value of an 'auto-netnography', where the basis of a netnography is largely autobiographical personal reflection on online community membership, as captured in fieldnotes and other subjective recordings of online experience. Significant portions of Annette Markham's (1998) *Life Online* are reflexive and auto-netnographic. Another example is that of Bruce Weinberg (2000), whose 'Internet 24/7 project', consisted of an early blog where he kept track of and analysed his experiences as an exclusively online shopper. Richard Kedzior and I have recently suggested that the auto-netnographic format can be very usefully applied to enhance our understanding of the subjective experience of 'being' an avatar in a virtual world environment (Kozinets and Kedzior 2009). We suggest that auto-netnography's deep subjective focus is useful because virtual worlds offer interesting characteristics, such as a sense of a new reality and a new body (characteristics that have been noted of many types of online community experience, including MUDs and MOOs).

Ideally, the experience one has as a netnographer will try to balance the reflexive, autobiographical, and subjective mode of the engaged cultural participant with the objectifying precision of the scientific observer. Inherent in the nature of ethnography and netnography, the researcher must constantly maintain a tension, tacking back and forth between the experientially close involvement with the members of online community and culture, and the more abstract and distanced worlds of theory, words, generality, and research focus.

In doing so, netnographic data collection will include the capture of three different types of data. The first are *archival data*, data that the researcher directly copies from pre-existing computer-mediated communications of online community members, data that she is not directly involved in creating or prompting. The prodigious amount of this information and the ease of its downloading can make handling it daunting. The researcher may require several levels of filtering for relevance. Second are *elicited data* that the researcher co-creates with culture members through personal and communal interaction. Researcher postings and comments, as well as e-mail and chat or instant messaging interviews, would be common procedures to elicit netnographic data. Third are *fieldnote data,* the fieldnotes that the researcher inscribes regarding their own observations of the community, its members, interactions and meanings, and the researcher's own participation and sense of membership. During the process of data collection, reflective data are usually reserved for the researcher's own purposes and are not shared with the community. These categories roughly follow Wolcott's (1992) categories of watching, asking, and examining or Miles and Huberman's (1994) categories of documents, interviews, and observations. Each of these types of data collection will be explained in turn. First, this chapter turns to a more general discussion of the basics of online data collection.

THE BASICS OF ONLINE DATA CAPTURE AND COLLECTION

This section will explain at a very fundamental level what is required in order to collect data from netnographic sites. Netnographic fieldwork is rather unique in that it is cultural, but it also involves the use of a computer networked through a server to other computers. Without becoming overly technical, this section will tell you how to use your computer's capabilities to capture netnographic data.

The netnographer has two basis choices to make when capturing data, and the type of data analysis she plans to pursue will dictate the choice. If the netnographer is going to code the qualitative data manually, using a pen-and-paper technique, or some variety of this technique using jottings on computer files or in a spreadsheet such as Microsoft Excel, then data collection should be limited to relatively small amounts of data, perhaps in the order of 1,000 pages of double-spaced text or less. This limitation may alter the boundaries of the online community or cultural field-site. It may also alter the focus of the netnography, which may be more suited to analysing only particular messages or threads within the community. In addition it may alter what data the netnographer chooses to actually save, rather than simply pass by or take brief notes or jottings on.

If the netnographer is going to use a qualitative data analysis software program to assist with coding and organizing the data, then data collection can be far more prolific, extending over 5,000 pages of double-spaced text. This freedom may extend the boundaries of the online community or cultural fieldsite. It may widen the focus of the netnography. It may also make the netnographer more able – or perhaps more prone – to collect data without a clear focus, or with a wider purview. We will return to a more detailed discussion of qualitative data analysis software in the next chapter of this book.

Consider the following example of manual netnographic data collection. In our co-authored study of Volkswagen consumers, which we coded and analysed entirely by hand, we initially read through a large number of messages about Volkswagen cars on our computer screens, making general notes about what we saw and where we found those data (Brown et al. 2003). We then focused in on threads and sites that had many references to the Volkswagen Beetle car. Again, we read many messages and took notes on them. During this pass, we saved some data in the form of postings and message threads. We then narrowed our focus once again to particular elements of Volkswagen Beetle car culture that were theoretically interesting and relevant to our central focus, such as those that we found relating to Walter Benjamin's theory. We examined a much smaller set of sites and newsgroups that we had previously identified, read the relevant messages and postings much more closely, and saved most of them as data files. We collected the files into one, large Microsoft Word file. Later, we printed some of these files and hand-coded them. As the project went on, we did most of our coding in the one large Microsoft Word data file on our computers' hard drive. We used the word processing program's search capabilities to look for repeat instances of our observations, which aided in coding as well as confirmation and disconfirmation.

In total, we had the equivalent of 560 double-spaced pages when printed in double-spaced 10-point font. Although this was a large amount of text, it was still quite amenable to the detailed hermeneutic reading one would give to a book or another text. As noted here, this text was already quite 'distilled'. That is, we had already read through, noted, thought about, and intellectually processed a large amount of data in the netnography that was not saved. The figures we reported on were only the amount of data that we saved and coded (not including our 20–30 pages of notes). These 560 pages represented 432 different postings that contained 131 distinct poster names.

Two basic ways to capture online data are to save the file as a computer-readable file, or as a visual image of your screen as it appears when you see the data. Both of these methods have advantages as well as drawbacks. When the communal communications are mainly textual, as they are with bulletin boards, newsgroups, forums, microblogs, and wikis, then saving the file as a computer-readable file is the best option. The files from Google Groups and Yahoo!Groups are already presented on-screen as text files. When the data contain many visual cues as well as text, as is the case in audio and visual sharing sites, virtual worlds, some blogs, and some areas of social networking sites, then various methods of screen capture are preferred. A third option, which combines both of the other options, is to save the file in a computer-readable format that roughly captures what you see on screen. If you will not be using an automated CAQDAS program to help you manage all of your documents, it is best to aggregate all of your data into (preferably) one large file in a word-processing program that you can later clean up and search. All of these formats – scanned images, HTML files, and downloaded text – can be aggregated together into a file.

The following details specifically what you need to do to collect data in this manner. As an example, consider that we are studying the way members of the public use online communities to discuss the relationship of capitalism with the environment.

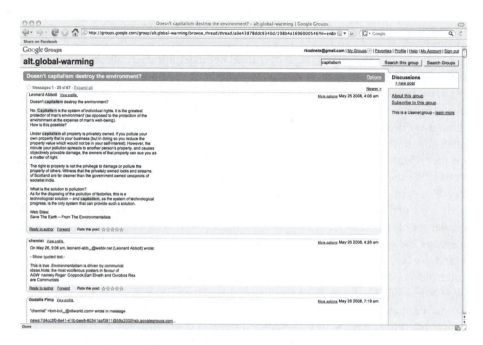

FIGURE 6.2   SCREEN CAPTURE OF NEWSGROUP THREAD*

Note: *saved in jpg image file format and displayed in a Firefox browser window

Using the search engine procedures outlined in Chapter 5, we find some interesting and relevant postings on the alt.global-warming newsgroup, which we access through the Google Groups website, using a Firefox browser on an Apple Mac computer running OS X.[8] In the browser window, the initial search yields a window that has been captured in Figure 6.2.

The image in Figure 6.2 has been captured using still-image screen capture software called 'Grab'. Still-image screen capture software programs are sometimes also called 'screen shot' software. There are many choices of screen capture software for Microsoft PC users, including Snagit, Screenhunter, Shutter, iQuick, Snapa, and Snapz Pro. Most of these programs have a very simple graphical user interface that works analogous to the operation of a camera. The researcher opens a page on their browser, and then opens the capture program. They select a capture option from the program menu, usually allowing them to select a field with their mouse, or to capture an entire window. They then press a particular button, and the image of the screen is captured. Captured screenshot images are stored in a compressed image file format such as bmp, jpg, or gif. The text that is included in them is therefore not readable as such by most computer programs, such as word processing or qualitative data analysis software.

It may also be beneficial to use full-motion screen capture software programs to record, moment-by-moment, what appears on the computer screen. Unlike the still images described above (and illustrated in Figure 6.2), these programs provide a moving picture that includes audio. Software such as Snapz Pro X, Camtasia, Cam

Studio, Replay Screencast, or Hypercam allows the netnographer to automatically record exactly what she is seeing and hearing on her computer screen in real time. She can capture various sequential online community searches, the sites that she clicks through, the messages and postings that she reads, as well as the images, sound files, and audiovisual files that she views on her computer. These data are saved as a digital video file (often an avi file, which is convertible to mpg, mov or even flv file formats) and events can be replayed at a future time, just like a DVD movie.

When data are collected in this way, the netnographer analyses the data by pausing or stopping events to note, code, or examine them further. Momentary details can easily be located and analysed. Also, you can easily fast forward or rewind to a particular place in the data. However, if you are going to spend a lot of time in your online community, as you should, recording every minute can require an investment in additional computer memory, or an extra hard drive. External memory is available relatively inexpensively in many countries. Even more important is the researcher time required. Reviewing all of this information can be very time-consuming. As with still screen captures, the text contained in these files is not in a form that word-processing or qualitative data analysis software can read, scan, and search as text. This suggests that the netnographer will still need to download text in a manner that maintains its readability as a text file.[9]

In order to download text as a text file, the netnographer has several options. The quickest initial way to save these data is to drag the computer mouse over the relevant area of text in the browser, highlight it, and then copy it (the command would be Edit-Copy in the menu or Control-C for those using Windows operating systems). Then, using a word processing program such as Microsoft Word, open a new document, paste the text, and save the file. The file can be saved in native doc file format or as a txt file. The process can also be performed using a browser. In many browsers, such as Firefox, you can save the entire browser view as a txt file. The relevant command is File-Save Page As … from the drop down menu. Another menu will appear, and in this you will choose 'Text Files' from the drop down menu next to 'Save as type …' If you are coding by hand or without the assistance of a software program, then choose the file format you are most comfortable handling. Depending upon which qualitative data analysis program you choose, different file formats may be required – almost all can read txt files.

The problem with this procedure quickly becomes obvious. Although it is targeted and thorough – you are only capturing the data that you identify – data collection quickly becomes tedious and time-consuming. If there are 50 separate postings in a message thread that you wish to capture, this entails a lot of dragging, dropping, copying, and pasting. The alternative is to capture as much of these data as is possible at once. In this case, the netnographer will locate the relevant data and choose 'Select all' from the Edit drop-down menu (on some browsers, this is a Control-A keystroke). A similar procedure of pasting into a document file would follow. However, this method nets significant amounts of extraneous data. The resulting file must be carefully edited in order to be legible to the average reader, although, for coding purposes, these 'messy' textual captures can be sufficient. The extraneous material is simply left uncoded. It does, however, clutter the document and make coding and comprehension considerably more challenging. A good option is to

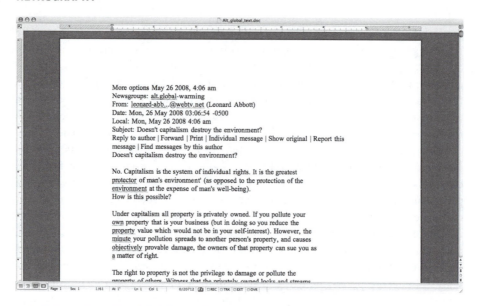

FIGURE 6.3   NEWSGROUP THREAD CAPTURED AS TEXT FILE*

Note: *saved in txt file format and displayed in a Microsoft OS X window

combine both approaches, capturing interesting smaller files using more targeted drag-and-drop techniques as well as selecting large amounts of data and placing them in single files. Unless the netnographer can identify good software solutions that enable one to automate the process of removing extraneous data, she should be prepared to spend considerable time 'cleaning up' these files. Figure 6.3 presents a scan of the alt.global-warming data presented earlier in Figure 6.2 after these had been copied and pasted into a Microsoft Word txt file, and cleaned of extraneous data.

The final option combines the text-readability of the word-processing doc or txt file with some of the on-screen formatting and graphical imagery of the web-page or posting. In this option, you save the messages or information as an html file, or as a complete web-page that is readable by your browser. The relevant command in Firefox to save your information as an html file is File-Save Page As … from the drop down menu. Another menu will appear, and in this you will choose 'HMTL' or 'Web-page, HTML' from the drop down menu next to 'Save as type …' Many qualitative data analysis programs will recognize, read, and search the text from html files. Depending upon how you have configured your browser, the html files may or may not save graphics – usually this will require a special command, such as 'Save as Web-page, Complete' or 'Save Related Graphics Files'. Figure 6.4 presents a scan of the alt.global-warming data presented earlier in Figure 6.2 after these had been saved using Firefox as an HTML web-page.

If visual files are important to your site or to particular types of data that you locate, then your best course of action is to save them as separate graphics files – or image captures. These images can later be incorporated into other files, or included in the overall body of data collected for your netnographic investigation. These various files will constitute your data set for analysis. They can be organized in various

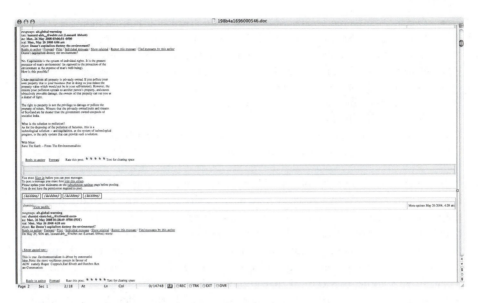

FIGURE 6.4   NEWSGROUP THREAD CAPTURED AS HYPERTEXT FILE*

Note: *saved in html file format and displayed in Firefox browser window

folders, and data can be placed into various tables depending upon the inclination of the netnographer. The tracking of these separate files can become challenging if there are many separate files and the netnographer is not using some automated system to combine or organize them. The basic principles, however, remain constant.

Now that we have learned these practical fundamentals of online data capture and collection, this chapter can proceed to discuss some of the more theoretical issues surrounding the netnographic collection of data.

A BRIEF WORD ABOUT SPAM

Netnographic newcomers are often amazed by the amount of 'spam' or unsolicited bulk messaging that can be found in many sites of online communities, such as newsgroups, forums, and even on wikis, social networking sites, and lists. No treatment of the topic would be complete without at least a mention of this circumstance. Spam, other forms of commercial connection, and the posting of pornographic photographs and links to pornographic sites, are a fact of life in the online world. They are the reality of online existence. Netnographers have at least three choices in the way that they treat spam, and these other difficulties.[10]

- *Option 1: Spam can be ignored.* Treat it like background noise or a minor annoyance. Scan items as you collect your data, but do not save them. Do not bother to mention it in fieldnotes.

- *Option 2: Spam can be accepted as a fact of life.* Treat it as culture members treat it. In most cases this will mean it will be ignored. Occasionally, when an item relates to something relevant to the community or the member, it may be attended to. When attended to, it would be saved in research archives and noted in fieldnotes.
- *Option 3: Spam can be examined.* Under some conditions, the spam might be a central topic for the community, or relate to a central theoretical area of netnographic study. In this eventuality, the spam would be read, coded, commented upon in fieldnotes, and later analysed. An example might be a study that focused on spam messages, or that focused upon community reactions to spam messages.

In general, most netnographers will find themselves taking option number 1 and ignoring the spam. Netnographers may have to shy away from communities where the spam-to-user-content ratio is too high, and where cultural communications are being choked out by commercial incursions. However, do not be too quick to jump to this conclusion. Vibrant, important online communities have coped and even thrived in spite of intense barrages of spam, and are likely to continue to do so for some time to come. It is critical that netnographers have an initial strategy guiding them in the way they treat spam messages, which they develop and adapt as needed during the progress of their investigation. Spam is important because, although it appears in almost every type of online community, it cannot be considered the same as culture members' interactions with one another, and cannot be collected and analysed as the same type of online community data.

ARCHIVAL NETNOGRAPHIC DATA

In this section, we will learn about the nature and treatment of archival cultural data. Netnographic data are different in several different ways from ethnographic data, in addition to the widespread presence of spam discussed above. One of the peculiarities is that these frequently involve large amounts of a type of conversational cultural data collected from archives. These data are unaffected by the actions of the netnographer. Archival cultural data provide what amounts to a cultural baseline. Saved communal interactions provide the netnographer with a convenient bank of observational data that may stretch back for years or, in some cases, well over a decade. Netnographers benefit from the prior transcription of posted text, images, and other messages. Collecting and analysing these archival data is an excellent supplement to cultural participation. These can be used analogously to the way that archival and historical data are used in ethnographies to extend and deepen the knowledge of the cultural context.

With the addition of vastly lower search costs than face-to-face ethnography, particularly when there are prevalent communities pertaining to one's research topic, observational data are plentiful and easy to obtain. Thus, dealing with instantaneous information overload is an important netnographic problem. It often means that the netnographer needs to be more judicious than traditional ethnographers about how the online fieldsite is defined, what data are saved, how data are sorted and presorted during collection, what data will not be included in the analysis, and what analytic tools and techniques will be brought to bear. Just as an entrée needs to be planned carefully, so also do strategies of data collection. Under these conditions, the netnographer's choices about which data to save and which communal paths to pursue become important.

The following general instruction may be helpful.

- Areas with significant data should be examined first for relevant areas of interest, and mainly those areas of interest downloaded or saved.
- Areas with smaller amounts of data may be saved or automatically archived in their entirety.
- Definitions of fieldsite and boundaries should be revisited in the early stages and related to data collection strategies.
- Data should be sorted into preliminary categories as they are initially read, and then re-sorted.
- Researchers using pen-and-paper or hermeneutic interpretation techniques should download judiciously, and focus on collecting smaller sets of data.
- Researchers using computer-assisted qualitative data analysis can download more prolific quantities of data, and focus on collecting larger sets of data.
- Data mining software should be used carefully, as it can obscure the cultural experience of netnography.

Because netnographers can anticipate large amounts of data, categories for interpretation emerge from the ground up, and research questions and foci shift during fieldwork. It is thus best to categorize and continually sort and re-sort the data as these are collected. This entails continuing to make new files and reclassifying the documents and other materials that exist saved in older files. Having macro datasets grouped into smaller sets can be helpful. As the researcher begins locating relevant themes or classification, this can guide the sub-grouping of the data collected. Specific folders and sub-folders can be used to classify particular observations, threads, postings, websites, or other data.

Data collection challenges the classifier, the librarian, and the order-seeker in all of us. David Weinberger (2007) has written an excellent book about the new classificatory possibilities emerging through the Internet as the collective intelligence of communities endlessly transforms disorder or 'the miscellaneous', as he calls it, into different forms of orderliness. The tagging, naming, sorting, and classification of digitally stored data that increasingly transpire, and even define, communal activities online are analogous to the coding and classifying analytic work of the ethnographer or netnographer. Netnographers have much to learn from these groups, their activities, and their tools. Tagging and sorting is a powerful skill for netnographers to practise and build, and may even be developed in concert with collective intelligence enabling 'Web 2.0' technologies, such as Wikipedia. The better you can get at organizing data as you collect them, the more methodical and systematic about data collection that you can become, then the better a netnographer you will be.

Non-Textual Cultural Data

It is also important to accustom yourself to the kinds of data that you will be selecting and saving, since you cannot save all of these. Remember that not all important information is carried in letters and numbers. Do not neglect visual and graphical data. Pay attention to background colours and font styles, as well as more overt graphical representations like drawings, emoticons, and photographs. Annette Markham suggests that participants' postings should be captured exactly as they appear on screen, in the original font, without any corrections of spelling, grammar, or punctuation. 'We literally reconfigure these people when we edit their sentences, because for many of them, these messages are a deliberate presentation of self' (Markham 2004, p. 153). Most blogs, forums, and bulletin boards automatically reformat messages into similar fonts. Where messages have divergent and significant styles, saving them as a screen capture may be warranted, as those visual data may be useful in the analysis stage. In general, however, saving text files in a basic text or html format will serve your research purposes well.

Visual data often convey information and emotional content elided by purely textual and even audio formats. Audio and audiovisual formats are increasingly common. If newsgroup members are repeatedly discussing or linking to certain YouTube videos then you should watch those videos. If they reveal interesting facets of the culture that you wish to pursue, you must save them for later analysis. Any type of expression that is relevant to community members – be it audiovisual, graphical, audio, photographic, or textual – is relevant to your analysis. As specified above, it should be saved in files, classified and sorted into folders and sub-folders as data.

ELICITED NETNOGRAPHIC DATA

In this section, we consider the elicitation of netnographic data, and how to handle it. There are many ways to elicit netnographic data, but these approaches can be classified into two basic strategies: communal interaction and interview. These two basic strategies can be mixed and matched in many different ways to produce a variety of interesting levels of engagement and community member insights.

My thesis research began with observations of bulletin boards such as rec.arts.tv. startrek. After a short time, however, it became obvious that a deeper engagement with the community was desirable. Not wanting to over-extend the hospitality of the bulletin boards, I initiated an online data collection strategy. In 1995, when *Star Trek: the Next Generation* was at its peak of popularity, I taught myself HTML programming. With this skill, I created, and then posted 'The *Star Trek* Research Web-page'. The web-page introduced me and my research to other fans, talking truthfully about my status as well as providing disclosure about my university affiliation and dissertation project (see Figure 6.5).

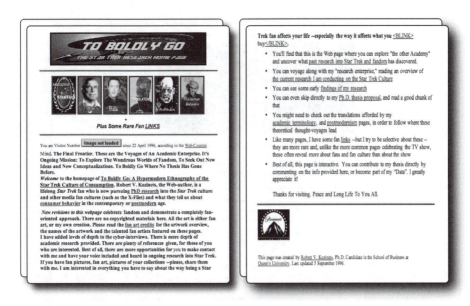

FIGURE 6.5   EXAMPLE OF RESEARCH WEB-PAGE

As a type of 'offering' to the wider *Star Trek* community, I provided a regular language review of extant research about *Star Trek*, the text, and its fan community. In the current Internet environment, a blog, an informative island in Second Life or another virtual world, or even a group on a social networking site would work equally well. The *Star Trek* Research Web-page reviewed scholarly work by people like Constance Penley, Henry Jenkins, and Camille Bacon-Smith. It contained pages of links to other *Star Trek*-related resources on the Internet. It was somewhat playful in its use of *Star Trek* fonts and graphics. In addition it contained a page that asked fans to answer a series of detailed questions. I positioned these questions as a 'cyber-interview' (see Figure 6.6).

The initiative was rewarding. Over the 20 months of fieldwork, the research web-page garnered e-mails from over 60 culture members in more then 20 different countries. It led to two research participants who could be categorized as assuming the role of 'key informants'. It also led me to Henry Jenkins, the famous MIT media scholar, who reached out to me through the web-page. Based on that initial contact, Professor Jenkins became a member of my dissertation committee and has continued to be a mentor and colleague ever since. Similar web-page strategies have been used successfully by a number of scholars, including Marie-Agnes Parmentier, a marketing scholar who studied with me. After experimenting with the blog format, Marie-Agnes eventually settled upon a research web-page for her dissertation research studying the online fan communities of *America's Next Top Model* (Parmentier 2009).

The key to this 'offering' strategy is that it offers actual content and communal connection before requesting cultural participation in the form of an interview.

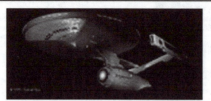

NEW AND IMPROVED CYBER-INTERVIEW!

It's Fun, It's Free and You Have A Chance To Include Your Voice In Star Trek Research!

My thesis research will be published as a dissertation available in its entirety from UMI university publishers. I will be adapting one or more articles from it for publication in top journals. It may even have a future beyond that if there is interest in publishing it as book chapters, or even as a book.

Here is **YOUR CHANCE** to be included, to let your voice ring out, to speak for yourself and for other Internet-using Star Trek fans. Be heard. Be famous. Let me know what you think.

Remember also that all your responses will be kept *strictly anonymous*. No one will ever be able to link you to what you said. But, if you'd like, I'd be happy to acknowledge you personally in the acknowledgements. I am also looking for your comments on the themes and ideas emerging in my research. If I'm wrong, please tell me, and I'll try to get it right.

I would greatly appreciate it if you'd take a few minutes to answer a few exploratory questions regarding Star Trek culture and what it means to you. Particularly in terms of how you buy things, and what kinds of things you buy. Thanks very much. I really appreciate it! And a great big THANK YOU to everyone who has answered so far. Many of you have become friends, co-researchers, and correspondents. This Web page is already a huge research success, with over a hundred cyber-interview already collected --thanks to all of you! But, like the Borg, I'm trying to be inclusive. I need to hear from everyone, to give everyone a chance to speak their mind and their opinions.

<BLINK>The Cyber-Interview</BLINK>

Please think about some or all of the following questions:

- ARE YOU A TREKKER? Do you identify yourself as a Star Trek fan, or even as a "Trekker"? Why? What does it mean to be a Star Trek fan, or Trekker? What

FIGURE 6.6   EXAMPLE OF ONLINE INTERVIEW REQUEST FROM RESEARCH WEB-PAGE

There are obviously many other ways to approach the community in search of research participation. In the previous chapter on making a cultural entrée we used as examples a number of good and not-so-good approaches. Posting insightful, relevant, timely, interesting, noteworthy questions to a particular, properly-targeted forum, or directly e-mailing very polite entreaties to particular people (such as bloggers) can offer a good foundation that a skilled interviewer can build upon. Good questions posted to a forum or newsgroup, on a blog, or on your own web-page can also yield excellent answers.

As with all interviews and survey research, having a clearly-worded question is important. Feedback that you receive through the early answers to your question can help you revise the questions later for added clarity (consistency in questions is not as important in depth interviews as it is in survey research). Respect the norms of the online community. Avoid inappropriate questions. Avoid going 'off topic'. Do not try to force community members to reveal sensitive information about themselves that they would not want exposed to the wider community, such as discussing dissent or other members in the public spaces of forums or boards. Do not repeat past research questions that have been posted by other researchers. In short, make your questions look as much as possible like the postings of other culture members, while being open about and true to the fact that you are conducting netnographic research.

Answers to postings become opportunities to continue the conversation. And this is the model you should adopt: *this is a conversation, not an interrogation*. You are the neophyte in the culture. You are here to learn from them.

In your communication, there should be genuine self-disclosure as well as the opportunity for others to disclose – there may even be genuine self-discovery. Contact with an online community can confer fulfilling benefits of meaningful knowledge and connection. Do not shy away from them. Reciprocate and give as well as take. Interact genuinely and respectfully. Do not act or conduct one-off, snatch-and-grab research. Treat community membership like a delicate relationship, a privilege, and not a right automatically granted to students or researchers.

A researcher becoming a member of an online community may have much to offer that community. We can provide research, connections, and perspectives that can help give culture members a sense of their own uniqueness. For example, the *Star Trek* Research Web-page allowed culture members to see how they had already been portrayed in academic research. The netnographer can become the 'go-to person' that participants come to depend upon for new insights and perspectives drawing from research and academic thought. They can provide a service, play an ongoing communal role. This requires the researcher to take the obligations and responsibilities of culture membership seriously.

Although this chapter separates online community interactions from online interviews, both means of eliciting data are in practice interconnected. For example, let us say you post a message online, then receive a reply on the forum to which you offer additional questions which are then answered, all on the forum. Is this an online interaction or an informal interview? What about a formally scheduled online interview in which you hold a discussion that you later continue in a public forum of the online community because it may be of wider interest? These categories of online and off-line, interview, observation, and participation are semi-permeable, at best. In research on consumer activism, I met people through interacting on online newsgroups whom I later interviewed over the telephone, then heard from again via e-mail weeks and even months later. Because interviews are such an important aspect of netnographic research, the next section of this chapter offers some guidelines and thoughts about this element of the approach.

NETNOGRAPHIC INTERVIEWS

You will learn about netnographic interviews, their conduct and their use, in this section. The interview's fraternal twin, conversation, permeates the online world. The worlds of forums and newsgroups, chat-rooms and virtual spaces, are already filled with the interpersonal dialogue of Q&A, the getting-to-know-you of social intercourse. Cultural participants expound and explore. They share their personal histories, spread rumours, and relate anecdotes. Collecting and decoding these free-form, free-wheeling conversations is a way of using archival data sources for netnography. The online interview is a more proactive venture.

The online interview is in many ways closely related to the online survey. Think of an open-ended survey conducted through some synchronous online medium, such as a chat window or room, or even an audiovisual program like Microsoft's NetMeeting or Apple's iChat. There is even an 'automated' interview software program called 'SelectPro' that enables researchers to conduct a fully automated interview to screen potential interviewees before actually interviewing them. The depth interview is a bit like a survey with far fewer questions and much more interaction, probing, and openness to the participant's unique perspective and input.

There are options and choices for the conduct of netnographic interviews. The advice in this chapter will help you to understand and make your decision among them. As with the in-person interview, the interview can be group-based or individual, formal or informal, structured or unstructured. You also have your choice of multiple formats to conduct the interview. A research web-page or blog can be used to reach out to potential participants. Other possible forums that might lend themselves to online interviewing would be social networking sites, chat-rooms and areas, and virtual worlds. With a 'blended' ethnography/netnography, you may even choose between online and face-to-face interviews, or combine them in various proportions. Because face-to-face and telephone-mediated interviewing is well-established, and there are many excellent books to guide the researcher in this area, this book will not offer much instruction about this approach. However, there most certainly is a place for the face-to-face interview within netnography. For example, a face-to-face or telephone interview with a few natural health bloggers may nuance and enhance a study of their social world by revealing aspects of it that are not captured in their blog texts alone.

Online interviewing has much in common with interviewing in general. It involves formally approaching a participant, suggesting an interview, and conducting a conversation from the frame of an interview, where the researcher's role is primarily that of the asker of questions (see Gubrium and Holstein 2001). The 'long' or 'depth' interview approach described by Grant McCracken (1988) is the preferred technique. This approach to interviewing requires the investment of considerable time and thus makes some real demands upon your interview participant. It also requires honed researcher acuity, a skill that requires some practice to develop. It begins with a series of grand tour questions that help to place your interviewee in their social and cultural milieu, and then narrows down to concerns more focal to the research. As with in-person interviews, the calibre of the questions and the nature of the interaction will determine the quality of the participant's response. Throughout the depth interview, the interviewer is probing and asking clarifying questions, building rapport, hoping for genuine disclosure, and staying open to interesting segues and elaborations.

Conducting an interview through your computer means that your communications are going to be shaped by the medium you use. Adaptation means that cultural communications are already adapted to particular online media. Adaptation and accessibility facilitate the sharing of documents or photographic images. Archiving entails that the interview can be automatically transcribed and saved. This means that the researcher can be freed from routine note-taking or transcription concerns to concentrate fully upon the body of the interview. However, this requires paying attention to data capture, as noted in the sections above. E-mail interviews can and should be saved in separate text files, and backed up for security on media such as flash drives. Chat interviews should be captured using one of the automated software programs, or with continual screen captures.

Anonymity also comes into play. Annette Markham (1998, pp. 62–75) offers some useful insights about conducting online interviews. The two chief differences that she elaborates are that 'online I see only the text – not the nonverbals, the paralanguage, the general mannerisms or demeanor of the participant' and 'because writing takes much longer than talking, being a good interviewer means being patient' (1998, p. 70). The following are five other ways to think about anonymity as you collect data, particularly in one-on-one personal online interviews. First, online identity is interlinked to other identifiers and therefore subject to increasing levels of accessibility. As many aspects of the Internet as social space are now interconnected, you can often link to people's MySpace and Facebook pages, YouTube postings, or Flickr albums that can give you some serious clues as to who you are talking to (but are never definitive). Secondly, identity can be formally verified. Just like an online dater, the researcher can use identity verification programs like Verisign and Veridate which charge a fee to validate or verify a person's identity. Third, communications can be chosen that reveal identifiers. The nature of online communications has changed a lot. Using Skype or a similar medium for an online interview can mean that you have a face-to-face link with someone. In many circumstances, this can be almost as good as an in-person interview for reading and recording social cues such as body language, and for getting the same general sense of gender, age, and ethnic disposition as you would in a face-to-face interview. Even a telephone call can disclose something different than a page of text, revealing, for example, accents, pauses, and so on. Fourth, you can ask your participants to identify themselves. Usually this means some sort of other commitment, such as offering financial remuneration: 'Provide your name and some basic demographic information for me before we conduct the interview and I will send your cheque to the address and name provided'. A tactic such as this one is going to need to be performed ethically, using established and approved informed consent protocols. Fifth, you can and should use analytic strategies that will give you sound results even in the absence of identifying information. We will discuss these strategies in the next chapter, where we detail data interpretation and analysis.

Matching the Interview to the Medium

Depending on your research focus, you may not need the sort of detailed understanding you can gain from long or depth interviews. Long interviews might also be difficult to obtain in certain sites, such as social networking sites or virtual worlds, where culture members are too busy to stop for the one to two hours that are required. As with in-person ethnography, a simple in situ conversation, or a quick exchange of information might suffice to inform your research question and focus.

Particular interview styles and desired outcomes also fit certain online community types better than others. The synchronous, real-time, abbreviated and superficial interaction of the chat-room – with its conversational tone and its unfettered nature – may be more suited to the informal interview that hopes for a quick insight through heat-of-the-moment disclosure. As anyone familiar with the medium can attest, the current text-based chat, as available in IM, Facebook, or MSN Messenger, provides a different conversational experience. It is linguistically distinct, abrupt, and less like conventional conversation or written text than an e-mail or a newsgroup posting. Over time, the chat style of text can offer some insights, but these insights may look less like the familiar textual verbatims that researchers are used to seeing (see, e.g., Cherny 1999; Giesler 2006; Markham 1998). Netnographers who use chat interviews will need to gain skills at extensively decoding this unique communicational style. Shoham (2004) conducted a study of Israeli chat-rooms for people in their 40s and 50s. He began with silent or passive observation of chat exchanges and then began to partake in chat exchanges and to conduct one-to-one virtual talks with chatters. In his research, he asserted that chat conversations enabled a newfound sense of community as well as providing a refreshing forum for a type of interactive expression that was freer and more flowing (for interesting theoretical conclusions on Napster and peer-to-peer systems as gift economies, see Giesler 2006).

In a predominantly visual or audiovisual community, such as on DeviantArt, Flickr, or YouTube, you may want to use the exchange of visual or even audiovisual information. Throughout all interaction forms, visual or graphical exchanges can offer participants a type of projective that reaches them on more of the tacit and unspoken level of understanding. Receiving and decoding such non-textual information can enable participants to access and express knowledge and feelings that are difficult to articulate verbally.

E-mail Interviews

Long-term interactions through e-mail offer a foundation of carefully considered answers often more appropriate to the aims of a formal interview. 'Persistent conversation' in any medium of online communication can lead to revelatory personal and emotional discovery (Chenault 1998). Because of the amount of time required, it can be difficult to get the requisite level of commitment and engagement in a chat-room or through a set of social networking site postings. E-mail conveys a sense of intimacy. However, it draws out the time necessary to establish rapport. Arguably, this amount of time also deepens and ripens the relationship. Coupled with researcher genuineness, trust-building and heartfelt confession, e-mail interviews – which can combine pen pal-like sociality with ongoing mentor–newbie tutelage – can provide interesting disclosure and enlightenment.

NETNOGRAPHIC FIELDNOTE DATA

Keeping Reflective and Observational Fieldnotes

This section provides guidance about the capture and treatment of the final type of netnographic data: fieldnotes. Netnography, like ethnography, involves the inscription of the experience of researcher participation. However, in netnography the nature of the fieldsite and the nature of participation change. This book presents netnography rather unproblematically. Yet, as the earlier methodological discussion touched upon, the traditional model of 'authentic' ethnography 'implies a process of face to face interaction leading to transcription and writing of notes, then upon return to the home territory, writing of the ethnography' (Beaulieu 2004, p. 154; see also Lyman and Wakeford 1999, pp. 361–63).

Thus, when the fieldsite is totally available in terms of access, it seems that there is no actual field.

> You do not go to [your Internet fieldsite]: you log in from where you physically happen to be. In doing this you are not making a visit in the usual sense; you are executing an electronically mediated speech act that provides access – an 'open sesame'. (Mitchell 1996, pp. 8–9)

For the ethnographer, this could be seen as a major problem. 'In a universe in which everything (and everybody) is produced and mediated by text, the [computers' memory] is the ultimate field recorder. Nothing escapes the panoptic gaze' (Stone 1995, p. 243). Schaap (2002, p. 30) presents his netnographic fieldsite, a MUD, as 'a whole world' that 'is literally a text, or better, "textual"'. In this case, where the online culture has already fully presented itself as text, telling its own story, what can be the contribution of the ethnographer?

Beaulieu (2004, p. 155) sums up the problem nicely: 'If access and transcriptions are no longer unique things that the ethnographer has to offer, what then is the contribution?' The answer is that netnography contributes by adding valuable interpretive insight, by building, through careful focus and analysis, what is available publicly on the Internet into a known and respected body of codified knowledge.

The answer to this query about contribution thus lies in our conceptualization of the actual 'field'. What we are studying are not texts online, but peoples' interactions through various technologically-mediated means. Ethnographers do not merely study the movements of bodies and vibrations in air – they study the meanings of acts and utterances. As Beaulieu (2004, p. 155) intimates when she sees Schaap's

(2002) anxious stance 'as a fetishization of the community as its own text', the online community may manifest through textual means, but it most definitively is not merely its texts. Access also is not so straightforward. If genuine participation as a culture member is held to be decisive, then mere access to online text is as material to netnographic understanding as the ownership of a set of encyclopedias is to the possession of encyclopedic knowledge.

Crucial to the consideration of netnographic expertise is the awareness that what becomes treated as 'data' or 'findings' is inseparable from the process of observation (Emerson et al. 1995, p. 11). In this combined process of acculturation and data collection, the keeping of fieldnotes can serve the critical function of recording and reflecting the all-important changes that occur outside the realm of the online text.

Because many netnographic observations of interactions are already in the process automatically transcribed, reflective fieldnotes become far more salient than observational fieldnotes in netnography. In reflective fieldnotes, netnographers record their own observations regarding subtexts, pretexts, contingencies, conditions and personal emotions occurring during their time online, and relating to their online experiences. Through these written reflections, the netnographer records her journey from outsider to insider, her learning of languages, rituals, and practices, as well as her involvement in a social web of meanings and personalities. These fieldnotes often provide key insights into what the online culture is and what it does. They are very useful to turn to in data analysis when asking why a particular graphic, photograph, message or posting was made by a particular person at a particular time. They help the netnographer decipher the reasons behind cultural actions, rather than offer the more typical recording or description of them.

It is also valuable to record observational fieldnotes written in the margins of downloaded data, elaborating upon subtleties noticed at the time but which are not captured in the text or data itself. These fieldnotes offer details about the social and interactional processes that make up the members of online cultures and communities' everyday lives and activities. It is best to capture them contemporaneously with the experience of those social interactions. Writing fieldnotes contemporaneously with interactive online social experiences is important because these processes of learning, socialization, and acculturation are subtle and our recollection of them becomes rapidly diluted over time.

Although the very visual nature of our online community experience may mislead us into thinking otherwise, social interaction online is not so much an event as a process. The unfolding of this process often contains much that is of interest to us as scholars. Initial impressions of communities, web-pages, and members' postings are important, as are key events or incidents. Record those impressions in your fieldnotes. Then contemplate your feelings. Use that contemplation to increase your sensitivity to the experiences of other culture members. If you feel shocked at a particularly questionable posting, do others feel this way as well? The entire process of reaction and observation is contextual. 'The ethnographer is concerned not with members' indigenous meanings simply as static categories but with how members of settings invoke those meanings in specific relations and interactions' (Emerson et al. 1995, p. 28). Because the when, where, and who questions of context are usually automatically recorded in netnographic work, what is even more important to capture in your fieldnotes is your own subjective impressions and expectations about the all-important why questions as they arise.

Netnography does not stop at the computer screen. My netnography of online coffee culture transformed the way that I consume coffee and serve coffee to others, and has had a permanent effect on the way that I relate to other coffee drinkers and the ways that they relate to me. During that netnography, I kept observational fieldnotes about my changing coffee habits, about conversations and meals at friends' and family's homes, about my shopping ventures, about my trips to Starbucks, to Peet's, and to local coffee houses. Even though I was interested in – and ended up writing almost exclusively about – the online community, I captured considerable data about the effect that the community had on my entire social experience, my relationships in person, with friends, with family, with my own tastebuds. The netnography was intended to capture the totality of my experience as an online community member. That meant that every aspect of my life affected by the meanings and social connections arising from my online community membership was relevant – indeed, I would suggest necessary – material for my reflective fieldnotes.

As you inscribe these observational fieldnotes of your lived cultural experience as a culture member, write as descriptively as possible:

> description calls for concrete details rather than abstract generalizations, for sensory imagery rather than evaluative labels, and for immediacy through details presented at close range. [Sociologist ethnographer Erving] Goffman (1989, p. 131) advises the fieldworker to write 'lushly,' making frequent use of adjectives and adverbs to convey details. (Emerson et al. 1995, p. 69)

In a netnography, these descriptions will be a combination of what is seen on the screen and what is experienced by the researcher. Although many of the on-screen manifestations of the 'events' that transpire through online interaction can be captured through screen captures and data downloads, what your fieldnotes should strive to capture are your own impressions as a culture and community member, the subjective meanings of interactions and events as they unfold over time. No memory stick, no screen capture software, can substitute for the finely tuned research instrument that is the mindful netnographer.

Accounting for Data

During data collection, some netnographers may wish to keep close count of the exact number of messages and web-pages read. Some reviewers and editors in my field request this sort of accounting. These encounters have resulted in actuarial passages such as the following:

> The volume of downloaded text amounted to 560 double-spaced, ten-point type size pages, which represents 432 postings containing 131 distinct e-mail addresses and user names (likely related to the number of distinct message posters). There

were 76 unique message-poster identifiers within the downloaded New Beetle messages and 55 unique poster identifiers included with the downloaded Star Wars messages. (Brown et al. 2003, p. 22).

In practice, this is a rather cumbersome set of measurements to make. How many distinct participants were involved? How many ongoing conversations were held? How many message threads were read over the period of immersion, and how many distinct user names do they represent? Answering these questions can require some impressive bookkeeping.

Somewhat easier to find and report on are public statistics about the number of members, number of visitors, and age of some online communities. It is important to realize – and to remind commenters and reviewers at times – that the strength of netnography is its particularistic ties to specific online consumer groups and the revelatory depth of their online communications. As with an ethnography, a netnography in the end must be able to describe and evoke a social world and the people who are members of it. Hence, interesting and useful conclusions could conceivably be drawn from a relatively small number of texts, if the researcher was a deep participant in the online community and/or community online, and if these messages contain sufficient descriptive richness and are interpreted with compelling analytic depth and insight.

As with the 'saturation' principle of grounded theory (Glaser and Strauss 1967; see also Fetterman 1998), data collection should continue as long as the investigation is still generating new insights on theoretically important topical areas. Data collection does not occur in isolation from data analysis. Data are endlessly converted and sorted as they are recorded. Data collection, as we have learned in this chapter, has pivotal implications for data analysis.

SUMMARY

Netnographic data collection is interconnected with participative online interaction and with ongoing data analysis, which is the topic of the next chapter. In this chapter, we learnt how characteristics of the data set, such as size, level of detail, and the presence of graphics and images, will drive data collection and data analysis. In general, netnographers must decide between saving data as text-readable files or as captured screen images. Engagement through communal interactions and interviews are the two basic approaches to the elicitation of netnographic data. Careful, reflective fieldnotes where netnographers record their own online experiences are also salient and important. In addition, the existence of spam is part of the reality of online fieldwork.

KEY READINGS

Chenault, Brittney G. (1998) 'Developing Personal and Emotional Relationships Via Computer-Mediated Communication', *CMC Magazine*, May, available online at: www.december.com/cmc/mag/1998/may/chenault.html

Emerson, Robert M., Rachel I. Fretz, and Linda L. Shaw (1995) *Writing Ethnographic Fieldnotes*. Chicago: University of Chicago Press.

Gubrium, Jaber F. and James A. Holstein (eds) (2001) *Handbook of Interview Research: Context and Method*. Thousand Oaks, CA: Sage.

Weinberger, David (2007) *Everything is Miscellaneous: The Power of the New Digital Disorder*. New York: Times Books.

7
DATA ANALYSIS

ABSTRACT

This chapter explains and illustrates two types of data analysis in netnography: analytical coding-based methods and hermeneutic interpretation. Guidelines for choosing and using a qualitative data analysis software package are also provided, along with general principles for the use of computers in data analysis. The final section presents interpretive strategies for dealing with the unique challenges of netnographic data.

> **Key Words:** CAQDAS, categorization, coding, grounded theory, hermeneutic interpretation, induction, interpretation, qualitative data analysis

ANALYSING AND INTERPRETING QUALITATIVE DATA: A BRIEF OVERVIEW

In this section, you will learn the basics of qualitative data analysis and induction. Netnography involves an inductive approach to the analysis of qualitative data. Analysis means the detailed examination of a whole by breaking it into its constituent parts and comparing them in different ways. Generally speaking, data analysis encompasses the entire process of turning the collected products of netnographic participation and observation – the various downloaded textual and graphical files, the screen captures, the online interview transcripts, the reflective fieldnotes – into a finished research representation, be it an article, a book, a presentation, or a report. As the metaphor frequently taught in graduate seminars holds, data are like a mineral raw material, close to the sensory level of experience and observation, which must be mined. In the ideal, with the intellectual fire of analysis and interpretation, 'raw' data become processed and refined, their essence extracted. They can then be cast into a theoretical form that brings us new understanding. In this chapter, you will learn about this refinement process.

Induction is a form of logical reasoning in which individual observations are built up in order to make more general statements about a phenomenon. Inductive data analysis is a way to manipulate the whole body of recorded information that you have collected over the course of your netnography. According to qualitative research scholars Matthew Miles and Michael Huberman (1994, p. 9) there are some qualitative data analytic processes that are generally common. These 'analytic moves arranged in sequence', named, and adapted to the needs of netnographers, are as follows:

- *Coding*: affixing codes or categories to data drawn from field notes, interviews, documents, or, in the case of netnographic data, other cultural material such as newsgroup or blog postings, Facebook wall scrawls or Twitter tweets, photographs, videos, and so on, drawn from online sources; during coding, codes, classifications, names, or labels are assigned to particular units of data; these codes label the data as belonging to or being an example of some more general phenomenon; categories for coding usually emerge inductively through a close reading of the data, rather than being imposed by prescribed categories.
- *Noting*: reflections on the data or other remarks are noted in the margins of the data; this form of annotation is also commonly known as 'memoing'.
- *Abstracting and Comparing*: the materials are sorted and sifted to identify similar phrases, shared sequences, relationships, and distinct differences; this abstracting process builds the categorized codes into higher-order, or more general, conceptual constructs, patterns or processes; comparing looks at the similarities and differences across data incidents.
- *Checking and Refinement*: returns to the field for the next wave of data collection in order to isolate, check, and refine the understanding of the patterns, processes, commonalities, and differences.
- *Generalizing*: elaborates a small set of generalizations that cover or explain the consistencies in the dataset.
- *Theorizing*: confronting the generalizations gathered from the data with a formalized body of knowledge that uses construct or theories; constructing new theory in close coordination both with the analysis of data as well as the existing relevant body of knowledge.

In the grounded theory framework presented by Strauss and Corbin (1990), two operations are useful for integrating the categories and constructs that have been defined and refined by the analyst during the act of coding. Selective coding increasingly moves constructs to higher and higher levels of abstraction, laddering them upwards and then specifying the relationships that link them together. Axial coding integrates coded data into theory by noting the contexts, conditions, strategies, and outcomes that tend to cluster together.

There are also more holistic ways to analyse data. Miles and Huberman (1994, pp. 8–9) suggest that there are at least three different approaches to qualitative data analysis, which they term interpretivism, social anthropology, and collaborative social research. Although social anthropologists might be in a 'quest for lawful relationships', others might be engaged in 'the search for "essences" that may not transcend individuals, and lend themselves to multiple compelling interpretations' (Miles and Huberman 1994, p. 9).

Consumer researcher Susan Spiggle (1994, p. 497) looks at the latter process as interpretation, suggesting that, 'In interpretation the investigator does not engage a set of operations. Rather, interpretation occurs as a gestalt shift and represents a synthetic, holistic, and illuminating grasp of meaning, as in deciphering a code'. Viewed in this way, data analysis becomes an act of code switching, of translation, of metaphor and trope (see Lakoff and Johnson 1980). As Thompson, Pollio, and Locander (1994, p. 433) note, the idea of hermeneutics, and especially the hermeneutic circle, has been considered 'a methodological process for interpreting qualitative data'. The process is

> an iterative one in which a 'part' of the qualitative data (or text) is interpreted and reinterpreted in relation to the developing sense of the 'whole.' These iterations are necessary because a holistic understanding must be developed over time. Furthermore, initial understandings of the text are informed and often modified as later readings provide a more developed sense of the text's meaning as a whole. (Thompson et al. 1994, p. 433).

Arnold and Fischer develop this fractal notion of the interrelation of the meaning of individual textual elements and of the global whole:

> the meaning of a whole text is determined from the individual elements of the text, while, at the same time, the individual element is understood by referring to the whole of which it is a part . . . Specific elements are examined again and again, each time with a slightly different conception of the global whole. Gradually, an ever more integrated and comprehensive account of the specific elements, as well as of the text as a whole, emerges. (1994, p. 63)

When constructing a hermeneutic interpretation, you should seek interpretations that are: 'coherent and free of contradiction', 'comprehensible' to the intended reading audience, 'supported with relevant examples', clearly related to 'relevant literature', 'enlightening' and '"fruitful"' in revealing new dimensions of the problem at hand' and yielding 'insights' that explicitly revise our current understanding, and that are also written in a prose style that is 'persuasive, engaging, interesting, stimulating, and appealing' and which uses allusions, metaphors, similes, and analogies (Arnold and Fischer 1994, p. 64). Thompson et al. (1994) further note that a good hermeneutic interpretation will delve into the social and historical contexts of the data for its explanations, providing a subtle, specific, nuanced cultural interpretation.

These two different analytic processes – analytic coding and hermeneutic interpretation – overlap in many interesting ways. Each must, in its own way, break down the text and then reassemble it as a new interpretation. As Miles and Huberman (1994) note, particular fields and scholarly traditions emphasize one form of analysis more than the other. However, in practice, the skilled netnographer

Google Groups

alt.coffee

Message from discussion Technique - the ████ (inni) method

View parsed - Show only message text

```
Path: archiver1.google.com!news2.google.com!news.maxwell.syr.edu!wn14feed!wn13feed!worldnet.at
From:
Newsgroups: alt.coffee
Subject: Technique - the  ███ (inni) method
Lines: 24
X-Priority: 3
X-MSMail-Priority: Normal
X-Newsreader: Microsoft Outlook Express 6.00.2800.1158
X-MimeOLE: Produced By Microsoft MimeOLE V6.00.2800.1165
Message-ID: <Ksgmb.19467$e01.:            >
NNTP-Posting-Host: 12.217.131.25
X-Complaints-To: abuse@mchsi.com
X-Trace: attbi_s02 1067               (Fri, 24 Oct 2003 21:03:38 GMT)
NNTP-Posting-Date: Fri, 24 Oct 2003 21:03:38 GMT
Organization: MediaCom High Speed Internet
Date: Fri, 24 Oct 2003 21:03:38 GMT

I realize part of the results may be due to my experience in pulling shots
or fluke of nature or or or...
I am using a Gaggia Espresso, a super Jolly Grinder, Panamanian Baru Green
roasted in Franken roaster
Anyway I read  ███████ s opinion of trying a low to no tamp, adjusting the
flow rate by a finer grind.
It does work, a nice tiger fleck crema (fairly thick) consistent shot time
(in the 20's)  good to excellent taste.
So as most things espresso are Italian I am dubbing this the  ███ (inni)
method....


--
The posting email address is not read or received
to contact me email me
```

FIGURE 7.1   ALT.COFFEE NEWSGROUP POSTING

Note: displayed (with alterations marked in blacked out and whited-out spaces) in original posting format

will use both of these methods. In the next section, we will apply these principles with a short, hands-on experience at using these methods to analyse netnographic data.

DATA ANALYSIS: A NETNOGRAPHIC EXAMPLE

We will continue learning about qualitative data analysis by applying the techniques of coding analysis and hermeneutics to a very small set of data – 112 words, to be precise. Consider first a single message posting, perhaps our introduction to a new online community and its culture. I show the message in its native format in Figure 7.1.

For ease of readability, I reproduce the entry here in text form, with a lot of the extraneous text removed, just as we explained in Chapter 6.[11]

BOX 7.1   DATA FOR DATA ANALYSIS EXAMPLE

Newsgroup: alt.coffee
From: '[Frank Rinetti]'
Date: Fri, Oct 24 2003 5:03 pm
Subject: Technique – the [Smith] (inni) method

'I realize part of the results may be due to my experience in pulling shots or fluke of nature or or or ... I am using a Gaggia Espresso, a super Jolly Grinder, Panamanian Baru Green roasted in Franken roaster. Anyway I read [John Smith]'s opinion of trying a low to no tamp, adjusting the flow rate by a finer grind. It does work, a nice tiger fleck crema (fairly thick) consistent shot time (in the 20's) good to excellent taste. So as most things espresso are Italian I am dubbing this the [Smith](inni) method ...'

We can use this as an exercise, a warm-up for your own analysis. It should not take you more than 10–20 minutes. So go get your pen or your keyboard ready, and then carefully read through that single posting a few times. First, try analytic coding on the entry. Follow the directions above. Now, code it, right on this page in the book. Assign your own labels and names to what you find to be interesting. See if you can locate a pattern in the data. Write yourself little notes on what you find. Abstract elements from the data, then compare and contrast them for their similarities and differences. Devise a generality to explain what you see in this one posting, which covers its consistencies.

Now, step back from what you have just done. Try a hermeneutic interpretation of this post. Consider, for a moment, the analysis that you have just performed and your starting point. Ask yourself about the deeper meaning of this posting. Ask yourself not what it says, but why the poster posted it. Do not aim for description. Aim for explanation. What is the poster of this message attempting to convey in this message? What is he conveying beyond the words that he is using? Why is he conveying this to the members of an online community? Why this online community? What does that say about the community? Remember that in your own data collection and analysis you will be conducting ongoing analyses and interpretations like this as a natural part of your data collection. The initial answers that we propose to these questions will be checked, cross-checked, and tested repeatedly against other new data that we collect in order to confirm or disconfirm them, or to bracket and nuance them.

Are you back? Did you give it a try? I would prefer to be there in person to discuss this with you, but this asynchronous textual interaction is going to have to suffice for now. I will begin by sharing my manual coding of the posting in Figure 7.2. I am using manual coding because it is relatively easy to reproduce in a book format, and also relatively easy to perform on a single, short posting. However, if there were hundreds or thousands of postings, you can see how manual coding would become challenging.

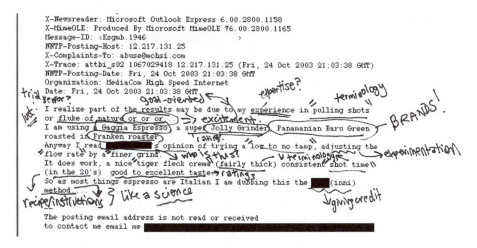

FIGURE 7.2   HAND CODING OF ALT.COFFEE NEWSGROUP POSTING

My coding uses a variety of terms that relate to the posting's professional, precise, quest-like pursuit: 'goal-oriented', 'expertise', 'recipe/instructions', 'trial & error', 'ratings', 'experimentation', and 'terminology'. They also try to pick up on some of the emotion conveyed in the posting, emotion that may be driving the quest-like pursuit: 'or or or ...' and the reference to a 'fluke of nature'. Repeatedly, I circle different brands, and place different pieces of terminology inside of quotation marks. These repeat instances are patterns that begin to tell a story. I write notes, questions to myself, as I memo on the paper about this posting. I link the codes with arrows, creating abstractions that can turn into generalizations. Combined with the other elements coded in the text, a consistent pattern seems to be unfolding about an emotion-driven, expertise-cloaked quest for a certain kind of cup of coffee, a quest that involved the combination of precise, scientific terms and ratings, and commercial brands.

Using this as the basis for my hermeneutic interpretation, I broaden and open my analysis. One of the first things we might notice about Frank's alt.coffee posting is that he is informing others and sharing his expertise, but he is also making many fine distinctions. This is where Frank's use of brand names comes in. He is not just using an espresso maker, it is 'a Gaggia Espresso'. It is not just any old coffee grinder, but 'a super Jolly Grinder'. It is not merely a roaster, but a 'Franken roaster'. And these are certainly not just any old coffee beans. They are 'Panamanian Baru Green'.

Frank's technical language also plays an important role. We can probably guess what he is talking about when he speaks about 'pulling shots' or a 'finer grind'. After all, this is coffee. But what is a 'low to no tamp'. And what is a 'flow rate'? What is a 'tiger fleck crema' and what might a 'consistent shot time (in the 20's)' mean?

These qualitative clues suggest that the newsgroup is used to display and to teach – and to teach in order to display – the specifics of coffee connoisseurship. As I discovered in my further investigation of this group (the later comparison and confirmation stages), but as is also evident in a close reading of the emphasis in Frank's posting, espresso is a central form of coffee. It turns out that, for this newsgroup, the authentic, precious, essential coffee is espresso, consumed without 'cow juice' or sugar.

From Frank's technical and specialized terms we quickly learn that, to make good espresso is a complicated affair. It involves attending carefully to the water, the grind, timing the shot, knowing your machine, maintaining the cleanliness of the filter and screen, proper use of the tamper ('low to no tamp'), the blend, the grind (in Frank's case, it is 'fine'), the ambient temperature, the age of the coffee, the degree of the roast, the air humidity, incoming water temperature, the flow of the water, the timing of the shot, and even such mystical elements as the mood of the barista (or coffee server), or the lucky 'fluke' of the one who 'pulls the shots'.

These categories are not merely functional considerations, but indications of social movement and status intended to manifest and demonstrate the 'distinction' or 'cultural capital' of upper-class tastes and abilities (Bourdieu 1984). There is an elite appeal to this conspicuous display of coffee knowledge. As Levy (1981) suggests, there are strong links between discernment, social class and the acculturated sense of taste. After all, consider the socio-economics of those who have the ability to invest this time and these resources in crafting the perfect cup of espresso, and in sharing this craftsmanship with others. The middle-class fascination with production, the expression of an intellectual need not only to consume coffee, but also to understand it, and to actively produce it, and then to share the knowledge and distinction that come from practising its production is a hallmark of deep devotion to a particular consumption orientation, such as is found in a range of subcultural, sport, music and media fan experiences.

'Who is this' John Smith?, my memo note wonders. Is it another member of the alt.coffee community? A little investigation ensues. It turns out that it is, for Mr Smith replies later that same day to Mr Rinetti's comment and politely declines credit for the method. He claims that the technique is common practice in Italy. As well, he had already partaken in a lengthy discussion of the technique on the alt.coffee group previously, a discussion in which he was only a minor contributor. This exchange indicates how the acculturation of the complexities of taste continues online. There is a subtle inculcation of coffee tastes being mapped in these coffeephile communications, which reference on another, giving and refracting credit. This sense of sharing, giving, and acknowledgment are very communal factors, and it can easily be seen how a desire for status and positive reinforcement would increasingly draw one into desiring deeper and more profound knowledge of coffee, expertise at coffee production, and experience at distinguishing various types of coffee. The role of brands also seems important. They are granted credit, but they are also important labels. They signify an element of the recipe that one must follow, but they also speak of the class, expertise, and taste of the recipe-giver.

This is the outline or beginning of a 'thick' interpretation that builds analytic coding together with a hermeneutic interpretation. I am interested to hear about what you made of this single posting, so feel free to share it with me. From one posting, we learn about the community's ritual practices, some of their central motivations and topical concerns, and the conversational practices that they use to build and maintain their community. Knowledge of these elements – as well as of coffee production – is a requirement for community members, as it is for the netnographer interested in studying the community.

This textual interpretation begins by breaking a text down into its constituent elements, classifying them, finding patterns among them that relate them, closely examining all of their elements, asking about the motivation behind them, testing and checking with further data, and then reading them for the culture that they represent. For further examples of the finished products of data analysis, researchers might choose to read any of the netnographic books and articles cited in this book in order to get a general feel for how online community and culture data become turned into published theoretical contributions.

The alt.coffee group has over 2,000 subscribers, and gathers over 700 message postings per month. Some of these postings can be quite lengthy and detailed. As mentioned above, if we were to expand our study to include a few thousand of these postings, and perhaps add in data from coffee-themed blogs, microblog feed, and social networking groups, a complete analysis would become challenging. It is at this point that the use of a software program to help organize and facilitate the task of coding and interpretation might be useful. We will learn more about this topic in the following section.

CONSIDERING MANUAL AND COMPUTER-ASSISTED QUALITATIVE DATA ANALYSIS METHODS

In this section, you will learn about the relative merits of manual and computer-assisted methods of qualitative data analysis in netnography. You will be faced with the tradeoffs that accompany this decision. You will then learn the fundamental principles and uses of computer software to assist in the analysis of qualitative data in netnography.

It is useful to begin with an overview of manual qualitative data analysis. If you are going to analyse data manually, this usually entails working with paper printouts, for example 30-page printouts of a long message thread or 15-page printouts of an online interview. If you store your netnographic data in paper form, it is going to take up a large amount of space. You will also need to catalogue your data and organize these so that you have access to them when you need it. You will need to code these, which may require different colours of highlighter, markers, or coloured pencils. As you analyse categories you may want to condense the information onto file cards, perhaps physically cutting off pieces of the texts and pasting or taping them onto file cards, which you can then organize and reorganize. These will be stored in file folders, alongside other file folders, in boxes and cartons, which will need to be carefully labelled so that you can find the documents you are looking for when you need to examine them.

There are times when the manual, on-paper, off-computer system can work effectively, such as when the dataset is quite small, the researcher is very familiar with the fieldsites, and the researcher is organized, has a good paper filing system, and prefers to work this way. However, using a pure paper method such as this for a netnography will very rapidly become unwieldy.

Some netnographers use computers for data storage, but do not use any of the sophisticated software packages for data analysis available. Instead, they use the tools at hand, such as Microsoft's powerful word-processing, spreadsheet, and database programs (see Hahn 2008).[12] These analysts save their files in word processing files, and use the word processing program to automate parts of the data analysis process. They organize their different downloaded data files into folders and then organize those folders into other folders. They code inside the computer files, perhaps in bold text, highlighting, or using different colours. They use comments in the paper to memo to themselves. They use the adequate search and find capabilities of word processing software to conduct text searches that aid them in their coding and classification. Then, different levels of coding and abstraction are organized using either the spreadsheet capabilities of a program such as Excel, or the even-more powerful database capabilities of a program such as Access. In some past research, I have used this 'semi-automatic' method. Like the manual system, it can work relatively well under conditions where the researcher is considering small datasets or has particularly suitable skills or preferences. Like the CAQDAS methods, it does require some computer literacy, and involves a learning curve to become familiar with the programs and the data entry procedures for coding and search.

The alternative to these methods is to employ software that assists the researcher in their analysis of qualitative data. Software used in this way has been termed Computer-Assisted Qualitative Data Analysis software, or CAQDAS, for short. The guiding and differentiating principle of CAQDAS is that it takes an inductive, bottom-up approach to the analysis of qualitative data. Such data could include text, graphics, photographs, sound files and music, videos, and any other type of non-numerical information. The qualitative approach to data analysis followed in these software packages is identical to the processes we have discussed above, except that these processes are automated. Contemporary software also comes with some sophisticated visualization abilities that are unique to these techniques, and that can assist in analysis and report presentation. In a netnography where the researcher is confronted with massive amounts of data, where different types of data must be combined, where the sorting and storage of the data present constant challenges, and where an ethnographic closeness to the data is carefully maintained by the netnographer, CAQDAS can be very useful.

How can the netnographer decide whether to use manual coding, such as on-paper, or a word processing program, or a dedicated qualitative analysis software program? She should consider the amount of data, size of fieldsite, conventions of the academic field, and the preferences and abilities of the researcher. The following basic guidelines to netnographic qualitative data analysis may be helpful in reaching this decision.

- Smaller scale or more bounded investigations of online communities and cultures (those with fewer or more limited constructs) may employ manual coding, categorization and classification, as well as hermeneutic interpretive analysis, in order to obtain their insights.

- Larger scale investigations, or investigations that uncover significant amounts of relevant data, may benefit from the efficiencies of computer-assisted qualitative data analysis, either through existing word processing and database programs or through dedicated CAQDAS programs such as NVivo and Atlas.ti.
- Researchers producing work for fields that value thick description and narrative depth may find hermeneutic styles of analysis more suitable.
- Researchers producing work for fields that affirm the value of statistical evaluations and structural accounts of ethnographic fieldsites may benefit from the precise coding and statistics calculating capabilities of CAQDAS.
- Researchers with impressive, developed, on-paper, filing skills may opt for manual data analysis and interpretation methods.
- Researchers who are organizationally challenged may benefit from the automated management of CAQDAS.
- Researchers who emphasize, or are concerned about, creativity or closeness to the data may prefer manual techniques.

LOOKING MORE CLOSELY AT COMPUTER-ASSISTED QUALITATIVE DATA ANALYSIS

In this section, we will learn more about computer-assisted qualitative data analysis, its principles, its uses, it benefits, and its drawbacks. We will also be introduced to a few of the current software program offerings.

In the previous section, we analysed one short piece of qualitative data, a message posting from the alt.coffee newsgroup. We conducted our analysis and interpretation by hand, on paper. But we could just as easily have performed it using a qualitative data analysis program. The same inductive principles would have applied. Instead of manually coding the words 'Gaggia', 'Jolly Grinder', and 'Franken' with the term 'BRANDS!' we would have used the program to tag the words. Instead of placing quotation marks around 'pulling shots', 'low to no tamp', and 'finer grind', these terms would have been labelled 'terminology'. Instead of memoing 'trial and error?', 'expertise?', and 'who is this', these terms would have been entered into the program as memos/comments. As we moved up to link 'brands' and 'terminology' with 'expertise' – and then to ask ourselves 'Is the use of brand names and terminology a signal of expertise?' – we would be both abstracting, and combining categories to form possible generalizations which could then be tested further. From higher-level analysis such as this, theories are constructed.

As we can see from this very simple example, the CAQDAS interprets data like any other form of qualitative analysis, by identifying and coding recurrent themes, concepts, ideas, processes, contexts, or other relevant constructs. It allows the researcher to construct categories for second-order coding and further analyses of relationships. As constructs are coded and relationships between them suggested and tested, explanations or theories can be developed and recorded by the program. All of the major software packages have functionality that allows for searching for particular keywords or related keywords as well as for the retrieval of coded materials.

Psychologists Eben Weitzman and Matthew Miles (1995, p. 5) suggest the following uses of computer software in qualitative research projects:

- recording fieldnotes
- correcting, extending, editing, or revising fieldnotes
- coding text to permit later retrieval
- storing texts
- organizing text
- searching and retrieving texts and making them available for inspection
- connecting relevant data segments to each other, forming categories, clusters, or networks
- writing reflective commentaries or 'memos' on the data as a basis for deeper analysis
- performing content analysis by counting frequencies, sequences, or locations of words and phrases
- displaying selected data in a reduced, condensed, organized format, such as in a matrix
- aiding in conclusion-drawing, interpretation, confirmation and verification
- building theory by developing systematic, conceptually coherent explanations of findings
- creating diagrams or graphical maps that depict findings or theories
- preparing interim and final reports.

CAQDAS can also be useful when working with a team. Many programs automatically calculate similarities and differences in coding. Many also facilitate the sharing of data across a computer network, so that two or more persons can code and work with the same set of data simultaneously. Three of the currently leading CAQDAS packages are ATLAS.ti 6.0, MAXqda2, and NVivo8, however other leading packages are HypeRESEARCH 2.8, QDA Miner 3.1, Qualrus, and Transana 2. There are many others, including some free packages (such as Weft QDA), some of which are online, and some that run on the Mac operating system (such as the TAMS/TamsAnalyser). As Lewins and Silver (2007) note, the major software packages all offer excellent capabilities in data storage, organization, coding, retrieval, and visualization (see also Bazeley 2007; Weitzman and Miles 1995). Almost all of them allow you to collect distinct types of netnographic data into a single project, including downloaded text files, saved digital photographs, links to videos, scans of handwritten reflective fieldnotes, and so on.

At any stage of your netnographic data analysis, CAQDAS offers an efficient and effective way to generate reports of your findings. Files can be easily saved, creating a snapshot of analyses, emerging or completed. For those who are still addicted to the feel of dead trees, a vast variety of printouts can be generated as the foundation for late night pen-and-paper coding exercises.

There are at least five great strengths of qualitative data analysis packages. First, most netnographic data are already in digital form, making their insertion into the program extremely straightforward. There are many search program that can automatically generate specific computer files by mining the Internet. The second strength of CAQDAS is that it encourages netnographers to think about their often vast and sprawling dataset as a whole. It is easy to become overwhelmed by large amounts of diverse data, and to focus on particular trees without seeing the forest. CAQDAS can be used to facilitate the bringing of your attention to the entire dataset. Third, they can assist the netnographer in keeping their project organized. Fourth, because they make access to the data quite easy, they can enable a virtuous closeness to the data during analysis. Fifth and finally, the visualization options can lead to interesting new creative thoughts. If you enjoy playing with your data and using these to spur your imagination, CAQDAS gives you more ways to play.

Computer-assisted methods can have drawbacks as well, and we set out five corresponding disadvantages here. First, with apparently unlimited file storage, researchers often find themselves tempted to collect every piece of data possible. This can lead not only to sorting and coding problems, but also to a wandering, unfocused project. Second, mechanical text searches become very easy to conduct, but include many unintended results, and can often miss many intended results. Text searches are not substitutes for careful coding, although researchers may be tempted to use them as such. Doing so not only results in messy categories and fuzzy theorizing, it also results in distance from your data, which is anathema to producing quality netnography. Third, computer files are vulnerable to loss in a way that paper simply is not. A single careless keystroke can erase months of careful data collection. Always carefully back up your project's dataset. Consider storing a copy on an online server as well. Fourth, computers may make it easy to fall into 'the coding trap' described by Richards (2005, p. 100). In the coding trap, the researcher conducts ever-increasing amounts of coding and classification, without theory ever seeming to emerge from the data. Fifth, software can help you to create too many ideas, too many categories. As the software enables you to create many new categories, you may be overwhelmed by these and find them stifling your creativity and your ability to use the data to say something new. Large bulks of data can be a barrier to thinking. There may be a trade-off between efficiency and creativity: just because computer software enables you to do something, such as unlimited searching or massive amounts of coding, does not mean that you should do it. In sum, the valuable lesson here is that the use of analytic tools must be guided not by software capabilities, but by the interpretive plans and directions of the netnographer. In the next section, we discuss some of those interpretive principles, in particular, those that are adapted to the contingencies of netnographic data.

ADAPTING THE PRINCIPLES OF DATA ANALYSIS TO NETNOGRAPHIC DATA

In this section, we will learn about some of the data analysis concerns particular to netnography. These concerns arise whether we are circling our data hermeneutically, or coding it intensely in a CAQDAS program. They occur because netnographic data are different from ethnographic data. We will then learn some analytic strategies to address them. The textual nature of the data and its disembodied quality have been considered problematic. Similarly, the anonymity of online interactions and the type of fluid identity play that they have been presumed to manifest have been troublesome to cultural analysts. Analysts have also been vexed by the ostensible dishonesty of online community members and the apparent lack of observability of their social processes. In this section, we will discuss these particular concerns before offering analytic strategies responsive to them.

CONCERNS WITH TEXTUALITY, (DIS)EMBODIMENT, AND IDENTITY IN NETNOGRAPHIC DATA

Netnographic data present challenges because they are textual and not unequivocally associated with particular people. The textual nature of much online communication has often been cast as a limitation of culturally oriented Internet research. This emphasis on the radical differences between online and face-to-face cultural environments tends to link the textuality of online communication to the disembodiment of the online experience. Similarly, there is still a widespread impression that online interaction is somehow not 'real' (see Kendall 2004).

However, it bears consideration that alteration, as technological mediation, is nothing new. The social fields we interact in exist quite concretely. The people at the other end of a social networking site or in virtual worlds are no less real than the people who talk to us on the telephone, author the books we read, or write us letters. It is true that textual communication omits many aspects of in-person communication, with its tonal shifts, pauses, cracked voices, downward turns of the eye, and so on. However, it may include other important symbolic expressions impossible to transmit through the body.

Within a textual reality, the anonymity that is sometimes advantageous at obtaining disclosure can also prevent us from having confidence that we understand the context of our communications. What age, sex, ethnicity is the person who is communicating with us? How can we compare difference in culture members? How do online and offline worlds relate? It can be difficult to definitively link the data one draws exclusively from an online community to particular genders, social classes, ages, and races.

How are researchers to confront these limitations in their research? The following sets of questions and suggestions may be helpful.

- Are particular aspects of identity important to your particular research study? Are they theoretically important?
    - For example, if you are conducting a study of a particular online community or culture (see Chapter 4), then the most relevant identity for your study may simply be that the person posts on the community and plays a particular role within it.
    - If links to other forms of identification are important, blended ethnography/ netnography can be a worthwhile option.

- Does the online community reveal aspects of identities?

    o   For example, online communities devoted to particular genders or gender issues, particular regions, particular religions, and so on, would very likely attract knowledgeable members of those groups.

    o   This knowledge and expertise is often not difficult to validate. There is a women's community that asks people in chat-rooms revealing questions about bra sizes that few men would be able to answer.

- Is this an online community where people customarily reveal other aspects of their identities?

    o   Many people on social networking sites use their real names and real pictures.

    o   Services such as FriendFeed link together different online media, facilitating the identification of particular people.

    o   We seem to be moving increasingly towards less and less anonymous communications.

CONCERNS ABOUT ARTIFICIALITY AND FALSIFICATION IN NETNOGRAPHIC RESEARCH DATA

Because netnographic data have the option of anonymity, or pseudonymity, concerns are raised about the ability of people to alter their identities, and present themselves untruthfully. This alteration of identity must affect our analysis. In addition, netnography seems to unfavourably compare with in-person ethnography, in that ethnography allows us to compare culture members' spoken perspectives on their actions with the actions that we as researchers actually observe (Tedlock 1991). Because netnography has been based primarily upon the observation of artefactually embedded, rather than physically uttered, discourse and action, it seems more limited than ethnography in this regard.

However, in her research on Internet relationships and sexuality, Whitty (2004) asserted that, although it is widely believed that people falsify self-related information on the Internet, the data suggest that this does not occur as frequently as previously presumed. She also suggests that these differences are contingent, for instance, that 'men tend to lie online more than women, typically exaggerating aspects of themselves, such as education, occupation and income, which are aspects men often tend to exaggerate off-line in order to attract women' (Whitty 2004, p. 206). Although men falsified in order to impress others and boost their own egos, women did it for safety reasons. Hope Schau and Mary Gilly met, in person, people who they had first contacted through their personal Internet web-pages. They asserted that the online representations were, generally speaking, accurate (Schau and Gilly 2003). This research suggests that online representation may not be a major concern, and that people online are not extravagant liars.

It is a social fact that we are constantly constructing and reconstructing ourselves through collective acts that display different aspects of ourselves in different social contexts. Therefore, as Taylor (1999) and Carter (2005) note, the study of participants' online personas and the fact that they are different from the personas they use in other social contexts is not problematic. It fails to be a predicament because this alteration of identity is a natural consequence of our social life *everywhere* and not simply some idiosyncratic tendency manifesting itself in life online. It merely needs to be analysed as such. Online anonymity should be considered a trade-off situation, where we gain insights in some areas as we lose them in others. 'The same freedom which inspires people to mischievously construct deliberate falsehoods about themselves and their opinions also allows them and others the freedom to express aspects of themselves, their ambitions and inner conflicts, that they would otherwise keep deeply hidden' (Kozinets 1998, p. 369). Our data analysis needs to emphasize this strength of anonymous or pseudonymous data: these are often more honest, rather than more deceptive.

Our data analysis strategies should also reflect the realization that, in fact, we do have both observation and discourse in netnography. We can observe how people act in their online postings. For example, 'George' might post many messages about how compassionate he is to people, and how much he gives to certain charities. However, we might also observe him attacking other members of the newsgroup ruthlessly. If we conduct interviews, we have culture members' reflections of their own and others' behaviour, just as we do in face-to-face interviews. What we are able to observe is how these participants 'acted' in their online postings and other representations. Our data analysis should reflect these options. This strategy leads directly to a particular approach to the analysis of netnographic data.

A PRAGMATIC-INTERACTIONIST APPROACH TO NETNOGRAPHIC DATA ANALYSIS

In this section, we will learn about a particular approach, founded in the philosophy of science, that confronts many of the analytic challenges associated with netnographic data (see also Kozinets 2002a, p. 64). This analytic stance is called a 'Pragmatic-Interactionist' approach because it combines the pragmatism of George Herbert Mead (1938) with the linguistic philosophy of Ludwig Wittgenstein (1953).

In Mead's (1938) interactionist approach, the unit of analysis is not the person, but the gesture, the behaviour or the act, which includes the speech act or utterance. When applied to the current context, Wittgenstein's (1953) linguistic philosophy might suggest that every interactive online posting is a social action, a communicative performance that can be conceived of as a 'language game'. If so, then every community 'player's' move in the social 'game' is a relevant observational event in and of itself. The idea behind this approach to data analysis is straightforward:

- Consider the online environment a social world.
- Assume that online environments have social and language games, with attendant rules, fields, winners, and losers.

- Treat online data as a social act.
- Seek to understand the meaning of these acts in the context of their appropriate social worlds.
- When appropriate, broaden the particular online social world to interact with other online social worlds as well as other social worlds that are not exclusively online, or not online at all.

Analyses of observations of players' acts might proceed with a consideration of the following netnographically-related social facts.

- The text of a particular blog posting has been written and was posted.
- A certain social networking group has been formed, and certain accounts have been linked to it.
- A certain photo was uploaded to a particular photo-sharing community, and received 37 comments.

An analyst following the Pragmatic-Interactionist approach does not necessarily need to know exactly 'who' is doing such things. She would initially be concerned with the observations of 'interactive acts' in the 'game' that is played on the online fields of community and culture. As this attention moves to the fields on which community and culture are played – rather than what the players do when they are not on the field – our analysis is altered. Netnographic data analysis then consists of contextualizing the meaning of the exchange and interaction in ever-widening circles of social significance.

Another of these alterations is that, as it considers the relationships between various online and off-line social worlds, netnographic data analysis must account for intervening communications occurring during the course of our investigation. It should attend to subtext, as well as to context and text in messages. Pay careful attention in your analysis of fieldnotes and data to the diverse and often convoluted processes through which members communicate with other community members. Understanding how members interact with the culture in general can pay off richly in understanding the complex lived experience of communal interaction.

In addition, as the diversity of the examples above indicates, it is not enough to simply gain fluency and 'translate' the various textual elements of online communities. Each photograph, each video, each tag, perhaps even each hypertext click of the mouse, is akin to a 'speech act', an utterance. We must be attuned to a new world where a choice from a drop down menu replaces a shrug, and a cursor's move replaces body language. '[T]hese and other aspects of participants' text-based interaction pose interpretive puzzles for the ethnographers in terms of their relationship to participants' presentation of self' (Garcia et al. 2009, p. 61).

Therefore, netnographic data analysis must include the graphical, visual, audio, and audiovisual aspects of online community data. Various aspects of visual data can be analysed: the use of moving graphical images or emoticons; the use of colour, type font, and graphic design; pictures and photographs; and layouts of pages and messages. Each aspect is a communication event of importance. Hine's (2000) analysis of websites is exemplary in this regard. She carefully interprets choice of photos, choice of arrangements for the photos, and use of backgrounds. She employs her visual analysis to reach conclusions about how online community members convey emotional messages about a famous murder case. Merely understanding the words that are exchanged online is only a part of the netnographer's job.

The formulation of generalizations is also important as we attend to various connections or disconnections of various online and offline communities and identities, the integration *vs.* separation of social worlds that we discussed previously in Chapter 4. It is not necessary to consider the results of every netnographic analysis of the community online to be representative of a general population of that community or culture, in the same way that a survey might be. As an inductive approach, netnography studies the world of phenomena for opportunities to build theoretical propositions or rich, thick, descriptions, comparisons, and classifications.

Media theorist Henry Jenkins's work is exemplary in this respect. Writing about the manifold cultural effects of digital technology on media consumption and production, he proposes and amply demonstrates notions of collective intelligence and a more participatory media culture. In his conclusion however, he asserts 'I do not mean for us to read these groups as typical of the average consumer ... Rather, we should read these case studies as demonstrations of what it is possible to do in the context of convergence culture' (Jenkins 2006, p. 247).

Netnographies can helpfully generate theory about new and emerging areas. Because we can look for unique or special instances – say of online communities that are using their technological interconnection to devise and foster more environmentally-friendly lifestyles and neighbourhoods – netnographies are also useful in the conduct of action research in which researchers seek to envision alternatives for social betterment (Ozanne and Saatcioglu 2008; Tacchi et al. 2004).

The analysis of netnographic data should be subtly attuned to the prevalent contingencies of the online cultural environment: the textuality of the data, the disembodied and anonymous nature of online interaction, the claims of dishonesty and the alleged difficulty of observability and verification. The fact that culture members adopt online personas is a natural consequence of social life. As a consequence, we can frame our analysis pragmatically, as concerned with observations of interactive acts in the communicative field of online community and culture. In particular, it is important that your analysis does not elide the many modalities of cultural communication such as the visual, audio, and audiovisual. Finally, analysis should be guided by a focus on theory, and that theory should be meticulously governed by an understanding of the inductive nature of netnography.

SUMMARY

The chapter has provided some concrete netnographic examples of coding, analysis and interpretation, techniques that accommodate an ecumenical range of views of the netnographic enterprise from the descriptive and poetic to the abstract and structural (see Chapter 9 for representation in netnography). In general, qualitative data analysis software can be helpful for managing, coding, and analysing large, complex datasets, but other methods usefully accommodate smaller, more descriptive and more bounded projects. The analysis of netnographic data must be subtly attuned to the prevalent contingencies of the online cultural environment: the textuality of the data, the disembodied and anonymous nature of online interaction, the claims of dishonesty and the alleged difficulty of observability and verification. Netnographic analysis is therefore framed pragmatically, concerned with observations of interactive acts in the communicative field of online community and culture – including cultural communications such as the visual, audio, and audiovisual – carefully inducted to form theory.

KEY READINGS

Arnold, Stephen J. and Eileen Fischer (1994) 'Hermeneutics and Consumer Research', *Journal of Consumer Research*, 21 (June): 55–70.

Kozinets, Robert V. (2006) 'Click to Connect: Netnography and Tribal Advertising', *Journal of Advertising Research*, 46 (September): 279–88.

Lewins, Ann and Christina Silver (2007) *Using Software in Qualitative Research: A Step-by-Step Guide*. Thousand Oaks, CA: Sage.

Miles, Matthew B. and Michael A. Huberman (1994) *Qualitative Data Analysis: An Expanded Sourcebook*, 2nd edition. Thousand Oaks, CA: Sage.

Spiggle, Susan (1994) 'Analysis and Interpretation of Qualitative Data in Consumer Research', *Journal of Consumer Research*, 21 (December): 491–503.

8
CONDUCTING ETHICAL NETNOGRAPHY

ABSTRACT

In this chapter, you will learn about ethical issues associated with the conduct of ethnography. You will also learn how other scholars have addressed these issues, and gain an understanding of how to address major issues such as informed consent, as well as the use and citation of online postings. This chapter is designed to help you responsibly conduct netnography in the complex online environment.

> **Key Words:** ethics, human subjects research, informed consent, Institutional Review Boards, Internet legal issues, Internet Research Ethics, online research ethics, research ethics

Research ethics is one of the most important and most complex topics in this book. It is the area of netnography that is the most uncertain, the most public, and that consequently tends to receive the most questions. Not only is netnography optionally as invasive and personal as ethnography, but in its conduct we also make lasting impressions, leaving our own tracks and trails leading to other people. We are conducting a type of outreach during which we have the opportunity to enlighten, to offend, and even to do harm. We represent our profession to community members and to the world. It is a chance to reveal ourselves and our colleagues as goodwill ambassadors, public servants, or ignorant exploiters. And each of us, ultimately, makes those choices and sticks with them on a daily, hourly, even minute-by-minute basis as we interact in the fields behind our computer screens.

With its mix of participation and observation, its often uncomfortable closeness, and its traditions of distanced description and cultural revelation, ethnographic inquiry already possesses some of the thorniest terrain for navigating research ethics. When we add to this the technological complexities and unique new contingencies of online interactions, these already-difficult issues become even more formidable.

Significant amounts of new research and literature have emerged to enlighten our perspective on what constitutes ethical netnography in the past decade. The stance provided by this chapter has therefore developed considerably from that offered in previously published works (e.g., Kozinets 1998, 2002a, 2006a). Its views have been informed by and benefited from the helpful work of a number of fellow scholars working in the areas of ethical philosophy, Internet legal issues, and online research ethics, whose work is cited and developed throughout this chapter. Although consensus on these issues is still emerging, we are now in an exceptionally good position to analyse the research ethics challenges facing the netnographer and to recommend protocols for ethical netnographic inquiry.

Although certainly not an exhaustive treatment of the topic, this chapter is intended to provide you with a good grounding in research ethics concerns as they relate to the conduct of netnography.[13] To dig deeper into questions about your particular project, you are encouraged to consult the various citations and resources mentioned in this chapter as you are required or inspired to do so. Additionally, you would be wise to check online, in journal articles, and in books for the most current and up-to-date thinking about these rapidly changing topics.

BOX 8.1   IS ETHICS REALLY IMPORTANT IN ONLINE RESEARCH?

In presentations of netnography, I often hear from students or fellow scholars who insist that, when people post things on the Internet, they already know that it becomes public knowledge. 'Why would we go to all that trouble just to confirm what we already know?'

It may be true at this point in history that most people do know that their online postings and information can be read in that form by members of the general public. However, the fact that people know that their postings are public does not automatically lead to the conclusion that academics and other types of researchers can use the data in any way that they please. A short example will suffice as I will develop this argument throughout this chapter.

In initial research on *X-Files* fans, I began downloading information from a public bulletin board (Kozinets 1997a). I thought it would be appropriate to ask people's permission before I directly cited them. When I did, everyone gave their permission except for one person. That one person had posted some information about their own UFO sighting and how it related to their relationship to the television show. They were likely a bit embarrassed because paranormal activities and experiences – especially those outside of the institutional context of organized religion – are stigmatized in our society. But because the data were so interesting

(Continued)

(Continued)

and so closely related to my paper's themes of consumption of conspiracy and the supernatural, I wrote to this person once again, repeating to them that they would be quoted using a pseudonym in the research, and that this would only be a research publication, not a mass publication. After my request to reconsider, this person declined.

At that point, it would have felt very wrong to include their data. If we do not ask, then others cannot refuse us permission. We can just take. However, we must consider carefully the ramifications of this ethical stance. This was a powerful personal illustration that not everyone who posts a message on a bulletin board wants it used in a piece of research, even if it will be used anonymously. This person probably did not know that search engine technology would shortly become so powerful that anyone wishing to enter their quotation could easily find it and locate their pseudonym. However, we must ask ourselves a follow-up question: should that person's wishes matter? Should they make the final determination?

Other researchers have asserted that members of online communities resist being studied. LeBesco (2004) reported that, in a single month, eight researchers tried to gain access to a particular online community site and all but one were rejected by the group. Bakardjieva (2005) reported her frustration with recruiting respondents through announcements on online newsgroups, a tactic she had to later abandon. In an article pithily titled 'Go Away', James Hudson and Amy Bruckman (2004) relate that people in chat-rooms reacted with hostility when they were aware of being studied by researchers. When these people were given the opportunity to become part of the research, only four out of 766 potential participants chose to do so. In summary, Johns, Chen, and Hall (2003, p. 159) reported that 'many list owners and newsgroup members deeply resent the presence of researchers and journalists in their groups'.

Knowing this, can we proceed on the assumption that culture and community members are automatically granting us their consent to use their words, images, photos, videos, and connections in our research? As we will learn in the remainder of this chapter, the answer is considerably more complicated that it seems.

IRE, IRB, AND NETNOGRAPHY

Internet Research Ethics (or IRE) is 'an emerging and fascinating research field', a sphere of inquiry that 'has been growing steadily since the late 1990s, with many disciplinary examinations of what it means to conduct research – ethically – in online or Internet-based environments' (Buchanan 2006, p. 14). Important guidelines have been advanced and developed through such leading organizations as the American Association for the Advancement of Science (Frankel and Siang 1999), the Association of Internet Researchers (see Association of Internet Researchers Ethics Working

Group 2002), and the American Psychological Association (see Kraut et al. 2004). Alongside a number of special issues, seminars, and conferences, three helpful edited volumes have been published (Buchanan 2004; Johns et al. 2003; Thorseth 2003).

The issues that IRE deals with are dynamic and complex; they touch upon philosophical matters, commercial interests, academic traditions of research practice and method, and institutional arrangements, as well as the oversight of legislative and regulatory bodies. As a whole, IRE's concerns stretch from legal issues such as 'liability for negligence' and 'damage to reputation' to conventional research ethics notions of 'informed consent' and 'respect', to larger, even social issues such as autonomy, the right to privacy, and the various differences in relevant international standards and laws.

It is onto this shifting, complex ground of moral, legal, policy- and method-oriented decisions that we now must step. For if we wish to conduct a netnography, we are going to have to answer to various institutional and regulatory bodies for the ethical standards of our research. In the United States, each university's Institutional Review Board, or 'IRB', governs and administers applicable research ethics standards. These IRBs in the United States are guided by the Code of Federal Regulations Title 45, Part 46, Protection of Human Subjects, which was inspired by the spirit of the Belmont report. In other countries, the names and protocols may be different. In a number of countries, academic research ethics are governed by Human Subjects Research Ethics Committees, which in turn tend to be regulated by government agencies and bodies that offer academic research grants. For research practitioners, various industry associations have codes of ethics or guidelines that govern the practice of ethical research. Every researcher is likely to be governed by at least two ethical research institutions and their codes.

Obviously, the aspiring and practising netnographer does not need to be concerned with the history or entirety of the Internet research ethics literature. As netnographers, what concerns us most are those topics and guidelines pertaining particularly to the online conduct of participant observational research and interviews. We must grapple with some difficult and obscure questions before we can make defensible decisions about how to conduct our netnography. Although it is far from an exhaustive list, you may want to consult Box 8.2 for a list of some relevant questions.

BOX 8.2

Conducting a netnography that is ethical and adapted to the unique environment of the Internet is far from simple. There are perplexing and difficult questions that scholars from philosophy, legal issues, and various academic departments are working to answer in an emergent field called Internet Research Ethics, or IRE. Some of the ethical questions that are relevant to netnographic inquiry include:

(Continued)

(Continued)

- Are online communities private or public spaces?
- How do we gain the informed consent of online community members?
- Who actually owns the online data posted on newsgroups or blogs?
- How do we deal with the information on corporate websites and other online forums? Can we use it in our research?
- Should we use conversations that we participate in or 'overhear' in chat-rooms? Are there different ethical rules for different online media?
- Do age and vulnerability matter online? In media in which identity is difficult to verify, how can we be sure about the age or vulnerability of research participants?
- Do international boundaries influence the way a netnographer collects data and publishes research?

These are vital questions. The answers will help us to formulate adaptable, yet directive, procedural guidelines for ethical netnography. Of course, like the Internet itself, these issues and acceptable protocols are constantly changing. You are obligated as a researcher to stay on top of the topics that are relevant to you and your research interests, and to make the decisions that you believe to be correct in consultation with your colleagues and relevant regulatory bodies (for academics in the USA, this would be your Institutional Review Board).

In the following sections, this chapter discusses four issues important to the understanding of netnographic research ethics. First, it covers whether netnographers should regard online communities as public or private spaces. Second, it discusses issues of informed consent. The section following will examine the need to avoid harm to culture members. In the fourth section, you will learn about the ethical complexities of presenting data from netnographic research participants.

The chapter then proceeds to discuss and describe four general procedural areas to address these issues: (1) identifying yourself and informing relevant constituents about your research, (2) asking for appropriate permissions, (3) gaining consent where needed, and (4) properly citing and crediting culture members. Although certainly not an exhaustive treatment of the topic, this chapter should give you the major ideas and procedures that you need in order to proceed ethically with your netnography, as well as the citations and resources you might require to dig deeper into questions about your own particular project.

THE PUBLIC *VS.* PRIVATE FALLACY

Much debate about Internet research ethics is concerned with whether we should treat computer-mediated interactions as if they took place in either a public or a private space. This spatial metaphor is commonly applied to the Internet and seems, in fact, to be a fundamental human cognition (Munt 2001). Another very common metaphor for understanding the Internet is to see the Internet as a text. Applied to the topic of Internet research ethics, these metaphors lead us to certain conclusions and encourage us to adopt certain procedures. If the Internet is a place, then is it like a public space? Is the capture of computer-mediated communications then similar to the transcription of conversation overheard in a public park? If the Internet is a text, then is the use of computer-mediated communications like the citation of or quotation from a published book?

The American Association for the Advancement of Science report on the ethical and legal aspects of human subjects research on the Internet (Frankel and Siang 1999) calls for the delineation of what is public and what is private in relation to the Internet. Others believe that 'technically there can be no such delineation' (Bassett and O'Riordan 2002, p. 243), and that it can become easy to conflate the metaphor for the object that it is supposed to describe. I tend to agree with Bassett and O'Riordan (2002) that only certain kinds of Internet experiences can be described in spatial terms. Oftentimes the Internet is used as a type of textual publishing medium, and culture members are fully aware of this public function.

As a result of these careful examinations of the guiding metaphors we use to direct our Internet research, a number of prominent scholars have concluded that not all Internet-based research benefits from applying a human subjects research code of ethics (e.g., Bassett and O'Riordan 2002; Bruckman 2002, 2006; Walther 2002). The models governing our codes of ethics need to be more flexible in the way that they analyse and acknowledge both spatial and textual understandings of computer-mediated communications – and perhaps adopt other metaphors as they are pertinent and useful.

According to the Code of Federal Regulations Title 45, Part 46, Protection of Human Subjects (2009), which governs Institutional Review Boards in the United States, human subjects research is research in which there is an intervention or inter-action with another person for the purpose of gathering information, or in which information is recorded by a researcher in such a way that a person can be identified through it directly or indirectly. Netnography, in which the netnographer participates online with community members, thus clearly fits into the human subjects research model. These participative interactions are therefore more like communications that happen in particular guarded places, with some reasonable expectation of privacy.

However, the research use of spontaneous conversations, if gathered in a publicly accessible venue, is not human subjects research according to the Code of Federal Regulations' definition. If the research involves collecting and analysing existing doc-uments or records that are publicly available, this research qualifies for a human subjects exemption. Much of the archival, observational research in a netnography would therefore be of this type.

Internet research pioneer Joseph Walther (2002) is quite clear about the research ethics implications of this observational form of investigation. Participants in online communities and cultures may not expect that their remarks are going to be read by others outside of the community; they may therefore react with anger that their communications might appear in a research publication. As noted above, some culture members (in my research, it has been only a tiny minority) have, when asked, resisted being included in research (see also Bakardjieva and Feenberg 2001; King 1996; McArthur 2001).

> However, it is important to recognize that *any person who uses publicly-available communication systems on the Internet must be aware that these systems are, at their foundation and by definition, mechanisms for the storage, transmission, and retrieval of comments.* While some participants have an expectation of privacy, it is extremely misplaced. (Walther 2002, p. 207; emphasis in original)

Analysing online community or culture communications or their archives is not human subjects research *if the researcher does not record the identity of the communicators and if the researcher can legally and easily gain access to these communications or archives.* Those are important conditions and, for instance, would indicate that content analysis and thematic analyses of online communications would, under some conditions, be exempt.

This suggests that, for research ethics purposes, we can regard the use of some types and uses of computer-mediated cultural interactions as similar to the use of texts. Jacobson (1999) notes that the recording of any written message or related document is protected in the United States by US copyright law. However, researchers are allowed to make 'fair use' of copyright materials, subject to certain restrictions, such as the length of the excerpt and the proportion of the original work quoted. In the USA, therefore, many of the otherwise restrictive effects of copyright may be waived as far as research purposes are concerned (Walther 2002). However, many of these fair use exemptions *are not* in effect in international law. Those nations' lack of fair use laws may well impede the ability of researchers outside the United States to conduct netnography. In addition, researchers seeking to make use of communal resources located on commercial websites may well run up against legal restrictions. Individual researchers are well advised to check into the relevant regulations pertaining to their countries.

The Internet is not really a place or a text; it is not either public or private. It is not even one single type of social interaction, but many types: chats, postings, comments on mass-trafficked blogs, sharings of soundclips and videos, telephone conversations shared using VOIP protocols. The Internet is uniquely and only the Internet. As we reason about it, we need to keep our guiding metaphors in mind.

CONSENT IN CYBERSPACE

Gaining the informed consent of research participants is a cornerstone of ethical research conduct. King (1996) recommended gaining additional informed consent from online research participants. Similarly, Sharf (1999) echoed this heightened sensitivity to the ethics of online fieldwork, even that which was purely observational. Yet, as Frankel and Siang (1999, p. 8) note, the 'ease of anonymity and pseudonymity of

Internet communications also poses logistical difficulties for implementing the informed consent process'.

In a major departure from traditional face-to-face methods like ethnography, focus groups, or personal interviews, netnography uses cultural information that is not given specifically, in confidence, to the researcher. The uniquely unobtrusive nature of the approach is the source of much of netnography's attractiveness as well as its contentiousness. If netnographers act in a manner found to be irresponsible and disrespectful by the public or officials, they could make it difficult for other researchers to conduct their research – a trend that that has already begun to develop – or even invite legal sanctions.

The analysis of archived messages does not, however, officially constitute human subjects social research. But netnography often goes further than unobtrusive observation and download. Netnographers are cultural participants; they interact. As Walther (2002, pp. 212–13) suggests, 'many kinds of human subjects social research that do involve some kind of interaction or intervention may also be exempt from IRB concern (that is, may apply for and be granted exemption from further review and oversight) due to the lack of harm the research presents' to those being researched. These categories of research that involve no risk would include research where activities were typical of normal day-to-day behaviour and where the research does not involve the collection of identity in association with response data.

In these cases, 'implied consent' may be an appropriate procedure. Online, implied consent occurs when research consent-related information is presented to the prospective research participant in an electronic, written form. The participant would signal their consent by agreeing to continue in the study, often by clicking an 'accept' button on a web-page and/or by providing data. Although questions have been raised about whether this approach can be valid without certain knowledge of the competency, comprehension, and even the age of the research participant, Walther (2002, p. 213) notes that many traditionally accepted methods such as mail and telephone surveys deal with the same sort of uncertain knowledge about whether people are actually who they say they are. In fact, there is no clear, indisputable link between face-to-face research and judgements of research participant competency and comprehension.

HARM ONLINE

Novel contexts seem to dichotomize judgements, and the opinions surrounding the new context of Internet research ethics are no exception. 'The early online data rush which treated every content found on the net as open to downloading, analysing and quoting has been countered by an ethical perfectionism leaving almost no space for research on virtual forums' (Bakardjieva and Feenberg 2001, p. 233). The same potential for harm present in face-to-face ethnographies – the revelation of cultural secrets, the hurtful portrayals of culture members, the disdainful treatment of customs – is present in netnography. Past methodological treatments have warned netnographers to be careful in considering the ethical concerns of privacy, confidentiality, appropriation, and consent (Kozinets 2002a, 2006a).

Culture members may well have strong feelings about the research use of their stored communications. Walther (2002, p. 215) opines that these issues warrant our careful consideration and further discussion, however, he suggests that they probably do not warrant 'the suspension of scientifically designed and theoretically motivated research'. Valid research uses of online community data are not the same as the 'spamming' of commercial entities, even though both may be seen as intrusions and interferences by online community members.

What about netnographies that write things about online community members, or the online community itself, that may not be positive or flattering? To provide a hypothetical example, what about a netnography of an online community devoted to a hip hop singer that ends up revealing that the community is also devoted to an appreciation of and education about illegal drugs such as heroin and cocaine?

As Bruckman (2002, p. 225; emphasis in original) notes, '*human subjects regulations do not prohibit us from doing harm to subjects*'. The relevant sections of the federal code relating to criteria for IRB approval of research suggest that risks to research participants should be minimized and that 'risks to subjects are reasonable in relation to anticipated benefits, if any, to subjects, and the importance of the knowledge that may reasonably be expected to result' (Protection of Human Subjects 2009). There is thus a consequentialist, utilitarian ethical philosophy guiding academic research practice – not a deontological one founded in the idea of doing no harm. Susan Herring (1996) notes that, as scholars, we are not bound to adopt research methods or voice research results in order to please our research participants. In an ideal situation, the netnographic researcher 'would carefully weigh the public benefit of making the revelation, and balance this against the potential harm to the subject' (Bruckman 2002, p. 225).

TO NAME OR NOT TO NAME, THAT IS THE QUESTION

As we noted above, in some ways participants in online communities can be seen to be creating and contributing to an ongoing, complex, and publicly available text. Technology scholar Amy Bruckman (2002, 2006) has probably gone furthest in analysing this state of affairs and drafting practical research ethics suggestions relating to it. There are a number of pertinent points. In the first case, culture members can and often have sought to undermine research anonymity by trying to identify the subjects of written accounts. Bruckman (2002, pp. 219–20) gives the example of Julian Dibbell's (1998) book, *My Tiny Life*, an ethnographic study of the LambdaMOO online community. 'After the book's publication, LambdaMOO members whom Dibbell studied collaborated to create a chart of who is who, and shared the chart openly with anyone interested' (Bruckman 2002, p. 220).

Secondly, online pseudonyms function exactly like real names and should be treated as real names.

Individuals often use the same pseudonym over time, and care about the reputation of that pseudonym. They may also choose to use a part or all of their real name as their pseudonym, or some other personal detail that is equally identifying. They may also routinely disclose information linking their pseudonym and real name. (Bruckman 2002, p. 221; see also Frankel and Siang 1999, Walther 2002).

Third, there are few defensible, practical solutions to the fact that a direct quote can be accessed through a full-text search in a public search engine. It is therefore a fairly simple procedure to enter the verbatim quote of culture members used in research publications into a public search engine and to then link that quotation with the actual pseudonym of a culture member (Kozinets 2002a, 2006a). If the pseudonym is to be treated as the real name, breaches of pseudonymity and thus anonymity are inevitable.

Fourth, there may be examples where culture members or culture leaders would like credit for their work. For example, if quoting a well-known blogger who is a member of an online community, why would a netnographer not cite them just as she would cite any other published author? Many bloggers would rather see their online work properly cited, just as that work would be credited were they to publish it in a book or article. Similarly, should we not consider some message posters, gatekeepers, and community members to be 'public figures', and accord them less power to control information about themselves (and more direct credit for their work) than so-called 'private people' who are not seeking power, influence, or attention in the same way?

Fifth, we should probably treat the recording of conversation in a chat-room, or activity and interaction in a virtual world, or other synchronous conversation and interaction differently from the way that we treat asynchronous communications that are more clearly intended as postings for mass and public communication.

Finally, old, binary distinctions between published and unpublished works are obsolete. Bruckman suggests that, in the Internet age, publishing is now a continuum: 'Most work on the Internet is "semi-published"' (2002, p. 227). Therefore, we are advised to treat the culture members we study in a netnography as 'amateur artists': 'in many ways, all user-created content on the Internet can be viewed as various forms of amateur art and authorship' (2002, p. 229).

LEGAL CONSIDERATIONS

Legal scholar, practising attorney, and professor, Tomas Lipinski (2006, p. 55; see also 2008) has published a valuable analysis of the potential legal issues pertaining to 'the protocols of ethnographers who use listserv, discussion board, blog, chat room and other sorts of web or Internet-based postings as the source of their data'. Although his approach favours a more observational and less interactive method, many of his conclusions still appear to apply to the more participative form of netnography that

I advance in this book. To summarize a complex set of topics, researchers who collect online community data from online sources and then 'publish' that information in some particular online venue, such as an online journal, or an online version of a journal, have significant protection from tort harm claims.

If the research is published in a traditional print medium, Lipinski (2006) suggests that researchers should be careful to only report true findings and not to deviate from standard research protocols. Those who do so are unlikely to be held liable for placing defendants in a false light, invading their privacy, defaming them, harming them, or in other ways acting in a negligent manner. Finally, because the conduct of academic research is so important to human understanding and public policy, Lipinski (2006) suggests that courts may treat this form of research as somewhat different from other types of investigation and other uses of online data, such as, for instance, marketing research.

Netnographic researchers 'who refrain from including not only the subject's name or pseudonym but also any information that might identify an individual' should be exempted from claims arising from invasion of privacy. In general, Lipinski (2006) suggests that researchers avoid identifying individual culture members through their real name, online pseudonym, or other identifying information, a suggestion that can be somewhat difficult in practice. However, even if the identification of culture members occurs, because the online forum is legally viewed as a public place, this should undermine claims of invasion of privacy.

These sections have provided necessarily brief overviews of four issues important to the understanding of netnographic research ethics: metaphors of private versus public and textual versus spatial, pragmatics of informed consent, consequentialist determinations of harm and benefit, and the pseudonymous complexities of quotation and citation. In the next section, we turn to some recommended procedures and solutions. Although not hard-and-fast rules or prescriptions, these guidelines are intended to help set standards so that netnographers can get on with the work of doing quality netnography. The four sets of guidelines are as follows. First, you must identify yourself and accurately inform relevant constituents about your research. Next, you must ask for the appropriate permissions. Appropriate consent must be gained. Finally you must properly cite and credit culture members.

Incorporating these suggestions into your research will mean making decisions that will alter every aspect of your netnography. Ethics is not a section of your research that can be simply 'tacked on' at the end by including a paragraph about IRB approval in a report's method section. It alters the research question you choose to pursue, the types of community that you will study, the specific approaches and methods you will use, the type of data you will and will not collect, the way you make your cultural entrée, the kind of questions you will ask community members, the type of fieldnotes you will keep and the type of analysis you will conduct, as well as markedly transforming the nature of your final report. Because of the persistent and accessible nature of online communications, ethics is involved from the very beginning of your decision to conduct a netnography until long after its final publication and distribution.

PROCEDURES FOR ETHICAL NETNOGRAPHY

Identifying and Explaining

The foundation of an ethical netnography is honesty between the researcher and online community members. Just as with in-person ethnography, the netnographer should *always* fully disclose his/her presence, affiliations and intentions to online community members during any research interactions. This obviously pertains to the research entrée, as well as to subsequent interactions.

Bruckman (2006) uses concrete examples from her graduate class on online community design in order to demonstrate procedures for studying online communities ethically. One of her instructions to students is for them to openly describe themselves as researchers. There must be absolutely no deception about what you are doing in the online community. It is highly recommended that the fact that you are conducting an online community study should appear prominently in your user profile. Some of the students in Bruckman's class who were studying on sites with customizable 3D avatars 'chose to dress themselves in white lab coats' (Bruckman 2006, p. 89). Another possibility would be to wear a t-shirt or a large button that proclaimed one's status as a researcher, or to have this as one's avatar, or in one's sig line. It is also important that the way the researcher reveals his or her presence should not be disruptive to the normal activity of the site.

Even if the practice of identity play, gender mixing, and other types of altered representation is common on the site, the researcher is more bound by codes of research ethics to disclose themselves accurately than they are by the practice of netnography to fit in as a culture member. Netnographers should *never, under any circumstances,* engage in identity deception.

When it comes to disclosing the research purposes of your netnographic investigation, the advice becomes vaguer. As with many types of studies, it could be counterproductive to reveal one's core themes and theoretical ideas as they are developing. It might also be off-putting to describe your research using complex theories and insider terminology that only fellow PhDs would appreciate. The guiding principle is to accurately and generally provide your research direction and focus. Not 'I am trying to see how Foucault's panopticon theory applies to a motherhood-based online community's monitoring of new mothers' behaviours' but 'I am interested in privacy and freedom in online communities'. Correctly phrased, the description of one's research focus and direction can and should serve as an excellent starting point for further discussion of the research topic. It could even help you to clarify your topic, and make it accessible to others outside of academe.

It is also highly desirable for the netnographer to offer some more detailed explanation about themselves in the research study. Because providing this information to an online forum in a series of ongoing posts or as a set of texts uploaded to a chat-room can be quite disruptive, I recommend using a separate web-page devoted to this purpose. Ideally, the web-page will be hosted on an official university (or other legitimate research entity) server and have links to the researcher's profile and perhaps other published works. As described in Chapter 5, I have found dedicated research web-pages to be a very helpful way to identify myself to online community members, inform community members about my research, contribute to the community by sharing information that might be of interest to them, and ask for interview participants.

The research web-page can also be a valuable way to provide online community and culture members with access to one's data and reports in order to solicit their comments. This procedure of 'member checking' can be a helpful way to gain additional insider feedback as well as another ethical check where community members are given additional opportunities to add their 'voice into their own representation' (see Kozinets 2002a). Member checks can also help to establish ongoing relations between researchers and online communities. In long-term research enterprises such as ethnography and netnography, this positive and trusting relationship offers benefits to all concerned.

So, from the beginning of the research through to its end, good netnographic research ethics dictate that the researcher: (1) openly and accurately identifies her or himself, avoiding all deception, (2) openly and accurately describes their research purpose for interacting with community members, and (3) provides an accessible, relevant, and accurate description of their research focus and interests. Finally, it is highly recommended that the netnographer set up a research web-page providing positive identification as well as a more detailed explanation of the research and its purpose, and perhaps should eventually share the initial, interim, and final research findings with online community members.

Asking Permission

Although notions of private or public space may be nebulous when applied in a general sense to the Internet, there are certain types of online communication where the expectation of privacy is more marked. Bulletin boards and newsgroups, such as those found on Usenet, possess a long history. With their FAQs and attention to newbies, they seem to be well aware that they are public modes of discourse with the potential to reach wide, general audiences. However, there are many websites requiring membership and registry. Chat rooms often fall into this category. Social networking sites and virtual worlds do as well. Lists and listservs are even more exclusive. When attempting to do research in these areas, asking for permission is clearly required.

In forums that are hosted on small Internet sites, a site's founder and/or administrator is a legitimate gatekeeper that the researcher should approach prior to contacting other users of the site. For larger sites, such as those contained on Yahoo! Groups, a group's moderator (but not Yahoo! management itself) would be an appropriate gatekeeper that the researcher would need to contact. Guild or clan leaders might be appropriate gatekeepers to approach before attempting to gain access to the wider membership of a massively multiplayer online game (or MMOG). However, not everyone who presents himself as a gatekeeper of an online community actually is one. Sometimes, it takes a bit of detective work by the netnographer to identify if there are any appropriate gatekeepers to approach relevant to the site they would like to study, who they are, and how best to approach them.

Using Commercial Sites for Netnography

As we now know it, the Internet is a hybrid form mixing public with commercial interests. Commercial websites often contain extremely interesting and useful material, and netnographers are often naturally attracted to them. For example, Nelson and Otnes (2005) conducted a netnography that studied several commercial bulletin boards devoted to helping brides plan their weddings. This is a very common practice. However, the ethical implications of these research-related uses of commercial websites have only rarely been considered.

In a very helpful article, Allen, Burk, and Davis (2006, p. 609) note that 'researchers are currently making substantial academic use of commercial Internet resources. Such research activity is important in developing our understanding of the many organizational aspects that are so deeply affected by the Internet'. However, these activities have not gone without notice and commercial sites have begun to use different sorts of legal means to limit individuals from access to online content. 'Academic research is not exempt from the legal arguments that have been successfully advanced' to limit and punish those who infringe on the content-related ownership rights of commercial sites (Allen et al. 2006, p. 609).

Acceptable and legal access terms for commercial websites are defined in their 'terms of service' or 'terms of use' agreements as well as and in conjunction with the robot.txt file located at the root directory of the web server (see Allen et al. 2006, pp. 602–3 for details). In fact, it turns out that many potential and popular sites for the conduct of netnographies have limitations written into their terms of service agreements.

For example, the terms of use for the popular social networking site Facebook seem to present a quite prohibitive contract.

> *Proprietary Rights in Site Content; Limited License.* All content on the Site and available through the service, including designs, text, graphics, pictures, video, information, applications, software, music, sound and other files, and their selection and arrangement (the 'Site Content'), are the proprietary property of the Company, its users or its licensors with all rights reserved. No Site Content may be modified, copied, distributed, framed, reproduced, republished, downloaded, scraped, displayed, posted, transmitted, or sold in any form or by any means, in whole or in part, without the Company's prior written permission, except that the foregoing does not apply to your own User Content (as defined below) that you legally post on the Site … Except for your own User Content, you may not upload or republish Site Content on any Internet, Intranet or Extranet site or incorporate the information in any other database or compilation, and any other use of the Site Content is strictly prohibited … Any use of the Site or the Site Content other than as specifically authorized herein, without the prior written permission of Company, is

strictly prohibited and will terminate the license granted herein. Such unauthorized use may also violate applicable laws including copyright and trademark laws and applicable communications regulations and statutes. (Facebook Terms of Use 2009, www.facebook.com/terms.php, accessed 1 February 2009)

Let us examine briefly what this would mean for netnography. Everything on the site – text, pictures, information and other files, that would constitute your potential netnographic data set – are owned by Facebook, and the company reserves all rights to them. The contract strictly and explicitly prohibits copying, reproducing, downloading, and republishing these data, which is what you would need to do in order to write and publish a netnography. Any other use of the content on the site other than what the agreement specifies, in this case, as a research project, is prohibited without the prior written permission of the company, and could end up in violation of the law. By agreeing to Facebook's terms of use, you are agreeing to abide by this contract.

Similarly, the content and associated forums of the Sony Pictures website contain a lot of material that is of potential interest to netnographers interested in fan or audience studies, as well as a variety of other topics related to consumer culture and media consumption. For instance, it contains the Spiderman fan boards and creative works exchanges, *The Young and the Restless* and *Days of Our Lives* fan bulletin boards, and a variety of other media-centred online communities. However, the Terms of Service agreement that one assents to in gaining access to the community is, again, restrictive.

Sony Pictures Entertainment grants you a non-exclusive, non-transferable, limited right to access, use and display the Site and the materials thereon for your personal use only, provided that you comply fully with this TOS … Except as otherwise provided herein, you may not reproduce, perform, create derivative works from, republish, upload, edit, post, transmit, or distribute in any way whatsoever, any materials from this Site or any other web site owned or operated by Sony Pictures Entertainment (the 'Site Materials') without the prior written permission of Sony Pictures Entertainment. (Sony Pictures Terms of Service, www.sonypictures.com/mobile/mazingo/terms_of_service.html, accessed 1 February 2009)

Because we must agree to these terms before gaining access to the online communities hosted on these sites, we seem to be locked into playing by the rules of these corporations. It would seem from all of this that performing a netnography of commercial sites can be problematic. Should it be avoided?

To answer this, consider the following. Allen et al. (2006, p. 607) specifically state that 'manual, non-automated access [by researchers] of information on publicly available web-pages [even ones belonging to corporations] should be acceptable without special permissions or actions'. Even though the website might not explicitly permit such acts as for research, the server load on the website is negligible and this sort of limited access for research purposes 'fits within normal website expectations' (2006, p. 607). Furthermore, strict enforcement of the terms of service agreements 'would virtually close commercial websites to any examination by academia' (2006, p. 607). Combined with what we know about fair use laws in the USA from Lipinski (2006,

2008), and the recognition that academic research is considered generally important to public policy and the public good, it appears that commercial sites are viable ones for netnography – if, *and this is a big if*, there are fair use laws in effect, as there are in the United States. However, the researcher would always be wise to consult with their appropriate IRB, Human Research Subjects Review Committee, or other regulative body and, when in doubt, to also check with a legal expert.

Although their article and corresponding advice were directed more at automated online data collection research than at netnographic approaches, Allen et al. (2006, p. 609) recommend two procedures that are applicable and appropriate to netnographic researchers seeking to study a community or culture placed on a commercial site. They recommend that the company be notified that the research is being conducted by sending a message to the appropriate group, persons, or person indicating the purpose and scope of the research. In addition, they recommend that the researchers provide a description of their research activity, preferably on 'a web-page that describes the research activity' (2006, p. 611). These two suggestions dovetail with the advice provided in the section above. Obviously, they would also work well together, as the notification contact could contain links to the descriptive research web-page – which could be the same page used to inform culture members. These notions of providing information and asking permissions lead us naturally to our next topic, that of gaining consent.

Gaining Informed Consent

As already noted in the section above, ethical standards in human subjects research require us to gain the permission of research participants where appropriate. However, it is also apparent that the archival research and download of existing posts does not strictly qualify as human subjects research. It is only where interaction or intervention occurs that consent is required. These guidelines are contingent upon the risk to the research participant and the level of identification of participants in the research. According to US federal regulations, researchers can request an exemption of informed consent documentation (which is *not* exemption from the consent itself) 'if the research presents no more than minimal risk of harm to subjects and involves no procedures for which written consent is normally required outside of the research context' (Protection of Human Subjects, US Federal Code Title 45, Section 46 (2000)). Many, but not all, participative netnographic studies will likely fall into this category of minimal risk of harm and no unusual procedures.

In general, as a netnographer interacts *normally* in the online community or culture, that is, as she interacts as other members do on the site but also takes fieldnotes of her experiences, there is no need to gain informed consent for those interactions. When these interactions occur as an asynchronous, persistent communication such as a posting on a bulletin board, then this material may be quoted subject to the guidelines on direct quotations that follow in the section below. With ephemeral, synchronous, real-time communication media such as chat or conversations in game spaces or virtual worlds, the researcher should never record those interactions without gaining explicit permission. It is currently a hotly debated topic whether it is ethical or even legal to record real-time interactions such as chat without permission (Bruckman 2006, Hudson and Bruckman 2004). To bring in another point, Bruckman (2006, p. 87) opines that in her experience, 'online interviews are of limited value'. Chat room interviews generally present very thin or superficial data and are of limited value in building theory or understanding. However, online interviews conducted using e-mail or a telephone-like link such as Skype, can be extremely valuable.

Interviews, whether conducted online or off, clearly fall into the area of an interaction and thus require informed consent. We must draw three levels of differentiation in order to proceed.

(1) Are the intended participants in the interview adults?
(2) Are the intended research participants members of a vulnerable population?
(3) Should the research be considered to have higher-than-minimal risk in some way?

If the intended research participants for the interview are not adults, are members of a vulnerable population, or where the research is higher risk, then traditional consent forms such as are used for in-person interviews or experiments are appropriate. For this research and these groups, it is best for the researcher to send the consent form electronically or through snail mail. The participants would then read and sign the form. They would be required to either mail it back through snail mail, fax it or, if permissible, send an appropriately signed digital copy. If the research participants are children, then the researcher would also need to gain the written permission of each child's parent or guardian on a consent form. An assent form would also need to be sent to the child to gain their assent. This form would need to be worded in a manner appropriate to the child's comprehension level at that particular age.

If the research participant is an adult, not a member of a vulnerable population, and the research is not high risk, then it may be possible for your appropriate regulatory body, be it an IRB or Human Research Subjects Review Committee, to permit you to use an online consent form. The consent form can be presented on a web-page with a button at the bottom that allows participants simply to 'click to accept' the terms of the form. Combining approved consent forms of my own with the useful example and suggestions of Bruckman (2006), I present a general format online consent form that you may wish to adapt to the particular needs of your own study and regulatory situation. See Appendix 1, at the end of this book, for that consent form.

Citing, Anonymizing, or Crediting Research Participants

Before beginning a netnography, the researchers and their relevant regulatory body should decide whether subjects' identities are going to be cloaked and if so, to what extent they will be protected. In anonymizing or crediting netnographic research participants' accounts, your goal is to fairly balance the rights of Internet users with the value of your research's contribution to society (Bruckman 2002, 2006; Hair and Clark 2007; Walther 2002). The ethics of citation or quotation are far from straight-forward. Online pseudonyms should be treated as real names (cf. Langer and Beckman 2005). They are often traceable to real names, and people often care about the reputation of their pseudonyms. A motivated person can easily trace a direct quote to its original online posting and thus locate a pseudonym. In fact, culture members often attempt to 'figure out' researcher-assigned pseudonyms. Finally, much of the work on the Internet can be considered to be 'semi-published' and the cre-ators of some online material may be public figures. We therefore may want to give the actual creators credit for the online material we use in our research.

We need to balance the following ethical considerations: (1) the need to protect vulnerable human participants who may be put at risk from the exposure of a research study, (2) the accessible and 'semi-published' qualities of much of what is shared on the Internet, and (3) the rights of individual community and culture mem-bers to receive credit for their creative and intellectual work. Listing names and dis-guising them both have issues in practice. Hiding denies credit where it is due. Providing actual names means that you are obligated to omit potentially damaging, yet theoretically valuable and insightful, information from your written accounts.

First and foremost, we must work with a solid understanding of the terms risk and harm. These determinations of risk should be guided in relation to strict ethical guidelines. The US Federal Code Title 45 regulations define minimal risk as mean-ing that 'the probability and magnitude of harm or discomfort anticipated in the research are not greater in and of themselves than those ordinarily encountered in daily life or during the performance of routine physical or psychological examinations or tests' (Protection of Human Subjects, 2009).

There are certain groups that are inherently vulnerable. For example if you are studying illicit or addictive drug use communities, pornographic communities, mari-tal infidelity sites, support groups for those with a serious disease, and other illegal, stigmatized, or marginalized groups, *these groups cannot be construed to be minimal risk.*

Risk is also a function of the goals and end result of your study. You may be studying an online community devoted to stockbrokers and discover that illegal animal import items are among the most profitable things that they trade. We must there-fore recognize that identification procedures must be decided on a case-by-case basis contingent upon the topic matter, the research purposes, and the research approach of your particular netnography. If the study is low risk, it would seem appropriate to give 'amateur artists' credit for their work if they desire it. In this case, the researcher would need to ask 'in my research, do you want me to list your pseu-donym, your real name, both, or neither?'

If the study is higher risk, providing either names or pseudonyms is not appropri-ate. As always in cases of research ethics, the degree of risk to the participant must be balanced against the potential benefits of the study. You may also want to take into account the degree to which your participant is a 'public figure'. In the higher risk case, before beginning the interaction with the participant, the researcher should explain the risks of the study and the fact that the research participant's work will not be credited. It is important that the researcher and their regulatory body make this determination, and not the research participant. For justification of this guideline, it might be instructive to look at Elizabeth Reid's (1996) study of an online site for survivors of abuse. In Reid's thesis study, some participants agreed to speak to her only on the condition that they would be named. She later wrote that this was a mistake and ended up putting her participants at risk; she was the one who should have made that determination, not the research participants.

Four Degrees of Concealment

Bruckman (2006, pp. 229–30) recommends four different levels of disguise on a continuum from 'no disguise' to 'heavy disguise'. She provides useful guidelines directing when each level of disguise should be adopted. To emphasize the researcher's protective actions, rather than the state of the participant, I have opted to use the metaphor of degrees of cloaking. The four degrees of concealment suggested in this section are: uncloaked, minimum cloaked, medium cloaked, and maximum cloaked.

Providing an *uncloaked* participant means using the online pseudonym or real name of the research participant in the research report. Real names should only be used with the explicit written permission of the individual, unless that person is undisputedly a public figure. In using real names, the researcher respects the individual's claim to copyright, and has also verified that the participant is the actual author of the work. When using real names, the researcher must be careful to omit material that could potentially be harmful to the individual if revealed. For instance, if a high-profile, underage, comic book fan artist reveals his frequent use of alcohol while composing his art, this should be left out of the written research account, even if it contributes to our understanding of his participation in the online comic book fan community.

In a *minimum cloaked* situation, the actual name of the online community or other group is given. Online pseudonyms, names, and other means of identifying the person are altered. Direct, verbatim quotes are used, even though a motivated individual could use them to identify the research participants. Group members might be able to guess who is being represented. In this case, the context of the research is so important to theoretical development that cloaking it would be detrimental to the creation of understanding. In the research reports, there should be no details that might be harmful to the community or to individual participants. In this way, the lack of anonymity is balanced by the lack of probable harm. With the alt.coffee examples presented in Chapter 7, a minimum cloaked identity situation is employed. The online community's name is given, but online pseudonyms and names are altered. These examples are mainly descriptive and instructive, and present minimal probability of harm to the community or its cited members.

Providing a *medium cloaked* identity is a concessionary accommodation. The level of security would be more than would be found in a minimum cloaked situation, but less than would be found under maximum cloaked conditions. Each situation might be different but would combine different aspects of the minimum and maximum cloaked conditions. For instance, the community might be named, but no actual names, pseudonyms, or direct verbatim quotes would be used. This situation might make sense where there was minimal-to-moderate risk to participants or the community, or where the risk to the participants and community had been determined to be acceptable, given the potential benefit of the research knowledge. Presumably the benefit in this case would accrue from theory development requiring the inclusion of the name of the community, or information that could be used to identify it. In one of the examples of weak communal entrée presented in Chapter 5, a medium cloaked identity strategy is used to depict the community posting. Because the critique given there could potentially be embarrassing to the student who posted the message, their identity is cloaked, the group is described in general terms but its name is not provided, and no direct quotes of any length significant enough to yield unique results in a search engine are given. The concern about embarrassment was weighed against the pedagogical utility of using this actual example and it was considered important enough to use it.

Finally, the *maximum cloaked* condition is intended to provide maximum security for research participants. In the maximum cloaked condition, the online community and its site are not named. All names, pseudonyms, and other identifying details are altered. There are no direct verbatim quotes used if a search engine could link those quotations to the individuals' original postings. Some indirect re-phrasings of original postings might be used, under the provision that these re-phrasings or re-statings are checked by the researcher by entering them into a search engine and ensuring that they do not lead to the original postings. Another possible course of action would be to have the original postings removed from online access – something that is usually only possible when control of the website lies in the researcher's hands. If the original posting is no longer accessible, then a direct quote can no longer be traced to the participant. However, the presence of automatic online archiving sites complicates assurances that the original posting is no longer available; it may have already been archived by a third-party (Hair and Clark 2007). Again, due diligence on the part of the researcher would be required.

In the maximum cloaked situation, some fictive details that do not change the theoretical impact of the paper may be intentionally introduced. For example, if studying an online community devoted to a high risk sport, one particular high risk sport might be changed to another one in order to protect research participant confidentiality.

Maximum cloaking means that the researcher does everything that they can to disguise research participants. It entails that even a dedicated and motivated person trying to determine the identity of a person in the research would be unable to do so. In the case of maximum cloaking, details that might be harmful to the research participants or to the online community itself may be revealed. The revelation of potentially harmful, disruptive, embarrassing, stigmatizing or even illegal materials can occur because the participants and the community have been so carefully anonymized. To provide a rather extreme example, in a study of online child pornography communities, the researcher would need to ensure that all identifying information was anonymized. In that case, having informants respond through a proxy server and having all IP addresses scrubbed, or IP logs turned off, could provide an extra level of cloaking to help ensure that participants in the research cannot be linked – even if the researcher was legally obligated to do so – to their real names or identities.

SUMMARY

Rather than providing a 'cookie cutter' solution to the complex ethical issues involved in conducting a netnography, this chapter presents information, procedures, and resources that will allow you first to understand the pertinent issues and then to choose a wise and ethical course of action for your research. Four difficult issues were presented as paramount to our understanding of netnographic research ethics: (1) whether online communities should be treated as public or private spaces, (2) how to gain informed consent from online community members, (3) the necessity of avoiding harm to online community members, and (4) how to portray data relating to netnographic research participants. Four general procedures address these issues: (1) identifying and informing, (2) asking permission, (3) gaining consent, and (4) citing and crediting. Incorporating these suggestions into your research will mean making decisions that will alter every aspect of your netnography, from its research focus to its final presentation – and thus ethical concerns should colour the way that each of the procedural chapters of this book are read and implemented. With the procedural chapters of this book now completed, we turn in the chapter following to a discussion of the (re)presentation of netnographic research and evaluations of its quality.

KEY READINGS

Bruckman, Amy (2002) 'Studying the Amateur Artist: a Perspective on Disguising Data Collected in Human Subjects Research on the Internet', *Ethics and Information Technology*, 4: 217–31.

Buchanan, Elizabeth (2004) *Readings in Virtual Research Ethics: Issues and Controversies*. Hershey, PA: Idea Group.

Johns, M., S.L. Chen and J. Hall (eds) (2003) *Online Social Research: Methods, Issues, and Ethics*. New York: Peter Lang.

Lipinski, Tomas A. (2006) 'Emerging Tort Issues in the Collection and Dissemination of Internet-based Research Data', *Journal of Information Ethics*, Fall: 55–81.

Walther, Joseph B. (2002) 'Research Ethics in Internet-Enabled Research: Human Subjects Issues and Methodological Myopia', *Ethics and Information Technology*, 4: 205–16.

9
REPRESENTATION AND EVALUATION

ABSTRACT

The evaluative standards for qualitative research and ethnography are unclear and this can cause considerable confusion. In this chapter, you will learn about the representational issues facing the netnographer ready to present or publish findings. Ten recommended evaluation standards are recommended for the assessment of the quality of a netnography.

Key Words: dependability, ethnographic authority, ethnographic interpretation, experimental ethnography, praxis, qualitative research evaluation, reflexivity, resonance, trustworthiness, validity

STANDARDS, EVALUATION, AND NETNOGRAPHY

Netnography is a specialized type of ethnography. It uses and incorporates different methods in a single approach focused on the study of communities and cultures in the Internet age. Qualitative online research such as netnography is 'essential in shaping our understanding of the Internet, its impact on culture, and culture's impacts on the Internet' (Baym 2006, p. 79). Yet there is far more to qualitative research than simply describing, recounting, or cataloguing people's words or actions.

What are the standards of excellence for qualitative research? Often, they have been critiqued as vague or unclear, especially when compared to the seemingly unambiguous evaluative standards of quantitative researchers. Although the relevance of a p-value of less than .05 can (and should) be debated, it is widely agreed that it is the convention through which the 'significance' and insignificance of many experimental and survey findings will be evaluated. Similarly, the principles of statistical sampling are widely agreed upon and dictate that large sample sizes, representative draws, and normal distributions are required in order to reach generalizable conclusions. Ethnographers, netnographers, and other qualitative researchers have no such clear and measurable standards of evaluation.

The general lack of qualitative standards can become even more of a problem when coupled with a new field such as Internet research. '[M]any internet researchers have the misguided sense that they are the first to discover an online phenomenon (a sense so strong that many apparently never bother to search existing literature to see whether this is the case)' (Baym 2006, p. 80). Many also tend to enter the field with the mistaken sense that research on the Internet or online communities is revolutionary. Over the last decade it has been stated *ad nauseum* that Internet research and the phenomena it treats are so different that they require an entirely new set of rules. A good historian of science will note that laypeople and scholars present at the birth of electricity, the railroad, the telephone, the television, and most of the other major innovations uttered similar pronouncements. But, as it inevitably turns out, our theories and techniques almost always can accommodate the new phenomena, be they global air travel or digital avatars in virtual worlds. In fact, shedding light on the similarities and differences with what has gone before – theoretically and substantively – is very often our objective as scholars and scientific thinkers.

Culturally-oriented studies of the Internet are still somewhat novel and standards in emerging areas such as this one can be difficult to discern because there is little agreement. This is compounded by the fact that we can not essentialize 'qualitative research' or 'ethnography' – or even 'netnography' – as one single approach or set of actions. There are not only many different techniques and research practices, but also many different schools. And each of these schools, approaches, and toolkits is inflected yet again by different scholarly fields, their journals, prominent centres of development, influential scholars, and so on. So no set of standards, given in its entirety, can be held to apply for every research circumstance. Although most of them are not substantially different from the standards for excellent ethnography or qualitative research in general, this chapter attempts to provide a brief overview of some evaluative standards that aspiring netnographers may find useful. Even if scholars do not agree with them and wish to cogently suggest alternatives (always a helpful and useful undertaking in science), it is helpful to begin with a lucid statement of expectations and criteria.

After opining about the generally low quality of much qualitative Internet research, and analysing five exemplary works of culturally-oriented Internet research, Nancy Baym concludes that there are

> at least six interrelated strengths they share: they are grounded in theory and data, they demonstrate rigor in data collection and analysis, they use multiple strategies to get data, they take into account the perspective of participants, they demonstrate awareness of and self-reflexivity regarding the research process, and they take into consideration interconnections between the Internet and the life world within which it is situated. (Baym 2006, p. 82)

These are excellent criteria, and a sound basis for the following discussion.

For over a decade, I have also been thinking, speculating, and writing about acceptable standards for qualitative research, ethnography, and netnography. Although this chapter flirts with essentializing qualitative research and netnography in stating such standards, I give them with the following provision: they are to be applied as needed. Not all of them are necessary, or even possible. Researchers can pick and choose which are most applicable to their work, their approach, their field, their publication or report outlet, and so on.

With that direction in place, the following sections provide ten defined, actionable, yet imperfect criteria to help guide the researcher. In order to thoroughly ground the standard-setting, the next section begins with some historical reflection on the nature of ethnographic evaluation. General aspects of the criteria are then related to these historical conventions. With some additional explanation and development, the ten new evaluative standards for netnography are then given.

CHANGING MOMENTS AND DEVELOPING STANDARDS: A VERY BRIEF HISTORY OF ETHNOGRAPHIC INQUIRY AND ITS STANDARDS

In order to understand and generate criteria for netnographic evaluation, we need to first understand the various historical standards that have come to signal quality ethnography. Denzin and Lincoln (2005) divide the history of ethnography in this century into eight cross-cutting, overlapping historical 'moments'. These are phases or stages that continue to influence our practice in the present. First was the *traditional* moment, lasting from the early 1900s until the post-World War II period, characterized by four 'classic norms in anthropology': objectivism, complicity with colonialism, social life structured by fixed rituals and customs, and ethnographies as monuments to a culture (Denzin and Lincoln 1994). From this phase we have gained many of the methodological conventions of ethnographic fieldwork, such as immersion in a fieldsite, learning and using the local vernacular, and collecting stories and traditional materials face-to-face from culture members. In addition, we have learned to judge quality in ethnographic texts by the awareness, inclusion, and detailing of these elements of fieldwork.

The next phase, the *modernist* moment or golden age, extended through the post-war years to 1970 and built on the canonical works of the traditional period, attempting to formalize qualitative methods and define the universal terms by which rigour could be judged. These evaluative terms drew on notions of validity developed in positivist or post-positivist social science, and thus are often referred to as post-positivist criteria. Much was learned in the effort to make commensurable radically different paradigms and approaches. However, the widespread experiment to make ethnography more scientistic was a failure. In the wake of this apparent disaster, a sort of rebirth of the method ensued.

The *blurred genres* moment, lasting from 1970 to 1986, was characterized by the emergence of a plethora of different paradigms, theories, methods, and strategies to employ in qualitative research. These included hermeneutics, symbolic interactionism, phenomenology, ethnomethodology, critical (Marxist or Marxian) theory, post-structuralism, semiotics, feminism, neopositivism, deconstructionism, ethnic paradigms, and historical, biographical, dramaturgical and documentary methods. Many of these methods were drawn from the humanities. It was during this period that Clifford Geertz (1973) suggested that the boundaries between the social sciences and the humanities had become blurred. The important epistemology and method of interpretivism was developed in this moment. Interpretivism is a school of thought devoted to the goal of understanding the complex world of lived experience from the point of view of those who live it, a phenomenological perspective (Schwandt 1994). The criteria underlying interpretive anthropology (Denzin 1997; Geertz 1973) favour grounded meanings, richly detailed or thick description, and use the metaphor of reading and interpreting a complicated text for the reading of a given culture.

The *crisis of representation* moment began in the mid-1980s and lasted until 1990. It was marked by the profound rupture accompanying the diffusion of several influential texts subverting the foundations of ethnographic representation (e.g., Clifford and Marcus 1986), and, through them, the legitimacy of ethnography as traditionally practised and ethnographic standards as conventionally applied. As Denzin and Lincoln (2005, p. 3) put it: 'Here researchers struggled with how to locate themselves and their subjects in reflexive texts'. In this moment, the ethnography's textual elements were underscored and the ethnographic enterprise acknowledged as one that involved not merely the transparent conduct of fieldwork and cultural learning, but also the loaded politics of writing and representation. The *postmodern* moment lasting from 1990 to 1995 was the first stage of a response to the critiques of the crisis. It was characterized by experimentation with new forms of, and standards for, ethnography and attempts to make ethnographic representations more 'evocative, moral, critical, and rooted in local understandings' (Denzin and Lincoln 2005, p. 3).

The seventh moment of *post-experimental inquiry* lasted from 1995 to 2000 and continued to refine and develop a response to the crisis. This moment brought a mature sophistication of research choices and greater levels of social consciousness into the evaluation of ethnographic texts. The eighth moment was the *methodologically contested present*, a time of great methodological and epistemological diversity as well as tension, conflict and retrenchment, as practices of inquiry were regulated to conform with 'conservative and neoliberal programs and [political and related policy] regimes' (Denzin and Lincoln 2005, p. 1116). The eighth and ninth moments (our *fractured future*, or present and near-future period), according to Denzin and Lincoln (2005, p. 1117), will be primarily concerned with four major issues in qualitative research: (1) reconnecting social science to social purpose, (2) creating indigenous social sciences to help meet the local needs of indigenous people, (3) decolonizing the academy, and (4) adapting to radical changes in the settings of Western social sciences and scientists.

We can use these eight or nine moments to understand developing notions about what is required of a netnography. Over the last century, we have seen approaches that have emphasized ethnography's portrayal of methodological rigour, phenomenological understanding, engagement with literature, the inclusion of post-positivist quasi-validity criteria, interpretivist thick description, reflexivity, moral and critical notions, and much more. Struggling with the challenges of the various ruptures, crises, and disjunctures has demanded that ethnographers develop technical agility and an openness to experimentation as well as, increasingly, a broadened sense of social consciousness and contribution. Although these factors are not used in every field, and cannot be applied against every ethnography or netnography, their widespread and growing acceptance means that all qualitative research scholars should at least be aware of them.

DEVELOPING NETNOGRAPHIC CRITERIA

We can consider that there are four basic evaluative positions for judging qualitative research: positivist, post-positivist, postmodern and post-structural (Denzin and Lincoln 1994, pp. 479–80; 2005). The positivist position suggests that one set of criteria – such as standard psychometric criteria of internal and external validity – should be applied to all scientific research, both qualitative and quantitative. The post-positivist position suggests that a set of criteria specific to qualitative research needs to be developed and utilized. These criteria can emphasize qualitative research's theory-generation, empirical grounding, generalizability, reflexivity, or its authenticity and critical approach (see, e.g., Guba and Lincoln 1989). The third position, the postmodern position, suggests that 'the character of qualitative research implies that there can be no criteria for judging its products' (Hammersley 1992, p. 58). Harry Wolcott (1990) comes from this position when he asserts that the concept of validity is, ultimately, absurd. He suggests that the term validity has been overspecified in one domain and thus becomes meaningless when reassigned to another. In quantitative research, validity has a set of corresponding technical microdefinitions, whereas in qualitative research, validity concerns description and explanation.

Finally, the post-structural position suggests that an entirely new set of criteria, separate from positivist and post-positivist traditions, needs to be constructed based on the particular nature of the qualitative research work under consideration and stressing such pragmatic and subjective criteria as subjective understandings, caring, feeling, and emotionality. Certain schools of feminist scholarship, cultural studies, ethnic studies, queer studies, and critical theory stress corresponding factors. Criteria based upon a post-structural position often focus on the differing constituents, interpretive communities, or audiences for the research (Altheide and Johnson 1994, p. 488), making the excellent point that evaluative standards vary between different audiences. Although evaluations and criteria are, ultimately, socially constructed, driven by consensus, and concerned with legitimacy and thus the exercise of power, they are nonetheless valuable and very difficult to dispense with.

In the following section this chapter builds on these sets of extant standards to develop a set of netnographic quality standards. It includes criteria harmonized with all four evaluative positions: positivist, post-positivist, postmodern and post-structural. The base level of criteria is formed from positivist and post-positivist positions. Since external 'validity' concerns are not an issue in naturalistic inquiry such as netnography, a coherent and internally consistent interpretation represents an analogue to positivist notions of 'internal validity'. The post-positivist relevant standards are those in which: netnographic method is represented as being adhered to, and accurately, relevant theoretical knowledge and domains are cited in the work, data are linked convincingly to theory, and those theoretical developments or descriptions represent an unambiguous advance in our knowledge and understanding of some community, culture, or related phenomenon.

The next set of criteria is drawn from the postmodern approach. Although these post-crisis and post-experimentation criteria recognize the constructed nature of netnographic representation, they focus on standards that emphasize the emotional connection that the representation is able to offer its readers and the lifelike qualities of that representation. The final three criteria actually combine a range of post-positivist, postmodern and post-structual concerns in their accentuation of the reflexivity and openness of the text, its pragmatic focus on social concerns, and the uniquely netnographic focus on the intertwining of online and off-line social worlds. The ten evaluative criteria and short attendant definitions are provided in Table 9.1, and full descriptions of each one follow in the sections below.

Some of these criteria – such as coherence and reflexivity – even contradict one another. These contradictions signal the unlikeliness and perhaps unworthiness of simple off-the-shelf solutions. They invite netnographers to probe and struggle in a focused and guided way, and to discover their own path. Each netnographer will

TABLE 9.1   NETNOGRAPHIC CRITERIA

Criterion Name	Definition ('the extent to which …')
Coherence	Each recognizably different interpretation is free from internal contradictions and presents a unified pattern
Rigour	The text recognizes and adheres to the procedural standards of netnographic research
Literacy	The text recognizes and is knowledgeable of relevant literature and research approaches
Groundedness	The theoretical representation is supported by data, and the links between data and theory are clear and convincing
Innovation	The constructs, ideas, frameworks and narrative form provide new and creative ways of understanding systems, structures, experience or actions
Resonance	A personalized and sensitizing connection with the cultural phenomenon is gained
Verisimilitude	A believable and lifelike sense of cultural and communal contact is achieved
Reflexivity	The text acknowledges the role of the researcher and is open to alternative interpretations
Praxis	The text inspires and empowers social action
Intermix	The representation takes account of the interconnection of the various modes of social interaction – online and off – in the culture member's daily lived experiences, as well as in its own representation

grow as a scholar as she wrestles with these issues, delves into her own philosophical foundations, gains a diachronic understanding of the multiple fields in which they obtain, and tries to forge together, in the manner of a bricoleur, a raggedy, makeshift solution, an unwieldy and precipitous craft that will get her from the point of launch to the point of discovery and back. The philosophies and criteria of different researchers need to be different, improved, and ever-changing. Build your own vessel. Stage your own show. Evaluate your own evaluations.

TEN CRITERIA TO EVALUATE AND INSPIRE NETNOGRAPHIC QUALITY

'Realist' ethnography is founded on the assumption of an objectively real social world that can be accurately captured in a text and transmitted to readers (Van Maanen 1988). The problems of representation presented by this view of ethnography will not simply vanish, nor are they likely to be facilely resolved. The tension between the concern for validity, authenticity, and certainty in the text will always be contradicted in an ongoing conversation with the sure knowledge that all texts are politically, historically, socially and culturally situated. Wise netnographers will be aware of the need to balance these tensions within the text. Thankfully, we have some shining role models for such work, such as Baym (1999), Hine (2000), Markham (1998), and many of the other netnographers cited in this text.

Until fairly recently, realist, post-positivist judgement standards have connected cultural and sociological research to a much larger body of objectivist-inspired scientific research. With the crisis of representation, much of this realist enterprise was questioned. However, in the post-crisis age, some of the more robust prior standards have survived increased scrutiny and are being reasserted by anthropologists (see, e.g., Fox 1991).

These new criteria are what remain of realist criteria after their confrontation with the crisis of representation. Atkinson (1992, p. 51) asserts that it would be wrong to consider the extreme perspective that there is 'nothing beyond the text'. Such a view, he says, 'capitulates the mistaken separation of Science and Rhetoric. It was wrong to celebrate science and ignore rhetoric. It is equally wrong simply to reverse the emphasis'. Deconstruction and post-structuralism are not simple relativist endeavours – they simply deny the possibility of ultimate referents. Thus, this first set of criteria pays homage to established realist principles of ostensibly 'objective' science.

Coherence

The first criterion is coherence, defined as the extent to which each recognizably different set of interpretations in the netnography is free from internal contradictions and presents a unified pattern. One important insight that a piece of interpretive research can afford its readers is that of a 'conceptual gestalt' that allows a reader 'to see a set of qualitative data as a coherent pattern or gestalt' (Thompson 1990). One excellent example of this is the netnography of the Apple Newton online community by Al Muñiz and Hope Schau. In their netnography, the researchers found motifs of deep brand meaning accompanying the brand and the community, including creation myths, the deification of Steve Jobs and demonization of Bill Gates, tales of miraculous performances, brand survival stories, and rumours of impending resurrection. Their integrative analysis suggests that these themes are present because of the enduring human link between community and mythic religious story-telling (Muñiz and Schau 2005). The observations and other collected netnographic data are integrated into one coherent pattern, an overriding argument freed from internal contradiction.

Coherence is a necessary but not sufficient condition enabling assertions about social interpretations to be posed as falsifiable theoretical statements. From this perspective, internal contradictions are undesirable because they undermine the persuasiveness of an ethnographic text, whereas a unified coherent interpretation inspires confidence in the research results. When an interpretation contains these contradictions, it is important that they – and likely the root phenomenon – be examined and resolved to shed further light on the phenomenon being interpreted. This attempt to reach individual interpretations that are free from contradictions, ones that seem reasonably complete within themselves, has been the basis of grounded theory and the constant comparative method (Glaser and Strauss 1967), negative case analysis (Lincoln and Guba 1985b), and the hermeneutic circle (see Arnold and Fischer 1994), as described in Chapter 7 in this book.

'Dependability' judgements have been based on the extent to which the interpretation was constructed in a way that avoids internal contradictions and contradictions with data, or the extent to which an interpretation 'avoids instability other than the inherent instability of a social phenomenon' (Wallendorf and Belk 1989, p. 70; Lincoln and Guba 1985b). These notions are related to the 'rhetorical' family of criteria suggested by Guba and Lincoln (1989), which include coherence, structural unity, and clarity.

Rigour

Rigour is the extent to which the text recognizes and adheres to the standards of netnographic research. Rigour means that the netnographer has done his or her methodological homework. It means that he or she understands what is required in order to conduct a netnography, following principled protocols of entrée, data collection, analysis and interpretation, research ethics, and representation itself. If we agree with Sally Jackson (1986) that all research methods are forms of arguments rather than signposts that point us towards the truth, then demonstrating that you are following the correct method is a way of suggesting that you have earned your place at the theoretical table and are ready to contribute to a substantive conversation.

Strategies of entrée must be carefully thought out and recounted to readers in a way that sensibly relates them to research questions, site choices, and theoretical conclusions. Data must be collected rigorously, not selectively. For example, if a netnography wishes to make claims about the general spiritual orientation of all Internet users, it is insufficient to present a study of one particular, church-oriented online community. Netnographic findings must be interpreted with a keen eye kept on how the data were collected and what they can be reasonably and logically held under the principles of induction to represent. The time periods under examination and observation are also relevant to one's findings. The netnographer who conducts a two-week study of a new virtual world island over the Christmas break cannot then proceed to make claims about what 'usually' happens in Second Life. With netnography, as with ethnography, quality evaluations are generally accorded to texts reflecting cultural immersion, prolonged engagement, internalization, and awareness of difference. In sum, quality netnography must constantly exhibit its familiarity with the accepted standards of netnography.

As Beaulieu (2004, p. 159) has noted, 'some prominent anthropologists have … discouraged students to undertake projects where the main field site would be "online"'. James Clifford (1997, p. 190) recounts Internet-based observational ('lurking') research on a group of exiled Afghans and asks what 'remains of classic anthropological practices in these new situations? How are the notions of travel, boundary, coresidence, interaction, inside and outside, which have defined the field and proper fieldwork, being challenged and reworked in contemporary anthropology?' As standards solidify, netnographers grapple with fundamental issues, and new research is conducted, the answers to these important questions are clarified.

Literacy

Knowledge is undeniably a cumulative enterprise, based upon historical foundations. In any research enterprise, an important first step is a thorough review of past scholarly literature in related areas. Increased credibility and insight are the usual consequences of a thorough, detailed literature search.

The literacy criterion is thus defined as the extent to which the netnographic text recognizes and is knowledgeable of literature and research approaches that are relevant to its inquiry. To be useful, research should be linked to central issues, problems and debates in its field. An exhaustive understanding of the constructs, issues, frameworks, problematics and contentious issues in a field, or related to a specific topic, is a key signal that one is communicating meaningfully to a given community of scholars. Because of the positivist and post-positivist belief in the cumulative structuring of knowledge, it is important for quality research to acknowledge and explicitly recognize scholarly tradition and literatures.

Meeting this criterion can of course be made more difficult by the fact that, as described in Chapters 2 and 5, research on online communities and cultural Internet phenomena is scattered across a wide range of disciplines, journals, conference proceedings, and working papers. Nonetheless, a good search engine and online reference search from any well-equipped university library can reveal a universe of new activity. To broaden the scope of a field, an invaluable contribution can be made by transcending the limits of one's own field and engaging in an interdisciplinary literature search, and by building the results carefully into one's netnography. In multidisciplinary fields such as Internet Research or Consumer Culture Theory, such cross-pollinating intellectual voyages are commonplace, and frequently yield consequential insights.

Groundedness

The fourth criterion is groundedness, defined as the extent to which: (1) the theoretical representation is supported by data, and (2) the links between data and theory are clear and convincing. Groundedness is not only a demonstration of the degree of empirical veracity, but a provision of sufficient and relevant evidence to back up the netnography's theoretical claims of contribution.

If we assume a social constructionist stance, we can state that shared meanings and meaning systems are knowable phenomena, although we can never know them with absolute certainty. Cultural knowledge must be grounded in detailed field knowledge of that culture, and in the data that fieldwork creates. The criterion of groundedness is based upon assessments of the adequacy of qualitative evidence, the extent to which the reader can determine that the research and theoretical representation are grounded in the netnographic data (see Spiggle 1994, p. 501). Similarly, it is related to post-positivist criteria of confirmability and dependability (Lincoln and Guba 1985b; Wallendorf and Belk 1989). Quality netnographies will therefore offer a strong sense of culture members' language, and will often liberally cite or quote from online texts and documents. Good ethnographies provide their readers with a sense that they have travelled to a different place and gotten to know and understand a group of people through their in-person interactions. Good netnographies similarly provide readers with a sense that they have made contact with a group of people, and gained an understanding of them through their online interactions.

Innovation

Once a penetrating review of past literature and theory on a topic or field has been conducted, quality research takes this a step further by seeking to extend current knowledge and create something previously unrealized. This contribution can be major or minor, but conventional standards across the sciences dictate that it be novel.

The criterion of innovation is therefore defined as the extent to which the constructs, ideas, frameworks and narrative form of the netnography provide new and creative ways of understanding systems, structures, experience or actions. Innovative ideas about online cultures and communities are likely to aid further inquiry best if they are connected to issues and settings that are prevalent in the literature. In the extreme, innovation is the ultimate criterion, the profound paradigm shift that allows the reader to understand the world in an entirely new and different way.

Paramount to innovation is the role of creativity and even artistry in the form of the netnography and its narrative. In the best netnographies, the quality of writing will not only make apparent the new knowledge advances propounded in the research findings, but will also include an evocativeness, a freshness and vividness in writing style. A good example of this fresh, evocative style is Brenda Danet's book *Cyberplay* (2001), where vivid graphics, a poetic spirit, and rich interpretation combine to create an enchanting portrayal of an online community's interactions. With technological advances, we have almost unlimited tools at our disposal to create strikingly original new examples of interactive, imaginative, hyperlinked, dynamic netnography, and to post them online – perhaps as an addition to published work in books and scientific journals.

Resonance

We must be careful in writing about other human beings to maintain and if possible enhance our understanding of each other, rather than portraying the cultural 'Other' as lifeless stereotypes captured in objectifying and moribund words. Resonance asks about the extent to which the netnography conveys to its readers a personalized and sensitizing connection with the online community or cultural phenomenon it studies. Is the work enlightening and evocative? Does it sensitize readers to the concerns and lifeways of others? Is there a phenomenological insight conveyed such that a more personal understanding or empathy is gained?

To explain the concept of resonance, Wikan quoted a 'professor-poet' in the Balinese village he studied:

> It is what fosters empathy or compassion. Without resonance there can be no understanding, no appreciation. But resonance requires you [and here he looked entreatingly at me] to apply feeling as well as thought. Indeed, feeling is the more essential, for without feeling we will remain entangled in illusions. (1992, p. 463; square brackets in original)

The ethnographic and, by extension, netnographic enterprise is about struggling to transcend our own illusory categories and to understand the categories of the community and culture we are focusing upon: 'To collapse and thus transcend the dichotomous self/other categories: finding the self in the other and the other in the self!' (Fernandez 1994: 155). This theme permeates the anthropological and sociological literature on ethnography.

A netnography sensitizes, personalizes and enlightens when it illuminates something previously unknown about a culture – such as that an online community plays a deep and important part in peoples' lives – and also when it makes an unfamiliar aspect of that culture seem intimate. A netnographic story is evocative and resonant when it touches our own lives, by making what is close and comfortable to us seem distant and bizarre. For example, Madge and O'Connor's (2006) netnography of socially-advantaged, technologically proficient, white heterosexual new mothers takes us into their world of fears and conservative limitations, liberatory hopes and restrictive concerns, and in the process, attends to the emotional life of culture members. Drawing particularly upon feminist scholarship, the evaluative standard of emotionality in research is an important one, closely related to resonance. Van Maanen (1988) and Ellis (1991) both note the important role played by emotion in fieldwork and suggest that it be more clearly incorporated into ethnographic writing.

Netnographies can and should also attend to the non-rational, non-verbal, emotional lives of both the culture members and researcher. By keeping emotions in the foreground of fieldnotes and cultural interactions, by not deprivileging feeling in favour of reason, and by not enforcing an orderly and 'objective' categorization scheme upon lived cultural experience, a measure of veracity can be obtained that remains absent from more barren accounts. Whether attempted through an interviewing technique such as 'creative interviewing' (Douglas 1985; see also Gubrium and Holstein 2001), through struggles to convey the emotional tone of voice of individual community members where observed and articulated by them, or through attempts to convey introspectively observed and felt emotions, resonance is found in the emotional pitch of the narrative.

Verisimilitude

In the moments following the crisis of representation, verisimilitude has often been proposed as an important – and occasionally the only – criterion for establishing the quality of a text. Verisimilitude simply refers to the text's ability to reproduce or simulate, and map, the 'real'. The importance of seeming realistic has been accentuated because of the importance of representation in ethnography's post-crisis moments.

On one level, in order to evoke a sense of reality, a netnography's narrative must be persuasive, credible, convincing, and believable. On another level, verisimilitude describes a text's relation to an objectively real world, and becomes almost indistinguishable from the realist criterion of groundedness detailed above. On its most sophisticated, 'surrealist', level, verisimilitude refers to the relationship of the text to consensually-derived standards of epistemological validity. A netnographic text thus establishes verisimilitude by resembling valid exemplars that are currently accepted by a relevant community of scholars. Verisimilitude is therefore defined as the extent to which a believable and lifelike sense of cultural and communal contact is achieved. The reader should feel through reading and experiencing the netnography as though they have actually contacted the community, culture, and its members.

Mikhail Bahktin's (1981) analysis of the 'polyphonic' novel may be relevant here. In polyphonic novels, there is a utopian textual enactment of heteroglossia through the representation of speaking subjects in a field of multiple discourses. When applied to cultural anthropology, the term refers to integrated, totalized, neatly-wrapped-up-and-explained cultural worlds or languages being forsaken in deference to the conception of culture as an open-ended, creative conversation between members of multitudes, diverse and fractious factions of intricately related and relating insiders and outsiders – a description that holds very well for much of what we see on the Internet.

A less extreme version of verisimilitude is achieved by simply presenting dialogue. Various netnographies have presented the dialectical processes of ethnography in the form of interviews, or a dialogue between two individuals (e.g., Cherny 1999; Markham 1998; see also Van Maanen's (1988) 'jointly told tale'). As in hermeneutics, a new reality is constructed through the 'fusion of horizons' of researcher and informant, whereby the 'textualized' world of the other is torn or opened and an interweaving of perspectives is actively undertaken. Some experimental ethnographies have addressed their concern with questions of resonance by sharing the political power of editing, writing and interpretation with inside members of a community. In practice, this can be a difficult but worthwhile pursuit. The wiki form possesses considerable potential to be involved in the co-construction of netnographic texts. For example, at the risk of coining another neologism, there might be 'wikinetnographies' in which culture members and a set of researchers use the online wiki form to jointly describe, portray, and understand a culture. As a wiki, the netnography would be an ongoing project that could be edited by anyone. It is very likely that innovative netnographies will soon be written using tools such as these.

Reflexivity

A key post-crisis ethnographic criterion is to deal openly with issues of reflexivity. This criterion applies equally well to netnography. One meaning of reflexivity is that the scientific investigator is a part of the setting, context, and culture that she is trying to understand and portray. Many groundbreaking analyses of reflexivity were published by symbolic interactionists, ethnomethodologists, and phenomenologists in the 1970s (Jorgensen 1989), as well as more recently by post-structural and post-modern scholars. Punch (1986) talks about 'coming clean' with the documentation of a study, and revealing to the reader such things as: problems with entrée and exiting the field; the political issues encountered on the site and the role played by the study; and the conflicts, ambiguities, and shady side of the understanding gained during the fieldwork.

Reflexivity is thus the extent to which the netnographic text acknowledges the role of the researcher and is open to alternative interpretations. The author of a netnography can no more hide behind the computer screen than the traditional ethnographer could be rendered invisible in their own cultural narrative. As participant-observers, netnographers play a part in the research process, captured in fieldnotes and through online interactions. As many of the examples in this book indicate, some of the most interesting occurrences in the world of netnography are occurring in the tension between the researcher and culture members, as online communities and cultures actively resist being studied. As the netnographic text is reflexive about these moments, its insights and ability to speak with authority about cultural membership are affirmed.

Related to this presence of the researcher in the netnographic text is an openness to the presence of others. The authoritative, monolithic, single, unified voice of the author has been increasingly interrogated in post-crisis anthropological writing.

Clifford (1988, p. 22) links the crisis in ethnographic authority – the use of a single overriding voice describing a 'culture' of the 'Other' – to the break-up and redistribution of colonial power in the decades after 1950, and the subsequent anthropological crisis of conscience.

In this vein, alternate forms of validity incorporating post-structural insights have been devised. Of interest to this research are Lather's (1993) concepts of reflexive, ironic, neopragmatic and rhizomatic validity. Reflexive validity refers to a text's self-subversive attempts to challenge its own validity claims. Ironic validity refers to presenting a proliferation of multiple representations and simulations of the real, revealing the strengths and limitations of each and arguing that no single representation is superior to another. Neopragmatic validity places dissensus, heterogeneity and discourse in the foreground, destabilizing the author's position as master of truth and knowledge. This dissensus and multivocal orientation comes somewhat naturally to the online community environment, with its cacophany of contending voices. Reflexivity reminds us not to smooth over conflicts and differences in our analysis and research representations, but to accurately convey them.

We can distinguish between relatively 'open' and relatively 'closed' netnographic texts. If the text neatly presents a closed argument, with all of its loose ends sewn up and portrayed as a final truth that leaves little or no room for active disagreement by readers, then this is a relatively closed text. Alternatively, a netnography where the facts and findings are presented along with the rationale and argument for drawing them into particular conclusions is an open text. Open texts allow and even encourage active, critical, responsive readership. In fact, the Internet may be changing the way we think about texts to an open model, where texts are always open to being critiqued, their claims questioned, their conclusions commented upon. The criterion of reflexivity is based upon a mature response recognizing the desirability of providing some acknowledgment of the researcher's own role in the conduct and analysis of fieldwork, portraying multiple voices and viewpoints, and welcoming other interpretations.

Praxis

The emancipatory, empowering, consciousness-raising ability to inspire social action is another criteria for ethnographic quality. Guba and Lincoln's (1989) evaluations of 'authenticity' invoke new criteria of:

- *Fairness*: the ability to deal even-handedly with research participants.
- *Ontological authenticity*: the ability of the research to enlarge personal constructions.
- *Educative authenticity*: the ability to lead to improved understanding of the constructions of others.
- *Catalytic authenticity*: the ability to stimulate to action.
- *Tactical authenticity*: the ability to empower action.

Guba and Lincoln (1989) note that these criteria overlap and extend the criteria often associated with research in the critical theory tradition (see also Lather 2001; Murray and Ozanne 1991; Tacchi et al. 2004).

The pursuit of praxis – practical action aimed at social betterment – guides the judgement of quality scholarship in the critical theory and feminist schools. Marcus and Fischer (1986) convincingly suggest that the submerged theme of ethnographic exploration has always been to use our understanding of the Other to engage in a 'cultural critique', whose essence is social criticism. In a wide variety of contexts, the ability of research to motivate and influence social betterment has been increasingly held to be a sign of research quality. 'Increasingly, the criteria of evaluation will turn … on moral, practical, aesthetic, political and personal issues – the production, that is, of texts that articulate an emancipatory, participative perspective on the human condition and its betterment' (Denzin 1994, p. 501). Lather (1993, 2001) calls this 'catalytic validity', the degree to which a research project empowers and emancipates.

With the impact and power of ICT altering our global society, it is incumbent upon netnographers to examine related phenomena with a pragmatic eye to their social implications. We cannot be deluded by 'ideologies of technology' accruing to online interactions and implying intrinsic utopian, efficient, and expressive possibilities, but must examine in situated contexts these powerful allusions (Kozinets 2008). All the same, we must continually strive to understand how technology might not only impassion, but actually empower, social action and activism, and to help through our scholarship to bring this about in positive ways. Attending to the criterion of praxis, defined as the extent to which the text inspires and empowers social action, may help provide some of these much-needed changes.

Intermix

The Internet and online interaction are becoming inextricable and unavoidable as a part of contemporary social life. The criterion of intermix asks the netnographic representation to take account of the interconnection of the various modes of social interaction – online and off – in culture members' daily lived experiences, as well as in its own representation. Earlier chapters such as Chapter 4, which explained the coordination of ethnographic research in face-to-face and online contexts, are salient to this criterion, which asks, fundamentally: how well has the intertwined online/off-line nature of contemporary social life been attended to where it is relevant to do so for this topic in this research?

We seem to be living in an age of 'technosociality', where individuals and communities are situated to various extents in delocalized information networks and constitute social relationships through technocultural processes (cf. Rabinow 1992). It therefore seems very likely 'that the internet will creep into ethnographies, as anthropologists follow their subjects, and are more or less forced to follow them online' (Beaulieu 2004, p. 159). Miller and Slater (2000, p. 8) 'treat virtuality as a social accomplishment rather than an assumed feature of the Internet' and see the 'capacity of communicative technologies to constitute rather than mediate realities and to constitute relatively bounded spheres of interaction' as 'neither new nor specific to the Internet'. They might assert that everything that is important happens in the mediations between science, technology, and society – in the intermix (see also Hakken 1999).

The notion behind the intermix criterion is that online and offline cultural worlds intermingle and that this very intermingling is among the most interesting and important areas that we must understand. Netnographers who relegate themselves merely to what they can download from postings in forums may miss much of what is interesting and critical about the phenomena they purport to study. Concepts of dematerialization, spatiality and place, textuality, inside and outside, and the field, need to be interrogated and investigated both ethnographically and netnographically, through savvy combinations of online and off-line fieldwork, marriages of computer-mediated and face-to-face interaction. The boundaries of this investigation, the places where netnographic tools and techniques can be marshalled and when they can be put down, are determined by the locus of research questions and the contributions a given netnography seeks to make. Many of the delineations in this book – such as the demarcation between studies of online communities and studies of communities online, and the general guide for the blending of ethnography/netnography – may be helpful to researchers who must draw the boundaries where netnographic data can stand alone and where these must intermix with data gathered from other approaches.

Finally, in the criterion of intermix I also seek to encapsulate an openness to using technological tools and online representation to both formulate and present netnographic projects or reports. In an examination of the epistemology of studies of Internet culture, Beaulieu (2004, p. 158) rightly notes that 'The overwhelming majority of [this research] is found in books and in journals, and only a very small portion of it has some web presence'. With a large variety of presentation formats online – web-pages and blogs, forum postings, social networking site links, videos, and wikis – we have many ways to share our research with the public at large as well as with the cultures and communities we seek to represent. Fascinating studies could be performed that would provide a living netnography through ever-growing hypertext links to cultural data, and their emerging and collaborative interpretation. Intermix thus entails attending to the various manifestations and interconnections of human social interaction as well as minding these manifestations and interconnections in the forms we use to represent online cultures and present our netnographies.

SUMMARY

The foregoing eight chapters of this book have been concerned with our knowledge of online communities and cultures, the different methods for studying them and, most especially, the procedures for conducting netnography. In this chapter, you learnt about the representational issues facing the netnographer ready to present or publish her findings. The ten criteria explained in this chapter represent a pragmatic, concrete, lucid, 'toolkit' orientation for the evaluation of netnography, but are also equivocal, ad hoc inventions, compromises intended to help start scholarly discussions and build ideas. Coherence, Rigour, Literacy, Groundedness, Innovation, Resonance, Verisimilitude, Reflexivity, Praxis, and Intermix – these ten criteria derive directly from an understanding of netnography's rootedness in the traditional ethnographic standards of the past and its present situation. We can now proceed to the final chapter of this book, which looks forward to netnography's future.

KEY READINGS

Baym, Nancy (2006) 'Finding the Quality in Qualitative research', in David Silver and Adrienne Massanari (eds), *Critical Cyberculture Studies.* New York: New York University Press, pp. 79–87.

Denzin, Norman K. and Yvona S. Lincoln (2005) *The Sage Handbook of Qualitative Research*, 3rd edition. Thousand Oaks, CA: Sage.

Geertz, Clifford (1973) *The Interpretation of Cultures.* New York: Basic Books.

10
ADVANCING NETNOGRAPHY:
The Changing Landscape

ABSTRACT

This chapter previews and suggests some of the exciting possibilities for the growth and adaptation of netnography. In it, you will learn about some theoretical areas and themes that may be of increasing importance, some thoughts about ongoing changes in the Internet and online environment, and a summary of related developments in netnography.

Key Words: adaptation of netnography, blog netnography, co-creation, communal–commercial relations, consumer empowerment, netnography, online communities, social media, social networking site netnography, virtual world netnography, Web 2.0

CONSIDERING NEW THEORETICAL DEVELOPMENTS USING NETNOGRAPHY

Netnography has been applied to research questions concerning many of the interests of social scientists, from human identity and sexual expression (Correll 1995, Turkle 1995), to online embodiment and pornography consumption (Slater 1998), to game-playing (McMahan 2003). The theoretical areas and topic matters it explores have varied widely. Netnography has been invoked to study personal web-pages (Schau and Gilly 2003), file-sharing communities (Molesworth and Denegri-Knott 2004), Dutch and Flemish online food culture (de Valck 2005, 2007), cross-cultural weddings (Nelson and Otnes 2005), brand communities (Füller et al. 2008; Muñiz and Schau

2005), musical instruments (Jeppesen and Frederiksen 2006), open source (Hemetsberger and Reinhardt 2006), digital camera discussion boards (Fong and Burton 2006), online fashion discussions (Thomas et al. 2007), consumer creativity and 'prosumption' (Füller et al. 2006; Kozinets et al. 2008), consumer resistance (Dalli and Corciolani 2008; Kozinets and Handelman 1998), and many other topics. There are nearly boundless opportunities emerging to study the ever-increasing varieties of online cultures and communities, as well as the ways that they interrelate with our existing, dynamic, and interacting systems of cultures, identities, and social arrangements. These opportunities will no doubt lead to advances in our theoretical understanding of ways that online communities function, and the role that online communities play in their members' lives and in society.

There have been several different theories presented throughout this book. Chapter 2 provided a retrospective on some early and essential theorizing about online communities, and attempted to update and develop this work. This section seeks to broaden the discussion of online communities and cultures, and suggest some future directions for it.

The first theoretical area concerns the relationship between communities and related commercial entities online. A key concern in my field of consumer research is the impact of commercial, consumer, or marketing culture upon contemporary society. This concern dovetails with the concerns of a significant number of cultural studies scholars, anthropologists and sociologists. For example, scholars of many disciplines interested in fan communities, whether they are fans of a television series, of book characters such as Harry Potter, or of music, have been aware of the social tensions between fans and entertainment companies since the mid-1990s. These tensions, and their associated legal conflicts, occurred due to alleged copyright and trademark law infringements on the Internet. The images and sound files used by fans on their websites were, technically and legally, the property of large entertainment conglomerates who, arguably, did not understand the developing communal nature of the Internet – and, again arguably, still do not.

On the other side of this divide sit the various initiatives by marketers and producers to utilize online communities and their conversations as part of the process of production, either as a form of marketing research (e.g., Kozinets 2002a), as new product developers (Füller et al. 2007, 2008; Kozinets 2002a; Kozinets et al. 2008; Tapscott and Williams 2007) or as a controlled, promotional part of the word-of-mouth marketing process (Kozinets 1999; Kozinets et al. 2010). The relationship between online communities and commercial enterprises in this domain has been cast in a polarized fashion, as either raging and opposed, or offering burgeoning partnerships.

Studies that situate online communities and cultures in relation to these long-standing and continually changing tensions between communities of consumers and commercial communities offer much of value. Although many studies touch upon the issue, it is still not well developed theoretically. A useful exemplar in this area is Campbell's (2005) study of gay men's affinity portals on the Internet. Campbell found that corporations were important actors creating and maintaining online communities. However, participation and a sense of belonging in these communities came at an important price. The community's existence depended upon their status as a type of commercial entity where consumers were under surveillance and commercially targeted by marketers. Campbell's sophisticated analysis did not view this simply as a form of negative exploitation, but more synergistically, as a type of dynamic social system, and one that needed to be carefully studied in order to be understood.

Reflected by and drawing upon academic scholarship such as the Frankfurt school, the critical theorists, the Situationists, and many critical postmodernists, are profound and deep-seated cultural discourses that run through much of Western society in which local communities and ways of life are cast in opposition to large corporations and their interests (see Kozinets 2001, 2002a, 2002b; Kozinets and Handelman 2004). This area of 'communal–commercial relations,' and the tensions, dialogues, paradoxes, uneasy compromises, and ongoing developments that constitute it, appear to be playing out increasingly in the realm of online community (see also Cova et al. 2007; Kozinets 2007).

Many of the core questions about communal–commercial relations relate to notions of ownership and intellectual property. As Chapter 8 demonstrated in the realm of research ethics, the ownership of posted materials is still highly contested territory. In studies seeking to examine online communities and cultures, this interrelationship of community, ethics, power, morality, and legal rights over ownership may well take centre stage. If we consider that, in their essences, learning and culture themselves are concerned with copying and imitation, emulation and acculturation, then these individualistic and private property related notions of ownership and rights can lead us to the centre of some explosive social conflicts. A number of recent books have heralded the flowering of creativity by members of online communities, such as Matt Mason's (2008) *The Pirate's Dilemma* and Tapscott and Williams's (2007) *Wikinomics* (see also Kozinets 2007). These books hold to a perspective that particular kinds of uses of information by online communities can be productive and helpful to companies.

Alternatively, we must inquire how these 'partnerships' benefit online communities, their members, and their cultures. Consumer anthropologists Sammy Bonsu and Aron Darmody studied 'consumer co-creation' in the virtual word of Second Life and conclude that:

> while consumers are genuinely empowered by co-creation practices, this empowerment that frees the consumer in a diversity of ways also offers significant avenues for entrapping the consumer into producing for the firm. In the end, co-creation is a veneer of consumer empowerment in a world where market power, in large measure, still resides in capital. (2008, p. 355; see also Zwick et al. 2008)

This perspective draws into question many of contemporary business's taken-for-granted assumptions regarding the 'utilization' of online communities. What are the effects of word-of-mouth marketing campaigns in the online community? Recent research suggests that they alter the dynamics, content, and social meaningfulness of the communal interactions (Kozinets et al. 2010). Should there be compensation to major community leaders and participants if their creative ideas are 'harvested' from online communications and used by a major corporation for new product development (Cova et al. 2007; Füller et al. 2007; Kozinets et al. 2008)? Where do the community's interests cease and corporate interests begin?

The social, political, and cultural ramifications of these ongoing experiments in corporate–community dynamics are in flux. In academia and in business, this social experiment is rarely being considered. We need a firmer sociological and anthropological grasp of a 'copy theory' that not only examines copyright and trademark ownership from the legalistic perspective of corporations, owners, and others with resources and power, but also from the grassroots, bottom-up perspective of the users of the systems of meaning that are partly or wholly 'owned': the culture and community members interacting and employing the many resources available to them, online and off, in social worlds of high fungibility and rapid transformation.

This realization is related to the next set of questions, which inquire into some of the wider implications of this grand social experiment. These are questions about the ownership and control of community as a type of public social space that turns or is being turned private, in order to serve specific interests and for particular ends. In addition, there are questions about the kinds of relations and communities that are being created.

This line of research might consider questions such as the following. What happens when an entire generation conducts much of their online socializing and community-building through commercial sites such as MySpace and Facebook? What are the implications of the various rules, gatekeepers, and norms present in online communities, particularly those with corporate backing? How is online community structured by corporations in ways different from how it is structured by grassroots participants? For example, consider communities like Bebo or eBay that 'exist', to a considerable extent, for market-based, commercial purposes. What happens to the social relations in a community like Facebook when the site is sold? Can a community be 'owned'? In what senses? What are the implications of this ownership for public policy? How does this ownership, and its restrictions, play out on the global stage? What happens when a major technology company based in one nation or region colonizes the online community interactions of other nations or regions? What happens as important and meaningful sources of community become structured along lines that benefit particular corporations, classes, ethnicities, languages, or nations? These questions are not merely of scholarly interest, but also of general concern to all thoughtful global citizens, particularly those who interact through online communities and cultures.

Perhaps it is in the public interest that some communities be commercially owned, and others remain a part of the public domain. Our current, essentialized understanding of these areas does not, as yet, foster such fine-grained distinctions, and hampers our decision-making ability. Our understanding of online communities and cultures will be greatly increased as we begin to probe the different social and expressive uses of the multifaceted online communications media. It is useful to remember that up until the fifteenth century, reading generally meant reading out loud, usually with an audience (Chartier 2001). The shift to silent reading had radical effects on society, changing reading from a communal to a personal act. Some suggested that the new solitary relationship between an individual and a text was one of the significant reasons leading to the notional separation of our private and public lives (Chartier 2001; Rettberg 2008). But as Rettberg (2008) notes, regarding the influence of blogging, there is a dual effect. As people moved away from public speech acts and into quiet reading, they apparently moved away from one another and retreated into private space. 'On the other hand, the fact that people unknown to one another could now read the same text allows for a new kind of impersonal connection between people. Today's niche communities online are in a sense a more fully evolved version of this' (2008, p. 40).

Chapter 4 suggests that online communities and interactions differ from in-person communications along four dimensions: adaptation, accessibility, anonymity, and archiving. There are three additional points to consider about these dimensions. First, they are each continua, not dichotomies. Second, specific qualities are arrayed differently for each particular communication medium. Third, they are dynamic, constantly changing and being merged into one another. Anonymity is not a polarity online, but a sliding scale that people adjust for different communicative uses and their relationships with different users. Accessibility, similarly, is controlled and titrated, with filters for particular content and particular people evident in advanced blog formats such as LiveJournal. Even technological adaptation is mutable, as community members increasingly have options allowing them to decide whether to use a longer personal form such as e-mail, an asynchronous and quasi-broadcast form such as a blog, or else an asynchronous textual form such as chat. Our relationships and messages drive the media choice, and the media continue to contain their own messages.

Our online community and cultural research will benefit from closer observation of the different contexts of communications. Why would you choose to communicate a personal message over Facebook rather than in an e-mail to someone's account? Why would you choose to microblog on Twitter rather than post a status update on your MySpace page? Why would you enter a short blog entry about another person's blog entry on someone else's own unpopular blog rather than the same short comment on that much more popular blog? Why would you want to converse one-on-one in a virtual world rather than have an audiovisual 'face-to-face' meeting using iChat or NetMeeting? Why would you post a link to a video with your own comments rather than a blog entry? We still know so little about people's online interactive choices and their social meanings and implications. This is yet another rich area waiting to be theorized.

The relationships between online communities and corporations. The wider social implications of online communities, their presence, their institutionalization, and their ownership. The different social and expressive uses of the different online communications media. These are three broad areas of theoretical inquiry that can be directly addressed using the netnographic research methods presented in this book.

THE EXPANSION OF THE INTERNET UNIVERSE

The expansion and incredible diversification of online communities and Internet 'space' are a lot like the Big Bang. We can make that analogy quite easily (see Kozinets 2005).

The Big Bang creation event is theorized by astrophysicists to have created our universe over 13.7 billion years ago. But it was only at the end of 1990 that the World Wide Web was invented, and credit for it must go Tim Berners-Lee, a scientist at CERN, the physics lab in Switzerland. The Web was not even truly opened to the general public until 1993 with the release of Mosaic, the first widely available graphical web browser. Online communities, of course, predated these developments, and today they continue to grow in size and influence, and radically alter their shapes and forms.

Just as life itself is remarkably promiscuous, with weeds pushing their way through cracks in the barren cement of city streets, so too does community start, inflect the tools of technology, and build its thriving hives of interactivity in and among the multifarious electronic offerings of the expansive Internet. We might, in this manner, think of the basic forms of Internet community – the board, the page, the ring, and the room – as the essential elements of online community. Clones, mutations, and amalgamations of these archetypes are spawned.

The netnographer's task is to be both an explorer and cartographer of this exciting new cultural terrain, and also an anthropologist, an explorer who respectfully and thoroughly studies the people who rise so quickly to inhabit and colonize these new online worlds. In Chapter 5, I provided some brief introductions and descriptions of a number of sites of online culture and community: bulletin boards, chat-rooms, playspaces, virtual worlds, lists, rings, blogs, wikis, audio/visual sites, social content aggregators, and social networking sites. Although each of these media merits a chapter in itself, or a journal article describing an adaptive netnographic approach, in this chapter we can share only a few introductory thoughts to help direct and develop ongoing research, and refer the interested reader to other citations and sources, as available.

THE NETNOGRAPHY OF BLOGS

The rise of blogs and the blogosphere is a fascinating phenomenon expertly charted in Jill Walker Rettberg's scholarly yet accessible (2008) book *Blogging*. From that book, it is clear that blogging has had and will continue to have a remarkable impact on social life, politics, corporate relations, and consumer resistance. The communally created information on blogs also offers the same sorts of insights and influences that have previously been ascribed to bulletin boards: targeted, precise, influential comments and feedback on particular lifestyles or other social arenas. Blogs thus offer a powerful opportunity to enter cultural lifestreams. They are a source of information that can contain rich, detailed, longitudinal data about individuals and their consumption practices, values, meanings, and beliefs.[14]

It seems clear that our netnographic approach should be different for blogs than for bulletin boards. Our entrée would likely be directed by different search engines, such as blogger.com and Technorati. In order to make our choice of sites, we might be influenced by those sites' ratings of different blogs' 'authority points' and the distinguishing characteristics that rate the impact of individual blogs among wider audiences. Participant-observation on the blog would need to be carefully considered; on some blogs, those with few comments, for example, the researcher's own postings might be disruptive to the regular flow of communal messages. Engagement might simply constitute regular readership. Responses that might otherwise be overly intrusive might be offered as comments or postings on the researcher's own blog or in other forums such as social networks.

More restricted forms of access, such as are found on LiveJournal and through other community blog formats, can be very helpful. Blogs would also require a more visual style of analysis than the textual elements of the average forum or bulletin board. Gaining permissions in order to perform an ethical netnography would also be necessary. Almost certainly, you want to contact the blog owner and tell them about your research. You would probably want also to ask them about their preferences for being cited in the research. When the research report is completed, you may want to post it online and suggest that the blogger also link to it and perhaps, if they are interested in doing so, comment upon it on their own blog. For some other very useful ideas about online ethnography using blogs, please consult Hookway (2008).

THE NETNOGRAPHY OF SOCIAL NETWORKING SITES

Social networking sites are another fascinating fieldsite for online community studies. An entrée into these communities can be as easy as joining a commercial service like Bebo or Orkut. Access to, and participation in, the many groups and interest activities – including online games – is relatively straightforward. Disclosure of one's identity as a researcher is critical in these early stages. This information should appear in one's profile and probably in other places, and is likely to temper or alter some of the responses received.

The variety of modalities for interactions on social networking sites provides a rich site for examining notions of communication, and their hybrid commercial–communal form makes them highly relevant for topics investigating this area. The seemingly endless jostling between social networking sites and their member bases over advertising and access makes for interesting case studies, and serve as fodder for impactful theorizing. The networks of people and the availability of data lend themselves to variegated methods for analysing and representing online community data. Many productive hybrids between social network analysis and netnography could be undertaken on such sites.

Social networking sites may not only be useful forums to study in themselves. For example, Kozinets (forthcoming) studies the relationships that Facebook users express to commercial brands in 'fan' groups. Social networking sites may also be useful for finding interested research participants. Groups can be used to publicize one's own research, leading people to a research web-page or to other modalities of contact. As we discussed in Chapter 8, the terms of service contract of some social networking sites can be restrictive, so following ethical procedures is an important concern. In addition, the netnographer would want to be very cautious about the ages of the participants in the research, ensuring adequate protocols are observed for appropriately gaining informed consent. In addition, the final report's usage of citations and attention to copyrights should be carefully considered.

THE NETNOGRAPHY OF VIRTUAL WORLDS

Even in this brief overview, we certainly cannot ignore virtual worlds. A large number of scholarly works have already taken an ethnographic approach to the study of virtual worlds (for an early example, see Taylor 1999). Virtual worlds are fascinating because of their members' apparent 'embodiment' as avatars. The real-time communications, entrée and subsequent interactions assume a form more similar in some ways to in-person ethnography than to the textual netnographies of bulletin boards. One's entrée in a virtual world means entering into a type of citizenry that cannot usually, by its nature, be inobtrusive or invisible. Gathering data becomes more like videography, with continuous capture and screen grabbing software solutions of considerable value.

In our research, Richard Kedzior and I have theorized that auto-netnography can be especially valuable in virtual worlds (Kozinets and Kedzior 2009). Auto-netnography is a more participative and autobiographical style of netnography that attends more closely to first-hand personal reflection as captured in fieldnotes. Because virtual worlds involve a 're-embodiment', a new sense of world or 'reworlding', and an ability to inhabit multiple worlds in multiple bodies or multiperspectivity, many of the most interesting aspects of the phenomena are experienced from a subjective point of view that is not easily captured through interactions or interviews with others. With its deep N of 1 not threatening or requiring the permission of other participants, auto-netnography may also simplify complex ethical research procedures.

In order to conduct ethical research in a virtual world, appropriate steps would need to be followed regarding permissions, self identification, the citation of others, and other procedures. Opportunities to engage and interact with other culture members in virtual worlds might transpire in that world in a specially-programmed 'location' sponsored by the netnographer, such as a 'research island'. Alternately, culture participants might be shepherded through synchronous in-world contact to other areas such as forums or blogs, or other types of interaction could ensue.

THE EXPANSION OF NETNOGRAPHY

The future for netnography has never looked brighter.

As these forms grow, change, and blend with multiplayer online games, wikis, mobile communications, and integrative media delivery services such as Feedster, we will see the continuous expansion of the boundaries of online community and culture. Our lives, as scholars, as consumers, as friends, as members, will become increasingly intertwined with them.

With a solid foundation of netnographic procedures in place, scholars and researchers can point towards legitimate techniques while building a consistent foundation of knowledge. Following common procedures will facilitate multi-person netnographies, where collaborators who may be dispersed geographically, disciplinarily, and even in time can utilize common signposts to harmonize their approach and speak with a consistent methodological voice.

There are even enticing possibilities for 'massively multi-person' netnographies, where dozens or even hundreds of netnographers, operating across multiple countries and disciplinary domains collect, analyse, and report findings about large-scale changes taking place across multiple communities and cultures of the Internet and ICT. There is still, however, much to be done to detail the differences in netnographic procedures required across different countries and regions. This book presents techniques skewed towards the North American, and particularly United States, context. Yet much of the Internet growth of the future and the growth of Internet research itself will come from outside that region. Adaptations of netnography for individual cultures, ethnicities, languages, regions, and nations are every bit as critical to the development of the technique as are adaptations of the approach for different and ever-changing forms of media.

Another area with prodigious potential is the combination of ostensibly observational 'data-mining' and content analytic techniques with the participative cultural orientation of netnography. Computational power can be enormously valuable in scanning the millions of conversations flowing across the Internet, filtering, classifying and sorting them into predesignated or emergent categories. The availability of advanced computer-assisted techniques can be quite seductive in that these can lead researchers to try to automate data collection and analysis, thus decontextualizing cultural data. Although seeming to classify the data, the abuse of these programs – or, indeed, of the ease of netnographic data collection using a search engine – must draw our attention and concern back to the importance of authentically understanding culturally embedded meanings. We cannot write about cultures we do not truly understand. And the ethnographer's creed is that we cannot truly understand a culture unless we have spent sufficient time within it to understand what membership means. This is not to discount multiple methods, by any means. Applying a systematic mixed methods approach can reveal many facets of a culture, such as its hidden social structures. But the grounding element, the core of these methods, should be cultural understanding if that approach is to be termed a netnographic one.

IN CLOSING: SURFING WITH ANTHROPOLOGISTS

We, this group, this community of wired anthropologists, have the ability to trace cultural interaction wherever it is manifested.

We, the netnographers of the network, the hunters and gatherers of urls and engines, scents and figures, gazes and captures. We cross oceans, not of water but of an infinity of rushing, roaring, crosscutting data streams. Digital detectives, bricoleurs in bits and bytes, we are constantly adapting, installing, programming, linking, questioning, interpreting, reflecting, noting. Following the intermix. Online and off. Offline and on. Asking permission in public from the public, for the public, to consent and assent to moments of dissent and eventful representation. Telling our tales with our tails on (the) line.

Hacking ourselves a new path through an ancient grove where flashing cupric cables grow like green vines up thick lush forest trees. Holding firm and strong to the bridge of old traditions, we chart our way into these new hollows, explore this new place, meet and learn from the people, for the people, as a person.

Our wiring is interactive, our DNA tribal. As cyborgs, we increasingly plug into networks to connect. Perhaps, as Erik Davis (1998, pp. 334–35) hints, we are on a 'network path' exploring 'a multifaceted but integral mode of spirit that might humanely and sensibly navigate the technological house of mirrors' into a matrix 'ablaze within entangling tongues', a realization of Jesuit paleontologist Pierre Tielhard de Chardin's (1959) 'noosphere'.

Our many cultures' and communities' feedback loops increasingly interconnect and gain feedback loops of their own. Your textual ideas morph into her photographic inspiration, his visuals are scanned into her graphical project, that graphic set to this music becomes the soundtrack to someone else's YouTube video grown famous through rating points, turned into a graphic novel and eventually shown on broadcast television with plans for an off-Broadway theatrical adaptation.

All of it discussed, all of it debated, all of it blogged and microblogged and promoted with lots of omgs and lols. And we will be there.

We will be a part of it. A part of the web, the webs of work that work through a newly socialized sociability, that stretch from the person next door to the distant global other, from the most passive lurker to the busiest business prosumer, reaching from the most inanely ridiculous video moments to the most sacred Scriptures that we share. Every blessed element of our culture will have strands leading to and from our online connectivity.

The Internet has changed our reality: the reality of being a member of society, a citizen, a consumer, a thinker, a speaker, a whistleblower, a blogger, a friend, a fan, an organizer, a doer. A scholar, a colleague, a parent, a student.

Perhaps you will be conducting your own netnography. Perhaps you will be reading and enjoying netnographies, or reviewing and evaluating them, or struggling to understand or work with them. Whatever your connection, I hope you find joy and inspiration from this new, thrilling area of human interconnection. For, just as important as our scientific rigour, perhaps, is our playfulness. Netnography – like ethnography – should be, much of the time, a joyous, boundless pursuit of discovery, new relations, and new relationships.[15]

See you online!

SUMMARY

In this short final chapter, we learnt about the trajectory of theory and practice in netnography as we previewed and suggested exciting possibilities for the method's ongoing growth and adaptation. Three broad theoretical areas and themes that are potentially of increasing importance are: (1) the relation between corporations and online communities; (2) the social implications of online communities, their presence, institutionalization, and ownership; and (3) the different social uses of different media of online interaction. Inquiries into particular sites of online culture and community require specific adaptations of netnography. This chapter overviews the adaptation of the approach to blogs, virtual worlds, and social networking sites. Many other sites of online community and modes of research are available to netnographers, presenting exciting opportunities to develop the method further.

KEY READINGS

Hookway, Nicholas (2008), '"Entering the Blogosphere": Some Strategies for Using Blogs in Social Research', *Qualitative Research*, 8: 91–113.

Kozinets, Robert V. (2005) 'Communal Big Bangs and the Ever-Expanding Netnographic Universe', *Thexis*, 3: 38–41.

Kozinets, Robert V. (2006) 'Netnography 2.0', in Russell W. Belk (ed.), *Handbook of Qualitative Research Methods in Marketing*. Cheltenham, UK and Northampton, MA: Edward Elgar Publishing, pp. 129–42.

Kozinets, Robert V. and Richard Kedzior (2009) 'I, Avatar: Auto-netnographic Research in Virtual Worlds', in Michael Solomon and Natalie Wood (eds), *Virtual Social Identity and Social Behavior*. Armonk, NY: M.E. Sharpe, pp. 3–19.

ENDNOTES

1   These electronically-mediated agglomerations of kindred spirits have been variously termed 'online', 'virtual', 'computer-mediated', or even 'e-communities' or 'e-tribes'. And although 'virtual community', was the term popular throughout most of the 1990s, it is currently in decline, most likely because of the connotation of the term 'virtual' as indicating that these communities were simulations, inauthentic mirror images, not actual or not real. In this book, I prefer to use the term 'online community' – although freely admitting that this term, like all the others, has its drawbacks and may well be superseded by a newer or better term.

2   Some might suggest, and I am sensitive to this perspective, that cyberculture cannot be essentialized and universalized into some form of culture that exists in a realm apart from other systems of meaning. It must always remain articulated with other aspects of culture, be they linguistic, material, or behavioural.

3   Although the report's authors do not provide details or analyse their research results, I would explain the contrast with Pew's earlier results of 84 per cent having online community activity as follows. First, the Digital Future Project's definitions of online community 'membership' are considerably more restrictive than those of the Pew Internet Report. Their questions specifically ask if the person is 'a member' of an online community, defining online community 'as a group that shares thoughts or ideas, or works on common projects, through electronic communication only' (The Digital Future Report 2008, p. 101). This emphasis on membership as well as the requirement for the group to meet exclusively through electronic communication – and also the somewhat surprising exclusion of the well over 100 million people globally connecting using social networking sites – likely makes regular 'online community membership' akin to a form of subscription, creating a higher standard. The 2001 Pew Internet Report, in contrast, simply asked about the activities and experiences that people had with more broadly defined online communities. This represented an easier standard to reach. Second, the Pew Internet Report was conducted in 2001, well before a lot of the 'mainstreaming' activities of the Internet and 'Web 2.0' had begun, such as blogging and social networking sites. I could conclude from this that the sample Pew drew from had considerably more experienced online users in it, and that these numbers represented people who had been online longer and whose experiences online had broadened to include more contact with other people. We may well see similar numbers take hold as experience and learning effects diffuse among the many newer users of the Internet captured in the Digital Future Project's surveys.

4   Of course, it is possible, and often desirable, to perform a post-structural netnography, such as that of Hine (2000) or Danet (2001). In a post-structural approach, relations and meanings are considered far more contingent and complex than they would be in a structural approach.

5   These procedures are, of course, a simplification guided by the rhetorical points I wish to convey and illustrate. Different ethnographies will have different types of concerns (e.g., auto-ethnography is not particularly concerned with site selection). However, these procedures are intended as a general framework in order to contrast and develop netnography.

6   In fact, much of my own published netnographic research to date has tended to focus on newsgroups (see Brown et al. 2003; Kozinets 2001, 2002a; Kozinets and Handelman 2004; Kozinets and Sherry 2005). For a while, as the academic record indicates, for online community researchers they were the main game in town.

7   Yes, the idea of dead tree hardcopies is more than a tad ironic. But to those over the age of 30, or deprived of a good Tablet PC, access to paper jottings can still be helpful.

8   The operating system and browser may not be entirely salient to the discussion, but they will explain why the graphical images represented in the figures look the way they do. They may also be of interest to those with a more technical inclination. The message thread, entitled 'Doesn't capitalism destroy the environment', has 67 messages by 17 authors. It can be found online at http://groups.google.ca/group/alt. global-warming/browse_thread/thread/a9e43878ddc9340d/198b4a1696000546?hl= en&lnk=gst&q=capitalism#198b4a1696000546, or, more simply, by entering the thread title into the Google Groups window and pressing 'Search Groups'.

9   Full-motion screen captures are most convenient when engaging in synchronous communications, such as with an online chat or audiovisual interview. The interviews or chats are automatically captured, and the netnographer can focus upon establishing rapport, attending to nuance, and asking insightful questions. Depending on your style and preferences as a researcher, full-motion screen capture software can also be useful to record general explorations of your fieldsite. The software does not substitute for keeping high-quality fieldnotes, although it can offer a very useful supplement to them.

10 I am not including online activism as a realistic option, although it did occur to me. Perhaps one day a courageous netnographer will engage in an influential campaign to rid the online world (or some small corner of it) of spam, beginning, from a participatory action research frame, a powerful social movement through netnography.

11 In addition, the pseudonyms and names in the message have been cloaked by replacing them with different pseudonyms or names. The reason for this is to abide by ethical research concerns. As Chapter 8 explains, this is a minimal form of cloaking used to mildly protect anonymity because the risk of harm to the community and individuals in it is considered to be minimal.

12 Any good software program can be used for these purposes, not just Microsoft's offerings. Hahn's (2008) book uses these examples, and so I stay with them. But your choices include many open source offerings, as well as the free and online Google suite of programs like Google Documents.

13 In the past, Kozinets (2002a, 2006a) recommended several ethical procedures involving full disclosure, gaining consent and permissions, and being cautious about the use of

direct quotations. Each of the specific procedures has been transcended by the updated suggestions and guidelines offered in this chapter.

14 For example, in Kozinets (2006a), I provide a brief example of a market-oriented netnography of a blog devoted to Barq's root beer, emphasizing the blog's rich and multifaceted world of individualized meanings, personalized stories, socio-historical and communal connections, and articulated practices. A much more detailed netnographic study of how bloggers react towards word-of-mouth marketing can be found in my co-authored research Kozinets et al. (2010).

15 To close this book, I would like to emphasize that sense of playfulness by citing a netnographic anthem that I recently composed for my blog. It is meant to be sung to the tune of a famous Beatles song. It is included in the book as Appendix 2. Why don't we hum it once and then sing it together, gently and mindfully, as we begin our preparation for once again dipping our toes into that ever-changing datastream, that echoing and burbling, ever-present and forever-captured mysterious place, that field that lives behind our screens?

GLOSSARY

Abstracting: sorting categorized codes into higher-order, or more general, conceptual constructs, patterns or processes; part of the process of qualitative data analysis.

Accessibility: the openness to participation and general availability of cultural inclusion in online communities and cultures; for example, almost all public newsgroups are open to the participation of new members, and available for anyone with Internet access to read; one of the four characteristic elements distinguishing online social experiences from face-to-face interactions.

Alteration: the transformation of social interaction that occurs due to communications and transactions being computer- or technologically-mediated, for example, by only allowing text or scanned images to be exchanged; one of the four characteristic elements distinguishing online social experiences from face-to-face interactions.

Anonymity: the liberating and complicating option of cultural participation under conditions where one's real name or identity is hidden; one of the four characteristic elements distinguishing online social experiences from face-to-face interactions; see also pseudonymity.

Archiving: the automatic saving and storing of records of cultural interactions; one of the four characteristic elements distinguishing online social experiences from face-to-face interactions.

Asynchronous communications: communications that are staggered in time, such as billboard, web-page, or forum postings, or e-mails; an asynchronous communication might spread out a short message or interaction over a period of days, weeks, or even months; contrasted with synchronous, or 'real-time', communications.

Audio/visual sites: online locations where participants asynchronously share and comment upon one another's graphical, photographical, audio, or audiovisual productions; a potential site of online community and culture.

Auto-netnography: adapted from auto-ethnography; a netnography composed mainly of autobiographical personal reflection on online community membership, as captured in fieldnotes and other subjective recordings of online experience.

Blended ethnography/netnography: research that combines the collection of online data and interactions with data and interactions collected through face-to-face contact.

Guidelines for blended ethnography/netnography include considerations of the research focus and question, the level of integration *vs.* separation, observation *vs.* verbalization, and identification *vs.* performance; see also online community research and research on communities online.

Blog: popular abbreviation for weblog; a special type of web-page that is, in the ideal, frequently updated, and which consists of dated entries arranged in reverse chronological order; a potential site of online community and culture.

Bulletin boards (or forums): predominantly text-based exchanges often organized around particular shared orientations or interests; bulletin boards tend to originate with interested individuals; a potential site of online community and culture; see also forums.

CAQDAS: acronym for Computer-Assisted Qualitative Data Analysis and its related software; computer programs that assist the researcher in their analysis of qualitative data. Useful for netnographic projects involving the management and analysis of large, complex, and/or diverse data sets.

Chat-rooms: a form of online communications in which two or more people share text, usually for social objectives, interacting synchronously – in real time – and usually without any fantasy role-playing (but often with a complex set of acronyms, shortcuts, and emoticons); a potential site of online community and culture.

Coding: affixing codes or categories to data drawn from fieldnotes, interviews, documents, or, in the case of netnographic data, other cultural material downloaded from the Internet or other ICT sites; categories for coding usually emerge inductively through a close reading of the data, rather than being imposed by prescribed categories; part of the process of qualitative data analysis.

Coherence: a criterion of netnographic quality where each recognizably different interpretation in a netnography is free from internal contradictions and presents a unified pattern.

Community: a group of people who share social interaction, social ties, and a common interactional format, location, or 'space'; in netnography, the 'space' is the 'cyberspace' of computer- or technologically-mediated communication; the boundaries of communal membership may be understood in terms of self-identification as a member, repeat contact, reciprocal familiarity, shared knowledge of some rituals and customs, some sense of obligation, and participation.

Computer-mediated communication(s), or CMC: any communication that takes place through a computer or network; CMC includes forums, postings, instant messages, e-mails, chat-rooms, as well as mobile text messaging.

Culture: a learned system of meaning, which includes beliefs, rituals and norms, behaviours, values, identities, and, in particular, languages that, in general, helps to organize and direct particular social formations.

Cyberculture: a distinct type of culture that developed along with digital information and communications technologies, in particular, the Internet; learned system of meaning, which includes beliefs, values, practices, roles, and languages, that helps to direct and organize particular online or technology-related social formations.

Entrée: the process of initial entry into a new culture or community; sometimes facililitated by a social contact; a successful entrée is often preceded by culture and community-specific research and investigation.

Ethnography: an anthropological approach to the research of culture based upon participant-observational techniques; ethnography's goals are a detailed and nuanced understanding of a cultural phenomenon, and a representation that conveys the lived experience of culture members as well as the meaning system and other social structures underpinning the culture or community.

Forums: predominantly text-based exchanges often organized around particular shared orientations or interests; forums tend to originate as a part of corporate or professional websites; a potential site of online community and culture; see also bulletin boards.

Full-motion screen capture software: computer programs that record, moment-by-moment, what appears on the computer screen, and can also include audio; useful for the collection of audiovisual data as well as for keeping detailed records of netnographic interaction and exploration.

Generalizing: elaborating a small set of generalizations to cover or explain the consistencies in the dataset; part of the process of qualitative data analysis.

Groundedness: a criterion for netnographic quality where the theoretical representation is supported by data, and the links between data and theory are clear and convincing.

Human Research Subjects Review Committee: one of the names given to the governing board or committee at a university or college level that must approve research on human subjects for its ethical appropriateness prior to the research being conducted; see also IRB.

ICT: abbreviation for Information and Communications Technologies; these would include the Internet; an umbrella term for any technological device or service that enables information-sharing and/or communications; ICT includes computer hardware and software, computer networks, satellite systems, and cellular phones as well as the Internet, television, and radio, as well as the various services and applications associated with them, such as instant messaging, specialty cable channels, and mobile computing.

Inductive data analysis: a form of data analysis in which individual observations are built up in order to gain a more general understanding of a particular phenomenon; netnographic data analysis is inductive.

Innovation: a criterion for netnographic quality where the constructs, ideas, frameworks and narrative form provide new and creative ways of understanding systems, structures, experience or actions.

Intermix: criterion for netnographic quality that judges the extent to which the netnography takes account of the interconnection of the various modes of social interaction – online and off – in culture members' daily lived experiences, as well as in its own representation.

Interpretivism: a school of thought devoted to the goal of understanding the complex world of lived experience from the point of view of those who live it; most applicable to netnography because of the related influence of interpretive ethnography.

IRB: Institutional Review Board; the name given in the USA for the governing board or committee at university or college level that must approve research on human subjects for its ethical appropriateness prior to the research being conducted; it is critical that netnographers submit and have their research proposal approved, as participative netnography is undoubtedly research on human subjects; see also Human Research Subjects Review Committee.

IRE: Internet Research Ethics; an emerging, important, and interdisciplinary research field that examines what it means to research ethically in Internet or online research environments.

Lists: groups of participants who collectively produce and share regular e-mails about a particular named topic or subject of mutual interest; a potential site of online community and culture.

Literacy: a criterion for netnographic quality where the netnography recognizes and is knowledgeable about the relevant literature and research approaches.

LOL: popular online acronym signifying 'laugh(ing) out loud'.

Member checks: consulting with culture members by providing a summary, parts, or all of an ethnography or netnography for their consideration and comments; simplified in netnography by online access; a recommended but not required procedure for netnography that can assist with researcher participation, the inclusion of culture members' voices and perspectives, and research ethics.

Memoing: see noting.

Microblogs: an extension of the blog utilizing small amounts of frequently updated text, distributed selectively and often across multiple platforms including mobile platforms; a potential site of online community and culture.

MMOG: massively multiplayer online game; also MMORPG, massively multiplayer online role-playing game.

Netnography: a type of online, or Internet, ethnography; netnography provides guidelines for the adaptation of participant-observation procedures – planning for fieldwork, making a cultural entrée, gathering cultural data, ensuring a high-quality ethnographic interpretation, and ensuring strict adherence to ethical standards – to the contingencies of online community and culture that manifest through computer-mediated communications.

Noting: making reflections on the data or other remarks noted in the margins of the data; part of the process of qualitative data analysis.

OMG: popular online acronym signifying 'oh my God'.

Online community: a community manifest through any form of computer-mediated communications; a group of people who communicate and share social interaction and social ties through the Internet or other computer mediated-communication, such as e-mail lists, forums, newsgroups, photo-sharing sites, blogs, virtual worlds, or social networking sites; levels of participation vary widely from largely passive subscribers to highly involved organizers.

Online community research (also research on online communities): the study of some phenomenon directly relating to online communities and online culture itself, a particular manifestation of them, or one of their elements.

Online interviews: the conduct of an interview through computer-mediation; often used to refer to synchronous, textual-based interviews such as those conducted through chat; less often used to refer to e-mail, audio, or audiovisual interviews conducted over the Internet, although all of these uses are technically correct.

Phenomenological: relating to the study of structures of consciousness as experienced from the first-person point of view; in netnography, a phenomenological approach seeks to understand and appreciate the content or meanings of members' experience in online communities and cultures.

Playspaces: communications forums where one or more people socially interact through the structured format of role- and game-playing; a potential site of online community and culture.

Praxis: a criterion for netnographic quality that judges the extent to which the netnography inspires and empowers social action.

Pseudonymity: regular cultural participation under conditions where one's real name or identity is replaced by a pseudonym; pseudonyms are often related or relatable to members' real names; under conditions of pseudonymity, culture members' pseudonyms become a persistent and real identifier.

'Pure' netnography: also know as a 'stand-alone' netnography; netnography conducted using only computer-mediated data and social interaction with no in-person or face-to-face data collection or interactional components.

Reflexivity: a criterion for netnographic quality that judges the extent to which the netnography acknowledges the role of the researcher and is open to alternative interpretations.

Research on communities online: studies that examine some extant general social phenomena whose social existence extends well beyond the Internet and online interactions, even though online interactions may play an important role with the group's membership.

Resonance: a criterion for netnographic quality that judges to what extent a personalized and sensitizing connection with the cultural phenomenon is gained.

Rigour: a criterion for netnographic quality that judges the extent to which the netnography recognizes and adheres to the procedural standards of netnographic research.

Rings: organizations of related web-pages that are linked together and structured by interest; largely obsolete; a potential site of online community and culture.

Social content aggregators: sites and services designed to help people communally discover and share Internet content, vote on it, and comment upon it; a potential site of online community and culture.

Social Network Analysis: an analytical method that focuses on the structures and patterns of relationships between and among people – as well as among organizations, states, and other entities; useful for determining structural relationships among and between online communities.

Social networking sites (or services; both abbreviated to SNS): a hybrid communications format that offers devoted individual pages, various interaction media, interest and activity groups, and communities made available to users through selective linkages; a potential site of online community and culture.

Spam: unsolicited bulk messages; almost every type of online community receives spam; netnographers need to learn how to deal with these messages, as they cannot be considered the same as culture members' interactions with one another.

Still-image screen capture software: computer programs that capture a snapshot-like graphical image of a computer screen, or part of a computer screen; also called 'screen shot' software; useful for the collection of still graphical, photographic, and other image-based data.

Synchronous communications: communications that occur in 'real-time', such as telephone calls, face-to-face conversations, and chat; contrasted with asynchronous communications.

Technoculture: a word given to represent the perspective that technology does not determine culture, and culture does not determine technology, but that they are co-determining, co-constructive social forces.

Theorizing: confronting generalizations gathered from the data with a formalized body of knowledge that uses constructs or theories; part of the process of qualitative data analysis.

Verisimilitude: a criterion for netnographic quality that judges the extent to which a believable and lifelike sense of cultural and communal contact is achieved.

Virtual community: another term for online community; a term popularized by Internet pioneer Howard Rheingold (1993, p. 5), who defined virtual communities as 'social aggregations that emerge from the net when enough people carry on ... public discussions long enough, with sufficient human feeling, to form webs of personal relationships in cyberspace'.

Virtual ethnography: a type of ethnographic study of virtual communities whose virtual nature is also to be considered necessarily partial and inauthentic because it only focuses on the online aspect of the social experience, rather than the entire experience; after Hine (2000).

Virtual worlds: a type of playspace that combines the synchronous, graphically-intense environment of the online game with the more open and grassroots social processes of many of the original dungeons; a potential site of online community and culture.

Wiki: a specialized, collaborative form of the web-page in which the page is designed so that it is open to contributions or modifications of its content; a potential site of online community and culture.

APPENDIX 1
ONLINE INFORMED CONSENT FORM TO BE USED ON RESEARCH WEB-PAGE

York University
Research Project Title: Studying Boycott Participants' Online Experiences
Principle Investigator: Dr Robert V. Kozinets

Online Research Consent Form
You are being asked to be a participant/volunteer in a research study.

Purpose:
The purpose of this research study is to examine the online experiences of boycott participants. We hope to learn more about the experiences of people who participate in boycotts as well as those who wish to participate in them, and to better understand the role of online interaction in those experiences and intentions. After the research is completed, the researcher hopes to publish the study in an academic journal, and may present it at academic conferences. A research web-page has been constructed to inform people about the research and is available at http://www.boycottresearchprojectonline.com/notthereyet/

Procedures:
If you decide to be part of this study, your participation will involve:

- consenting to an interview to be conducted in person, over the telephone, or through e-mail
- that interview taking approximately two hours
- the same interview focussing on your boycott-related online and personal experiences
- in the case of a face-to-face interview, the session being audiotaped; a telephone interview being audiotaped; an e-mail interview being saved for future reference.

Risks
The following risks may occur as a result of your participation in this study:
There are no foreseeable risks or discomforts in this study. The risks involved are no greater than those involved in daily activities such as speaking on the telephone or using e-mail. Because some of the topic matter related to boycotts may be sensitive, there is a chance that your recollections may become personal and emotional.

Benefits
The following benefits to you are possible as a result of participating in the study:
You are not likely to benefit in any way from participating in the study. However, your participation in the study will contribute to our understanding of boycotts and of online experience.

Compensation
There is no compensation for your participation in this research.

Confidentiality
The following procedures will be followed in order to keep your personal information confidential:
To protect your confidentiality, your name will not appear in any publications. You will be assigned a pseudonym (a fake name) that will be used instead of your name to disguise your participation. In the case of quotes about things you have done online (such as posts on newsgroups or forums, blog entries or comments), this disguise could be vulnerable. Using a search engine, a motivated person could break it. A person could take a quotation from the research and use a search engine to find the actual page online. They could therefore break the pseudonym disguise assigned in the research and trace the original posting. We do not anticipate uncovering sensitive information about you in this research. In case it does, other strong precautions will be used to protect your confidentiality.

The data that we collect about you will be kept private to the extent allowed by law. To make sure that this research is being conducted in the proper way, York University's Human Subject Review Committee may have access to the research records.

In the case of electronic communications in online consent, you should be aware that this form is not being run from a 'secure' https server, such as the kind used to handle credit card transactions. There is therefore a small possibility that responses could be viewed by unauthorized parties, such as computer hackers.

Costs to You
Research participants should incur no cost as a result of consenting to be interviewed.

Participant Rights

- Your participation in this study is voluntary. You are under no obligation to participate in the study.
- You have the right to change your mind and leave the study at any time without giving any reason and without any penalty.

- Any new information that might make you change your mind about being in the study will be provided to you.
- You will be given a copy of this consent form to keep.
- You do not waive any of your legal rights by signing or agreeing to this consent form.

Questions about the Study or Your Rights as a Research Participant

- If you have any questions about this research study, you may contact Dr Robert Kozinets at telephone no. (777) 545–4975.
- If you have any questions about your rights as a research subject, you may contact Ms Rita Jones, York University Human Participant Review Committee coordinator at (777) 545–4999.

Have you read the information on this page and do you agree to participate? (Select one)

☐ I have read and understand this information and agree to participate.
☐ I do not want to participate.

E-mail address: ☐_____☐
(required to confirm identity)

┌─────────────┐
│ **SUBMIT** │
└─────────────┘

APPENDIX 2
A POEM/SONG ABOUT THE
CONDUCT OF NETNOGRAPHY

Sung to the tune of *Come Together* by The Beatles (ASCAP 1969)

click together

here come old *H@Kk_Ur!*
he go surfin' all nightly
he got flickr eyeball he read global braindump
he got ten servers in his big RV
must be influential he just post what he please

he shop all naked he got ebay football
he got twitter finger he one second lifer
he say 'i friend you, you friend me'
All Is Information and It Got To Be Free
click together online community

he blogospheric he big technorati
he got google goggles he shoot youtube picture
he got cloudware clickstream on his page
look him up in facebook he make maximum wage
click together online community

he carpal tunnel he wear warcraft diaper
he got wiki widget he one porno filter
he say 'web plus web is two point oh'
got to be a broker he net portfolio
click together online community

REFERENCES

Adams, Tyrone L. and Steven A. Smith (eds) (2008) *Electronic Tribes: Virtual Worlds of Geeks, Gamers, Shamans, and Scammers*. Austin, TX: University of Texas Press.

Allen, Gove N., Dan L. Burk and Gordon B. Davis (2006) 'Academic Data Collection in Electronic Environments: Defining Acceptable Use of Internet Resources', *MIS Quarterly*, 30(3) (September): 599–610.

Altheide, David L. and John M. Johnson (1994) 'Criteria for Assessing Interpretive Validity in Qualitative Research', in Norman K. Denzin and Yvonna S. Lincoln (eds), *Handbook of Qualitative Research*. Thousand Oaks, CA: Sage. pp. 485–99.

Andrews, Dorine, Blair Nonnecke and Jennifer Preece (2003) 'Electronic Survey Methodology: A Case Study in Reaching Hard-to-Involve Internet Users, *International Journal of Human–Computer Interaction*, 16(2): 185–210.

Andrusyszyn, Mary Anne and Lynn Davie (1997) 'Facilitating Reflection through Interactive Journal Writing in an Online Graduate Course: A Qualitative Study', *The Journal of Distance Education*, 12(1), available online at: www.jofde.ca/index.php/jde/article/viewArticle/266 (accessed 15 January 2009).

Arnold, Stephen J. and Eileen Fischer (1994) 'Hermeneutics and Consumer Research', *Journal of Consumer Research*, 21(June): 55–70.

Arnould, Eric J. and Melanie Wallendorf (1994) 'Market-Oriented Ethnography: Interpretation Building and Marketing Strategy Formulation', *Journal of Marketing Research*, 31(November): 484–504.

Association of Internet Researchers Ethics Working Group (2002) *Ethical Decision-Making and Internet Research: Recommendations from the AOIR Ethics Working Committee*, available online at: www.aoir.org/reports/ethics.pdf

Atkinson, Paul A. (1992) *Understanding Ethnographic Texts*. Newbury Park, CA: Sage.

Atkinson, Paul A., Amanda Jane Coffey, Sara Delamont, John Lofland and Lyn H. Lofland (2001) *Handbook of Ethnography*. Thousand Oaks, CA: Sage.

Bahktin, Mikhail (1981) 'Forms of Time and the Chronotrop in the Novel', in Michael Holquist (ed.), *The Dialogic Imagination*. Austin: University of Texas Press. pp. 259–442.

Bakardjieva, Maria (2005) *Internet Society: The Internet in Everyday Life*. London: Sage.

Bakardjieva, Maria and Andrew Feenberg (2001) 'Involving the Virtual Subject', *Ethics and Information Technology,* 2: 233–40.

Bassett, Elizabeth H. and Kate O'Riordan (2002) 'Ethics of Internet Research: Contesting the Human Subjects Research Model', *Ethics and Information Technology*, 4: 233–47.

Baym, Nancy K. (1995) 'The Emergence of Community in Computer-Mediated Communication', in Stephen G. Jones (ed.), *Cybersociety*. Thousand Oaks, CA: Sage. pp. 138–63.

Baym, Nancy K. (1999) *Tune in, Log on: Soaps, Fandom, and Online Community.* Thousand Oaks, CA: Sage.

Baym, Nancy (2006) 'Finding the Quality in Qualitative Research', in David Silver and Adrienne Massanari (eds), *Critical Cyberculture Studies.* New York: New York University Press. pp. 79–87.

Bazeley, Patricia (2007) *Qualitative Data Analysis with NVivo.* Thousand Oaks, CA: Sage.

Beaulieu, Anne (2004) 'Mediating Ethnography: Objectivity and the Making of Ethnographies of the Internet', *Social Epistemology,* 18(2–3; April–September): 139–63.

Beaven, Zuleika and Chantal Laws (2007) '"Never Let Me Down Again": Loyal Customer Attitudes Towards Ticket Distribution Channels for Live Music Events: a Netnographic Exploration of the US Leg of the Depeche Mode 2005–2006 World Tour', *Managing Leisure,* 12(2&3), April: 120–42.

Belk, Russell W. (1987) 'ACR Presidential Address: Happy Thought', in Melanie Wallendorf and Paul Anderson (eds), *Advances in Consumer Research, Volume 14.* Provo, UT: Association for Consumer Research. pp. 1–4.

Beninger, J.R. (1987) 'Personalization of Mass Media and the Growth of Pseudo-Community', *Communication Research,* 14: 352–71.

Berkowitz, S.D. (1982) *An Introduction to Structural Analysis: the Network Approach to Social Research.* Toronto: Butterworth.

Bhattacharya, Himika (2008) 'New Critical Collaborative Ethnography', in Charlene Nagy Hesse-Biber and Patricia Leavy (eds), *Handbook of Emergent Methods.* New York: Guilford Press. pp. 303–22.

Biocca, Frank (1997) 'The Cyborg's Dilemma: Progressive Embodiment in Virtual Environments', *Journal of Computer-mediated Communications,* 3(2), September, available online at http://jcmc.indiana.edu/vol3/issue2/biocca2.html/

Bodley, John H. (1994) *Cultural Anthropology: Tribes, States and the Global System.* Dubuque, IA: William C. Brown.

Bonsu, Samuel K. and Aron Darmody (2008) 'Co-creating Second Life: Market–Consumer Co-operation in Contemporary Economy', *Journal of Macromarketing,* 28(4): 355–68.

boyd, danah (2007) 'Why Youth (Heart) Social Network Sites: The Role of Networked Publics in Teenage Social Life', in David Buckingham (ed.), *Youth, Identity, and Digital Media.* Cambridge, MA: MIT Press.

Bourdieu, Pierre (1984) *Distinction: A Social Critique of the Judgement of Taste,* translated by Richard Nice. London: Routledge and Kegan Paul.

Brown, Stephen, Robert V. Kozinets and John F. Sherry, Jr (2003) 'Teaching Old Brands New Tricks: Retro Branding and the Revival of Brand Meaning', *Journal of Marketing,* 67(July): 19–33.

Brownlie, Douglas and Paul Hewer (2007) 'Culture of Consumption of Car Afficionados: Aesthetics and Consumption Communities', *International Journal of Sociology and Social Policy,* 27(3/4), January: 106–19.

Bruckman, Amy (2002) 'Studying the Amateur Artist: a Perspective on Disguising Data Collected in Human Subjects Research on the Internet', *Ethics and Information Technology,* 4: 217–31.

Bruckman, Amy (2006) 'Teaching Students to Study Online Communities Ethically', *Journal of Information Ethics,* Fall: 82–98.

Buchanan, Elizabeth (2006) 'Introduction: Internet Research Ethics at a Critical Juncture', *Journal of Information Ethics,* 15(2): 14–17.

Buchanan, Elizabeth (2004) *Readings in Virtual Research Ethics: Issues and Controversies.* Hershey, PA: Idea Group.

Campbell, Alex (2006) 'The Search for Authenticity: an Exploration of an Online Skinhead Newsgroup', *New Media & Society,* 8(2): 269–94.

Campbell, John Edward (2004) *Getting It On Online: Cyberspace, Gay Male Sexuality and Embodied Identity.* New York: Haworth Press.

Campbell, John Edward (2005) 'Outing PlanetOut: Surveillance, Gay Marketing, and Internet Affinity Portals', *New Media & Society*, 7(5): 663–83.

Campbell, John Edward and M. Carlson (2002) 'Panopticon.com: Online Surveillance and the Commodification of Privacy', *Journal of Broadcasting and Electronic Media*, 46(4): 586–606.

Carey, James W. (1989) *Communication as Culture.* New York: Routledge.

Carter, Denise (2005) 'Living in Virtual Communities: an Ethnography of Human Relationships in Cyberspace', *Information, Communication & Society*, 8(2)(June): 148–67.

Chartier, Roger (2001) 'The Practical Impact of Writing', in D. Finkelstein and A. McCleery (eds), *The Book History Reader.* London: Routledge.

Chenault, Brittney G. (1998) 'Developing Personal and Emotional Relationships Via Computer-Mediated Communication', *CMC Magazine*, May, available online at: www.december.com/cmc/mag/1998/may/chenault.html

Cherny, Lynn (1999) *Conversation and Community: Chat in a Virtual World.* Chicago: University of Chicago Press.

Clerc, Susan J. (1996) 'DDEB, GATB, MPPB, and Ratboy: The X-Files' Media Fandom, Online and Off', in David Lavery, Angela Hague and Marla Cartwright (eds), *Deny All Knowledge: Reading The X-Files.* Syracuse, NY: Syracuse University Press.

Clifford, James (1997) 'Spatial Practices: Fieldwork, Travel, and the Discipline of Anthropology', in Akhil Gupta and James Ferguson (eds), *Anthropological Locations: Boundaries and Grounds of a Field Science.* Berkeley, CA: University of California Press, 185–222.

Clifford, James (1988) *The Predicament of Culture.* Cambridge, MA: Harvard University Press.

Clifford, James and George E. Marcus (eds) (1986) *Writing Culture: The Poetics and Politics of Ethnography.* Berkeley: University of California Press.

Cohn, Deborah Y. and Vaccaro, Valerie L. (2006) 'A Study of Neutralisation Theory's Application to Global Consumer Ethics: P2P File-Trading of Musical Intellectual Property on the Internet', *International Journal of Internet Marketing and Advertising*, 3(1): 68–88.

ComScore (2001, January 16) 'ComScore Networks Study Reveals Inaccuracies in Consumers' Ability to Accurately Recall their On-line Buying Behavior and Offers New Solution', available online at: www.comscore.com/news/pr_comscore_study.htm (accessed 17 September 2002).

Correll, Shelley (1995) 'The Ethnography of an Electronic Bar: the Lesbian Café', *Journal of Contemporary Ethnography*, 24(3), October: 270–98.

Couper, M.P. (2000) 'Web-based Surveys: A Review of Issues and Approaches', *Public Opinion Quarterly*, 64: 464–94.

Cova, Bernard, Robert V. Kozinets and Avi Shankar (eds) (2007) *Consumer Tribes.* London: Butterworth-Heinemann.

Creswell, John W. (2009) *Research Design: Qualitative, Quantitative, and Mixed Methods Approaches*, 3rd edition. Thousand Oaks, CA: Sage.

Crumlish, Christian (2004) *The Power of Many: How the Living Web is Transforming Politics, Business, and Everyday Life.* Hoboken, NJ: Wiley.

Daft, Richard L. and Robert H. Lengel (1986) 'Organizational Information Requirements, Media Richness and Structural Design', *Management Science*, 32(5): 554–71.

Dalli, Daniele and Matteo Corciolani (2008) 'Collective Forms of Resistance: The Transformative Power of Moderate Communities: Evidence from the BookCrossing Case', *International Journal of Market Research*, 50(6): 757–75.

Danet, Brenda (2001) *Cyberpl@y: Communicating Online.* Oxford and New York: Berg.

Davis, Erik (1998) *Techgnosis: Myth, Magic + Mysticism in the Age of Information.* New York: Harmony Books.

Davison, K.P., J.W. Pennebaker and S.S. Dickerson (2000) 'Who Talks? The Social Psychology of Illness Support Groups', *The American Psychologist*, 55: 205–17.

Denzin, Norman K. (1994) 'The Art and Politics of Interpretation', in Norman K. Denzin and Yvonna S. Lincoln (eds), *Handbook of Qualitative Research*. Thousand Oaks, CA: Sage. pp. 500–15.

Denzin, Norman K. (1997) *Interpretive Ethnography: Ethnographic Practices for the 21st Century*. Thousand Oaks, CA: Sage.

Denzin, Norman K. and Yvonna S. Lincoln (1994) *Handbook of Qualitative Research*. Thousand Oaks, CA: Sage.

Denzin, Norman K. and Yvonna S. Lincoln (2005) *The Sage Handbook of Qualitative Research*, 3rd edition. Thousand Oaks, CA: Sage.

De Valck, Kristine (2005) *Virtual Communities of Consumption: Networks of Consumer Knowledge and Companionship*, ERIM PhD Series: Research in Management.

De Valck, Kristine (2007) 'The War of the eTribes: Online Conflicts and Communal Consumption', in Bernard Cova, Robert V. Kozinets and Avi Shankar (eds), *Consumer Tribes*. Burlington, MA: Elsevier/Butterworth-Heinemann. pp. 260–74.

Dibbell, Julian (1998) *My Tiny Life: Crime and Passion in a Virtual World*. New York: Henry Holt and Company.

DiMaggio, Paul, E. Hargittai, E. Neuman and J.P. Robinson (2001) 'Social Implications of the Internet', *Annual Review of Sociology*, 27: 307–36.

Douglas, Jack D. (1985) *Creative Interviewing*. Beverley Hills, CA: Sage.

Dubrovsky, Vitaly, Sara Kiesler and Beheruz Sethna (1991) 'The Equalization Phenomenon: Status Effects in Computer-mediated and Face-to-face Decision Making Groups', *Human–Computer Interaction*, 6: 119–46.

Ellis, Caroline (1991) 'Emotional Sociology', *Studies in Symbolic Interaction*, 12: 123–45.

Emerson, Robert M., Rachel I. Fretz and Linda L. Shaw (1995) *Writing Ethnographic Fieldnotes*. Chicago: University of Chicago Press.

Escobar, Arturo (1993) 'The Limits of Reflexivity: Politics in Anthropology's Post-Writing Culture Era', *Journal of Anthropological Research*, 49(4): 377–91.

Escobar, Arturo (1994) 'Welcome To Cyberia: Notes on the Anthropology of Cyberculture', *Current Anthropology*, 35(3)(June): 211–31.

Fernandez, James W. (1994), 'Culture and Transcendent Humanization: On the "Dynamic of the Categorical"', *Ethnos*, 59(3–4): 143–67.

Fetterman, David M. (1998) *Ethnography: Step-by-Step*. Thousand Oaks, CA: Sage.

Fong, John and Suzan Burton (2006) 'Online Word-Of-Mouth: A Comparison of American and Chinese Discussion Boards', *Asia Pacific Journal of Marketing and Logistics*, 18(2): 146–56.

Fournier, Susan and Lara Lee (2009) 'Getting Brand Communities Right', *Harvard Business Review*, April: 105–11.

Fox, Fiona E., Marianne Morris and Nichola Rumsey (2007) 'Doing Synchronous Online Focus Groups with Young People: Methodological Reflections', *Qualitative Health Research*, 17(4), April: 539–47.

Fox, Richard G. (1991) 'Introduction: Working in the Present', in Richard G. Fox (ed.), *Recapturing Anthropology: Working in the Present*. Santa Fe, NM: School of American Research Press. pp. 1–16.

Frankel, Mark S. and Sanyin Siang (1999) 'Ethical and Legal Aspects of Human Subjects Research on the Internet', *American Association for the Advancement of Science (AAAS)*. Washington, DC, available online at: www.aaas.org/spp/dspp/sfrl/projects/intres/report.pdf/

Füller, Johann, Gregor Jawecki and Hans Mühlbacher (2007) 'Innovation Creation by Online Basketball Communities', *Journal of Business Research*, 60(1): 60–71.

Füller, Johann, Kurt Matzler and Melanie Hoppe (2008) 'Brand Community Members as a Source of Innovation', *Journal of Product Innovation Management*, 25(6) (November): 608–19.

Gaiser, Ted (1997) 'Conducting On-Line Focus Groups: A Methodological Discussion', *Social Science Computer Review*, 15: 135–44.

Garcia, Angela Cora, Alecea I. Standlee, Jennifer Bechkoff and Yan Cui (2009) 'Ethnographic Approaches to the Internet and Computer-Mediated Communication', *Journal of Contemporary Ethnography*, 38(1), February: 52–84.

Garton, Laura, Caroline Haythornthwaite and Barry Wellman (1999) 'Studying On-Line Social Networks', in Steve Jones (ed.), *Doing Internet Research: Critical Issues in Methods for Examining the Net*. Thousand Oaks, CA: Sage. pp. 75–105.

Geertz, Clifford (1973) *The Interpretation of Cultures*. New York: Basic Books.

Giesler, Markus (2006) 'Consumer Gift Systems', *Journal of Consumer Research*, 33 (September): 283–90.

Glaser, Barney G. and Anselm L. Strauss (1967) *The Discovery of Grounded Theory: Strategies for Qualitative Research*. New York: Aldine Publishing Company.

Goffman, Erving (1989) 'On Fieldwork', *Journal of Contemporary Ethnography*, 18: 123–32.

Gossett, Loril M. and Julian Kilker (2006) 'My Job Sucks: Examining Counterinstitutional Websites as Locations for Organizational Member Voice, Dissent, and Resistance', *Management Communication Quarterly*, 20(1)(August): 63–90.

Greenbaum, Thomas L. (1998) *The Handbook for Focus Group Research*. New York: Lexington Books.

Grossman, Lev (2006) '*Time's* Person of the Year: You', *Time Magazine*, 13 December, available online at: www.time.com/time/magazine/article/0,9171,1569514,00.html/

Guba, Egon G. and Yvonna S. Lincoln (1989) *Fourth Generation Evaluation*. Newbury Park, CA: Sage Publications.

Guba, Egon G. and Yvonna S. Lincoln (1994) 'Competing Paradigms in Qualitative Research', in Norman K. Denzin and Yvonna S. Lincoln (eds), *Handbook of Qualitative Research*. Thousand Oaks, CA: Sage. pp. 105–17.

Gubrium, Jaber F. and James A. Holstein (eds) (2001) *Handbook of Interview Research: Context and Method*. Thousand Oaks, CA: Sage.

Gumpert, Gary and Robert Cathcart (1985) 'Media Grammars, Generations, and Media Gaps', *Critical Studies in Mass Communication*, 2: 23–35.

Hahn, Chris (2008) *Doing Qualitative Research Using Your Computer: A Practical Guide*. London: Sage.

Hair, Neil and Moira Clark (2007) 'The Ethical Dilemmas and Challenges of Ethnographic Research in Electronic Communities', *International Journal of Market Research*, 49(6): 781–800.

Hakken, David (1999) *Cyborgs@Cyberspace?: An Ethnographer Looks at the Future*. New York, London: Routledge.

Hammersley, Martyn (1992) *What's Wrong with Ethnography? Methodological Explorations*. London: Routledge.

Haythornthwaite, Caroline (2005) 'Social Networks and Internet Connectivity Effects', *Information, Communication & Society*, 8(2), June: 125–47.

Haythornthwaite, Caroline, Barry Wellman and M. Mantei (1995) 'Work Relationships and Media Use: a Social Network Analysis', *Group Decision and Negotiation*, 4(3): 193–211.

Hemetsberger, Andrea and Christian Reinhardt (2006) 'Learning and Knowledge-building in Open-source Communities: A Social-experiential Approach', *Management Learning*, 37(2), 187–214.

Herring, Susan (1996) 'Linguistic and Critical Analysis of Computer-Mediated Communication: Some Ethical and Scholarly Considerations', *The Information Society*, 12: 153–60.

Herring, Susan C. (2001) 'Computer-mediated Discourse', in D. Schiffrin, D. Tannen and H. Hamilton (eds), *The Handbook of Discourse Analysis*. Oxford: Blackwell Publishers. pp. 612–34.

Hiltz, Starr Roxanne (1984) *Online Communities: A Case Study of the Office of the Future*. Norwood, NJ: Ablex Publishing Company.

Hiltz, Starr Roxanne and Murray Turoff (1978) *The Network Nation: Human Communication via Computer*. Reading, MA: Addison-Wesley.

Hine, Christine (2000) *Virtual Ethnography*. London: Sage.

Hobbs, Dick (2006) 'Ethnography', in Victor Jupp (ed.), *Sage Dictionary of Social Research Methods*. London: Sage.

Hoffman, Donna L., Thomas P. Novak and Alladi Venkatesh (2004) 'Has the Internet become Indispensable?', *Communications of the ACM*, 47(7), July: 37–42.

Holeton, Richard (1998) *Composing Cyberspace: Identity, Community, and Knowledge in the Electronic Age*. New York: McGraw-Hill.

Hookway, Nicholas (2008) '"Entering the Blogosphere": Some Strategies for Using Blogs In Social Research', *Qualitative Research*, 8: 91–113.

Howard, P.E.M, L. Rainie and S. Jones (2000) 'Days and Nights on the Internet', *American Behavioral Scientist*, 45: 383–404.

Howard, Philip N. (2002) 'Network Ethnography and the Hypermedia Organization: New Media, New Organizations, New Methods', *New Media & Society*, 4(4): 550–74.

Hudson, James M. and Amy Bruckman (2004) '"Go Away": Participant Objections to Being Studied', *The Information Society*, 20(2): 127–39.

Hughes, Jerald and Karl R. Lang (2004) 'Issues in Online Focus Groups: Lessons Learned from an Empirical Study of Peer-To-Peer Filesharing System Users', *Electronic Journal of Business Research Methods*, 2(2): 95–110.

Jackson, Sally (1986) 'Building a Case for Claims about Discourse Structure', in D.G. Ellis and W.A. Donohue (eds), *Contemporary Issues in Language and Discourse Processes*. Hillsdale, NJ: Erlbaum. pp. 129–47.

Jacobson, David (1999) 'Doing Research in Cyberspace', *Field Methods*, 11(2): 127–45.

Jenkins, Henry (1992) *Textual Poachers: Television Fans and Participatory Culture*. New York: Routledge.

Jenkins, Henry (1995) '"Do You Enjoy Making the Rest of Us Feel Stupid?": alt.tv. twinpeaks, The Trickster Author and Viewer Mastery', in David Lavery (ed.), *'Full of Secrets': Critical Approaches to Twin Peaks*. Detroit: Wayne State University Press. pp. 51–69.

Jenkins, Henry (2006) *Convergence Culture: Where Old and New Media Collide*. New York and London: New York University Press.

Jeppesen, Lars Bo and Lars Frederiksen (2006) 'Why Do Users Contribute to Firm-Hosted User Communities? The Case of Computer-Controlled Music Instruments', *Organization Science*, 17(January–February): 45–63.

Johns, M., S.L. Chen and J. Hall (eds) (2003) *Online Social Research: Methods, Issues, and Ethics*. New York: Peter Lang.

Jones, Stephen G. (1995) 'Understanding Community in the Information Age', in Stephen G. Jones (ed.), *Cybersociety: Computer-mediated Communication and Community*. Thousand Oaks, CA: Sage. pp. 10–35.

Jones, Steve (1999) 'Studying the Net: Intricacies and Issues', in Steve Jones (ed.), *Doing Internet Research: Critical Issues in Methods for Examining the Net*. Thousand Oaks, CA: Sage. pp. 1–27.

Jorgensen, D.L. (1989) *Participant Observation: A Methodology for Human Studies.* Newbury Park, CA: Sage.

Kanayama, Tomoko (2003) 'Ethnographic Research on the Experience of Japanese Elderly People Online', *New Media & Society*, 5(2): 267–88.

Kavanaugh A. and S. Patterson (2001) 'The Impact of Community Computer Networks on Social Capital and Community Involvement', *American Behavioral Scientist*, 45: 496–509.

Kendall, Lori (1999) 'Recontextualizing "Cyberspace": Methodological Considerations for On-line Research', in Steve Jones (ed.), *Doing Internet Research: Critical Issues and Methods for Examining the Net.* Thousand Oaks, CA: Sage. pp. 57–74.

Kendall, Lori (2004) 'Participants and Observers in the Online Ethnography: Five Stories about Identity', in M.D. Jones, S.-L.S. Chan and G.J. Hall (eds), *Online Social Research: Methods, Issues, and Ethics.* New York: Peter Lang. pp. 125–40.

Kiesler, Sara, D. Zubrow, A.M. Moses and V. Geller (1985) 'Affect in Computer-mediated Communication: An Experiment in Synchronous Terminal-to-Terminal Discussion', *Human-Computer Interaction*, 1: 77–104.

Kiesler, Sara, Jane Siegel and Timothy McGuire (1984) 'Social Psychological Aspects of Computer-mediated Communication', *American Psychologist*, 39(10): 1123–34.

King, Storm (1996) 'Researching Internet Communities: Proposed Ethical Guidelines for the Reporting of Results', *The Information Society*, 12: 119–28.

Kivits, Joëlle (2005) 'Online Interviewing and the Research Relationship', in Christine Hine (ed.), *Virtual Methods: Issues in Social Research on the Internet.* Oxford: Berg. pp. 35–50.

Kluckhohn, Clyde (1949) *Mirror for Man.* New York: Wittlesey House/McGraw-Hill.

Komito, Lee (1998) 'The Net as a Foraging Society: Flexible Communities', *Information Society*, 14(2): 97–106.

Kozinets, Robert V. (1997a) '"I Want To Believe": A Netnography of *The X-Files'* Subculture of Consumption', in Merrie Brucks and Deborah J. MacInnis (eds), *Advances in Consumer Research*, Volume 24. Provo, UT: Association for Consumer Research. pp. 470–5.

Kozinets, Robert V. (1997b) 'To Boldly Go: a Hypermodern Ethnography of *Star Trek* Fans' Culture and Communities of Consumption', unpublished PhD dissertation, Queen's University, Kingston, Canada.

Kozinets, Robert V. (1998) 'On Netnography: Initial Reflections on Consumer Research Investigations of Cyberculture', in Joseph Alba and Wesley Hutchinson (eds), *Advances in Consumer Research*, Volume 25. Provo, UT: Association for Consumer Research. pp. 366–71.

Kozinets, Robert V. (1999) 'E-Tribalized Marketing? The Strategic Implications of Virtual Communities of Consumption', *European Management Journal*, 17(3): 252–64.

Kozinets, Robert V. (2001) 'Utopian Enterprise: Articulating the Meanings of *Star Trek's* Culture of Consumption', *Journal of Consumer Research*, 28(June): 67–88.

Kozinets, Robert V. (2002a) 'The Field Behind the Screen: Using Netnography for Marketing Research in Online Communities', *Journal of Marketing Research*, 39 (February): 61–72.

Kozinets, Robert V. (2002b) 'Can Consumers Escape the Market? Emancipatory Illuminations from Burning Man', *Journal of Consumer Research*, 29(June): 20–38.

Kozinets, Robert V. (2005) 'Communal Big Bangs and the Ever-Expanding Netnographic Universe', *Thexis*, 3: 38–41.

Kozinets, Robert V. (2006a) 'Netnography 2.0', in Russell W. Belk (ed.), *Handbook of Qualitative Research Methods in Marketing.* Cheltenham, UK and Northampton, MA: Edward Elgar Publishing. pp. 129–42.

Kozinets, Robert V. (2006b) 'Netnography', in Victor Jupp (ed.), *The Sage Dictionary of Social Research Methods*. London: Sage. pp. 193–5.

Kozinets, Robert V. (2006c) 'Click to Connect: Netnography and Tribal Advertising', *Journal of Advertising Research*, 46(September): 279–88.

Kozinets, Robert V. (2007) 'Inno-tribes: *Star Trek* as Wikimedia', in Bernard Cova, Robert V. Kozinets and Avi Shankar (eds), *Consumer Tribes*. Oxford and Burlington, MA: Butterworth-Heinemann. pp. 194–211.

Kozinets, Robert V. (2008) 'Technology/Ideology: How Ideological Fields Influence Consumers' Technology Narratives', *Journal of Consumer Research*, 34(April): 864–81.

Kozinets, Robert V. (forthcoming) 'Brand Fans: When Entertainment + Marketing Integrate Online', in Tracy Tuten (ed.), *Enterprise 2.0*. Westport, CT: Praeger.

Kozinets, Robert V. and Jay M. Handelman (1998) 'Ensouling Consumption: A Netnographic Exploration of The Meaning of Boycotting Behavior', in Joseph Alba and Wesley Hutchinson (eds), *Advances in Consumer Research*, Volume 25. Provo, UT: Association for Consumer Research. pp. 475–80.

Kozinets, Robert V. and Jay M. Handelman (2004) 'Adversaries of Consumption: Consumer Movements, Activism, and Ideology', *Journal of Consumer Research*, 31 (December): 691–704.

Kozinets, Robert V. and Richard Kedzior (2009) 'I, Avatar: Auto-netnographic Research in Virtual Worlds', in Michael Solomon and Natalie Wood (eds), *Virtual Social Identity and Social Behavior*. Armonk, NY: M.E. Sharpe. pp. 3–19.

Kozinets, Robert V. and John F. Sherry, Jr (2005) 'Welcome to the Black Rock Café', in Lee Gilmore and Mark van Proyen (eds), *Afterburn: Reflections on Burning Man*. Albequerque, NM: University of New Mexico Press. pp. 87–106.

Kozinets, Robert V., Andrea Hemetsberger and Hope Schau (2008) 'The Wisdom of Consumer Crowds: Collective Innovation in the Age of Networked Marketing', *Journal of Macromarketing*, 28(December): 339–54.

Kozinets, Robert V., Kristine de Valck, Andrea Wojnicki and Sarah Wilner (2010) 'Networked Narratives: Understanding Word-of-mouth Marketing in Online Communities', *Journal of Marketing* (March).

Kraut, R., J. Olson, M. Banaji, A. Bruckman, J. Cohen and M. Cooper (2004) 'Psychological Research Online: Report of Board of Scientific Affairs' Advisory Group on the Conduct of Research on the Internet', *American Psychologist*, 59(4): 1–13.

Kraut, R., S. Kiesler, B. Boneva, J. Cummings, V. Helgeson and A. Crawford (2002) 'Internet Paradox Revisited', *Journal of Social Issues*, 58: 49–74.

Krueger, R.A. (1994) *Focus Groups: a Practical Guide for Applied Research*, 2nd edition, London: Sage.

Lakoff, George and Mark Johnson (1980) *Metaphors We Live By*. Chicago, IL: University of Chicago Press.

Langer, Roy and Suzanne C. Beckman (2005) 'Sensitive Research Topics: Netnography Revisited', *Qualitative Market Research: an International Journal*, 8(2): 189–203.

Lather, Patti (1993) 'Issues of Validity in Openly Ideological Research: Between a Rock and a Soft Place', *Interchange*, 17: 63–84.

Lather, Patti (2001) 'Postmodernism, Post-Structuralism and Post (Critical) Ethnography: of the Ruins, Aporias and Angels', in P. Atkinson, S. Delamont, A.J. Coffey, J. Lofland and L.H. Lofland (eds), *Handbook of Ethnography*. London: Sage. pp. 477–92.

Laurel, Brenda (1990) *The Art of Human–Computer Interface Design*. Reading, MA: Addison-Wesley.

Lazar, J. and Preece, J. (1999) 'Designing and Implementing Web-based Surveys', *Journal of Computer Information Systems*, 34(4): 63–7.

LeBesco, Kathleen (2004) 'Managing Visibility, Intimacy, and Focus in Online Critical Ethnography', in M.D. Johns, S.-L.S. Chen and G.J. Hall (eds), *Online Social Research: Methods, Issues, and Ethics*. New York: Peter Lang. pp. 63–79.

Lewins, Ann and Christina Silver (2007) *Using Software in Qualitative Research: A Step-by-Step Guide*. Thousand Oaks, CA: Sage.

Lévy, Pierre (2001) *Cyberculture*, translated by Robert Bononno. Minneapolis, MN: University of Minnesota Press.

Levy, Sidney J. (1981) 'Interpreting Consumer Mythology: A Structural Approach to Consumer Behaviour', *Journal of Marketing*, 45(Summer): 49–61.

Li, Charlene and Josh Bernoff (2008) *Groundswell: Winning in a World Transformed by Social Technologies*. Boston, MA: Harvard Business Press.

Lincoln, Yvonna and Egon G. Guba (1985a) 'Judging the Quality of Case Study Reports', *Qualitative Studies in Education*, 3(1): 53–9.

Lincoln, Yvonna and Egon G. Guba (1985b) *Naturalistic Inquiry*. Beverly Hills, CA: Sage.

Lincoln, Yvonna S. and Norman K. Denzin (1994) 'The Fifth Moment', in Norman K. Denzin and Yvonna S. Lincoln (eds), *Handbook of Qualitative Research*. Thousand Oaks, CA: Sage. pp. 575–86.

Lipinski, Tomas A. (2006) 'Emerging Tort Issues in the Collection and Dissemination of Internet-based Research Data', *Journal of Information Ethics*, Fall: 55–81.

Lipinski, Tomas A. (2008) 'Emerging Legal Issues in the Collection and Dissemination of Internet-Sourced Research Data: Part I, Basic Tort Law Issues and Negligence', *International Journal of Internet Research Ethics*, 1(1) January: 92–114, available online at: www.uwm.edu/Dept/SOIS/cipr/ijire/ijire_1.1_lipinski.pdf/

Lyman, Peter and Nina Wakeford (1999) 'Going into the (Virtual) Field', *American Behavioral Scientist*, 43(3): 359–76.

Lysloff, René T.A. (2003) 'Musical Community on the Internet: an On-Line Ethnography', *Cultural Anthropology*, 18(2), May: 233–63.

Macek, Jakub (2005) 'Defining Cyberculture (v. 2)', translated by Monika Metyková and Jakub Macek, available online at: http://macek.czechian.net/defining_cyberculture.htm (accessed 8 January 2009).

Maclaran, Pauline, Margaret Hogg, Miriam Catterall and Robert V. Kozinets (2004) 'Gender, Technology and Computer-Mediated Communications in Consumption-Related Online Communities', in Karin M. Ekström and Helene Brembeck (eds), *Elusive Consumption: Tracking New Research Perspectives*. Oxford: Berg. pp. 145–71.

Madge, Clare and Henrietta O'Connor (2006) 'Parenting Gone Wired: Empowerment of New Mothers on the Internet?', *Social & Cultural Geography*, 7(2)(April): 199–220.

Mann, Chris and Fiona Stewart (2000) *Internet Communication in Qualitative Research: a Handbook for Researching Online*. London and Thousand Oaks, CA: Sage Publications.

Marcus, George E. and Michael Fischer (1986) *Anthropology as Cultural Critique*. Chicago: University of Chicago Press.

Markham, Annette N. (1998) *Life Online: Researching Real Experience in Virtual Space*. Walnut Creek, CA: Altamira.

Markham, Annette N. (2004) 'Representation in Online Ethnographies: a Matter of Context Sensitivity', in M.D. Johns, S.-L.S. Shannon and G.J. Hall (eds), *Online Social Research: Methods, Issues, and Ethics*. New York: Peter Lang. pp. 141–55.

Markham, Annette N. and Nancy K. Baym (2008) *Internet Inquiry: Conversations about Method*. Thousand Oaks and London: Sage.

Mason, Matt (2008) *The Pirate's Dilemma: How Youth Culture is Reinventing Capitalism*. New York: Free Press.

Matei, Sorin and Sandra Ball-Rokeach (2003) 'The Internet in the Communication Infrastructure of Urban Residential Communities: Macro or Meso-Linkage?', *Journal of Communication*, 53(4): 642–57.

Maulana, Amalia and Giana M. Eckhardt (2007) 'Just Friends, Good Acquaintances or Soul Mates? An Exploration of Website Connectedness', *Qualitative Market Research: An International Journal*, 10(3): 227–42.

McArthur, Robert L. (2001) 'Reasonable Expectations of Privacy', *Ethics and Information Technology*, 3: 123–8.

McCracken, Grant (1988) *The Long Interview*. Beverly Hills, CA: Sage.

McDougal, Robert (1999) 'Subject Fields, Oral Emulation and the Spontaneous Cultural Positioning of Mohawk E-Mail Users', *World Communication*, 28(4): 5–25.

McKay, H.G., R.E. Glasgow, E.G. Feil, S.M. Boles and M. Barrera (2002) 'Internet-based Diabetes Self-Management and Support: Initial Outcomes from the Diabetes Network Project', *Rehabilitation Psychology*, 47: 31–48.

McKenna, Katelyn and Gwendolyn Seidman (2005) 'You, Me, and We: Interpersonal Processes in Electronic Groups', in Yair Amichai-Hamburger (ed.), *The Social Net: Human Behavior in Cyberspace*. Oxford: Oxford University Press.

McKenna, K.Y.A. and J.A. Bargh (1998) 'Coming Out in the Age of the Internet: Identity Demarginalization through Virtual Group Participation', *Journal of Personality and Social Psychology*, 75: 681–94.

McLuhan, Marshall (1970) *Culture is our Business*. New York: McGraw-Hill.

McMahan, Allison (2003) 'Immersion, Engagement and Presence: A Method For Analyzing 3-D Games', in M. Wolf and B. Perron (eds), *Video Game Theory*. London: Routledge. pp. 60–88.

Mead, George Herbert (1938) *The Philosophy of the Act*. Chicago: University of Chicago Press.

Meyer, Gordon and Thomas, Jim (1990) 'The Baudy World of the Byte Bandit: A Postmodernist Interpretation of the Computer Underground', in Frank Schmalleger (ed.), *Computers in Criminal Justice*. Bristol: Wyndham Hall. pp. 31–67.

Miles, Matthew B. and A. Michael Huberman, (1994) *Qualitative Data Analysis: An Expanded Sourcebook*, 2nd edition. Thousand Oaks, CA: Sage.

Miller, Daniel and Don Slater (2000) *The Internet: An Ethnographic Approach*. New York: Berg.

Mitchell, William J. (1996) *City of Bits: Space, Place, and the Infobahn*. Cambridge, MA: MIT Press.

Molesworth, Mike and Janice Denegri-Knott (2004) 'An Exploratory Study of the Failure of Online Organisational Communication', *Corporate Communications*, 9(4): 302–16.

Muñiz, Albert M. Jr. and Hope Jensen Schau (2005) 'Religiosity in the Abandoned Apple Newton Brand Community', *Journal of Consumer Research*, 31(4)(March): 737–47.

Munt, Sally R. (ed.) (2001) *Technospaces: Inside the New Media*. London: Continuum.

Murray, Jeff B. and Julie L. Ozanne (1991) 'The Critical Imagination: Emancipatory Interests in Consumer Research', *Journal of Consumer Research*, 18(September): 129–44.

Myers, D. (1987) 'Anonymity is Part of the Magic: Individual Manipulation of Computer-mediated Communication Context', *Qualitative Sociology*, 10: 251–266.

Nelson, Michelle R. and Cele C. Otnes (2005) 'Exploring Cross-Cultural Ambivalence: a Netnography of Intercultural Wedding Message Boards', *Journal of Business Research*, 58: 89–95.

Nelson, Michelle R., Heejo Keum and Ronald A. Yaros (2004) 'Advertainment or Adcreep: Game Players' Attitudes toward Advertising and Product Placements in Computer Games', *Journal of Interactive Advertising*, 5(1), available online at: www.jiad.org/article52/

Newhagen, J.E. and S. Rafaeli (1996) 'Why Communication Researchers Should Study the Internet: a Dialogue [on-Line]', *Journal of Computer-mediated Communication*, 1(4), available online at: http://jcmc.indiana.edu/voll/issue4/rafaeli.html

Olaniran, Bolanle (2004) 'Computer-Mediated Communication in Across-Cultural Virtual Teams', in Guo-Min Chen and William Starosta (eds), *Dialogues among Diversities*. Washington, DC: NCA. pp. 142–66.

Olaniran, Bolanle (2008) 'Electronic Tribes (E-Tribes): Some Theoretical Perspectives and Implications', in Tyrone L. Adams and Steven A. Smith (eds), *Electronic Tribes: Virtual Worlds of Geeks, Gamers, Shamans, and Scammers*. Austin, TX: University of Texas Press. pp. 36–57.

Ozanne, Julie L. and Bige Saatcioglu (2008) 'Participatory Action Research', *Journal of Consumer Research*, 35(3): 423–39.

Paccagnella, Luciano (1997) 'Getting the Seats of Your Pants Dirty: Strategies for Ethnographic Research on Virtual Communities', *Journal of Computer-Mediated Communications*, 3(June), available online at: http://jcmc.indiana.edu/vol3/issue1/paccagnella.html/

Parmentier, Marie-Agnes (2009) 'Brands as Resources for Virtual Communities of Consumption', unpublished HEC Montreal Working Paper.

Penley, Constance and Andrew Ross (eds) (1991) *Technoculture: Cultural Politics*. Minneapolis, MN: University of Minnesota Press.

Pew Internet Report (2001) 'Online Communities: Networks that Nurture Long-distance Relationships and Local Ties', *Pew Internet & American Life Project*, available online at: www.pewinternet.org/report_display.asp?r=47/

Price, Linda L., Eric J. Arnould and Patrick Tierney (1995) 'Going to Extremes: Managing Service Encounters and Assessing Provider Performance', *Journal of Marketing*, 59(April): 83–97.

Protection of Human Subjects, US Federal Code Title 45, Section 46 (2009), available online at: www.hhs.gov/ohrp/humansubjects/guidance/45cfr46.htm (accessed 3 February 2009).

Punch, Maurice (1986) *The Politics and Ethics of Fieldwork*. Beverly Hills, CA: Sage.

Rabinow, Paul (1992) 'Artificiality and Enlightenment: From Sociobiology to Biosociality', in J. Crary and S. Kwinter (eds), *Incorporations*. Cambridge, MA: Zone. pp. 234–52.

Reid, Elizabeth (1996) 'Informed Consent in the Study of On-Line Communities: a Reflection on the Effects of Computer-Mediated Social Research', *The Information Society*, 12: 169–74.

Rettberg, Jill Walker (2008) *Blogging*. Cambridge, UK: Polity Press.

Rheingold, Howard (1993) *The Virtual Community: Homesteading on the Electronic Frontier*. Reading, MA: Addison-Wesley.

Rice, Ronald E. (1984) 'Evaluating New Media Systems', in Jerome Johnstone (ed.), *Evaluating the New Information Technologies: New Directions for Program Evaluation*. San Francisco, CA: Jossey-Bass.

Rice, Ronald E. and E.M. Rogers (1984) 'New Methods and Data for the Study of New Media', in R.E. Rice (ed.), *The New Media, Communication, Research, and Technology*. Beverly Hills, CA: Sage Publications. pp. 81–99.

Rice, Ronald E. and G. Love (1987) 'Electronic Emotion: Socio-emotional Content in a Computer-mediated Communication Network', *Communication Research*, 14: 85–108.

Richards, Lyn (2005) *Handling Qualitative Data: A Practical Guide*. London: Sage.

Sack, Warren (2002) 'What Does a Very Large-Scale Conversation Look like? Artificial Dialectics and the Graphical Summarization of Large Volumes of E-Mail', *Leonardo*, 35(4): 417–26.

Schaap, F. (2002) *The Words That Took Us There: Ethnography in Virtual Ethnography*. Amsterdam: Aksant Academic Publishers.

Schau, Hope Jensen and Mary C. Gilly (2003) 'We Are What We Post? The Presentation of Self in Personal Webspace', *Journal of Consumer Research*, 30(4)(December): 385–404.

Schivelbusch, Wolfgang (1986) *The Railway Journey: The Industrialization of Space and Time in the 19th Century*. New York: Berg.

Schlosser, Ann (2005) 'Posting Versus Lurking: Communicating in a Multiple Audience Context', *Journal of Consumer Research*, 32, September: 260–5.

Schouten, John W. and James H. McAlexander (1995) 'Subcultures of Consumption: An Ethnography of the New Bikers', *Journal of Consumer Research*, 22(June): 43–61.

Schwandt, Thomas A. (1994) 'Constructivist, Interpretivist Approaches to Human Inquiry', in Norman K. Denzin and Yvonna S. Lincoln (eds), *Handbook of Qualitative Research*. Thousand Oaks, CA: Sage. pp. 118–37.

Scott, John (1991) *Social Network Analysis: A Handbook*. London: Sage.

Sharf, Barbara (1999) 'Beyond Netiquette: The Ethics of Doing Naturalistic Discourse Research on the Internet', in Steve Jones (ed.), *Doing Internet Research: Critical Issues and Methods for Examining the Net*. London: Sage.

Shea, Virginia (1994) 'Core Rules of Netiquette', *Educom Review*, 29(5): 58–62.

Sherblom, John (1988) 'Direction, Function, and Signature in Electronic Mail', *Journal of Business Communication*, 25: 39–54.

Sherry, John F. Jr (1991) 'Postmodern Alternatives: The Interpretive Turn in Consumer Research', in H. Kassarjian and T. Robertson (eds), *Handbook of Consumer Theory and Research*. Englewood Cliffs, NJ: Prentice-Hall. pp. 548–91.

Shields, Robert (ed.) (1996) *Cultures of the Internet: Virtual Spaces, Real Histories, Living Bodies*. London: Sage.

Shimanoff, Susan B. (1988) 'Degree of Emotional Expressiveness as a Function of Face-needs, Gender, and Interpersonal Relationship', *Communication Reports*, 1(2): 43–53.

Shoham, Aviv (2004) 'Flow experiences and image making: An online chat-room ethno-grapy', *Psychology and Marketing*, 21(10): 855–82.

Short, John, Ederyn Williams and Bruce Christie (1976) *The Social Psychology of Telecommunications*. New York: Wiley.

Silver, David (2006) 'Introduction: Where Is Internet Studies?', in David Silver and Adrienne Massanari (eds), *Critical Cyberculture Studies*. New York and London: New York University Press. pp. 1–14.

Sirsi, Ajay K., James C. Ward and Peter H. Reingen (1996) 'Microcultural Analysis of Variation in Sharing of Causal Reasoning about Behavior', *Journal of Consumer Research*, 22(March): 345–73.

Slater, Don (1998) 'Trading Sexpics on IRC: Embodiment and Authenticity on the Internet', *Body & Society*, 4(4): 91–117.

Sohn, Changsoo (2001) 'Validity of Web-Based Survey in IES Related Research as an Alternative to Mail Survey', *AMCIS 2001 Proceedings. Paper 318*, available online at: http://aisel.aisnet.org/amcis2001/318

Spiggle, Susan (1994) 'Analysis and Interpretation of Qualitative. Data in Consumer Research', *Journal of Consumer Research*, 21(December): 491–503.

Sproull, Lee and Sara Kiesler (1986) 'Reducing Social Context Cues: The Case of Electronic Mail', *Management Science,* 32: 1492–512.

Stone, Allucquère Rosanne (1995) *The War of Desire and Technology at the Close of the Mechanical Age*. Cambridge, MA: MIT Press.

Strauss, Anselm L. (1987) *Qualitative Analysis for Social Scientists*. Cambridge: Cambridge University Press.

Strauss, Anselm and Julie Corbin (1990) *Basics of Qualitative Research: Grounded Theory Procedures and Techniques*. Thousand Oaks, CA: Sage.

Sudweeks, Fay and Simeon J. Simoff (1999) 'Complementary Explorative Data Analysis: the Reconciliation of Quantitative and Qualitative Principles', in Steve Jones (ed.), *Doing Internet Research: Critical Issues in Methods for Examining the Net*. Thousand Oaks, CA: Sage.

Sunderland, Patricia L. and Denny, Rita M. (2007) *Doing Anthropology in Consumer Research*. Walnut Creek, CA: Left Coast Press.

Tacchi, J., G. Hearn and A. Ninan (2004) 'Ethnographic Action Research: A Method for Implementing and Evaluating New Media Technologies', in K. Prasad (ed.), *Information and Communication Technology: Recasting Development*. Knoxville, TN: B.R. Publishing Corporation. pp. 253–74.

Tapscott, Don and Anthony D. Williams (2007) *Wikinomics: How Mass Collaboration Changes Everything*. New York: Penguin.

Taylor, T.L. (1999) 'Life in Virtual Worlds: Plural Existence, Multi-Modalities, and Other Online Research Challenges', *American Behavioral Scientist*, 43(3): 436–49.

Tedlock, Barbara (1991) 'From Participant Observation to the Observation of Participation: The Emergence of Narrative Ethnography', *Journal of Anthropological Research*, 47: 69–94.

Tesch, R. (1990) *Qualitative Research: Analysis Types and Software Tools*. New York: Falmer.

The Digital Future Report (2008) 'Surveying the Digital Future, Year Seven', *USC Annenberg School Center for the Digital Future*. Los Angeles, CA: Figueroa Press.

Thomas, Jane Boyd, Cara Okleshen Peters and Holly Tolson (2007) 'An Exploratory Investigation of the Virtual Community MySpace.com: What Are Consumers Saying About Fashion?', *Journal of Fashion Marketing and Management*, 11(4): 587–603.

Thompson, Craig J. (1990) 'Eureka! And Other Tests of Significance: A New Look at Evaluating Interpretive Research', in Marvin E. Goldberg et al. (eds), *Advances in Consumer Research*, 17. Provo UT: Association for Consumer Research. pp. 25–30.

Thompson, Craig J., Howard R. Pollio and William B. Locander (1994) 'The Spoken and The Unspoken: A Hermeneutic Approach to Understanding Consumers' Expressed Meanings', *Journal of Consumer Research*, 21(December): 432–53.

Thomsen, Steven R., Joseph D. Straubhaar and Drew M. Bolyard (1998) 'Ethnomethodology and the Study of Online Communities: Exploring the Cyber Streets', *Information Research*, 4(1), July, available online at: http://informationr. net.ezproxy.library.yorku.ca/ir/4-1/paper50.html

Thorseth, May (2003) *Applied Ethics in Internet Research*. Trondheim, Norway: Programme for Applied Ethics, Norwegian University of Science and Technology.

Teilhard de Chardin, Pierre (1959) *The Phenomenon of Man*. New York: Harper and Row.

Tucker, William T. (1967) *Foundations for a Theory of Consumer Behavior*. New York: Holt, Rinehart and Winston.

Tulloch, John and Henry Jenkins (1995) *Science Fiction Audiences: Watching Doctor Who and Star Trek*. London and New York: Routledge.

Turkle, Sherry (1995) *Life on the Screen: Identity in the Age of the Internet*. New York: Simon & Schuster.

Van den Bulte, Christophe and Stefan Wuyts (2007) *Social Networks and Marketing*. Cambridge, MA: Marketing Science Institute.

Van Maanen, John (1988) *Tales of the Field: On Writing Ethnography*. Chicago: University of Chicago Press.

Vroman, Kerryellen and Joann Kovacich (2002) 'Computer-Mediated Interdisciplinary Teams: Theory and Reality', *Journal of Interprofessional Care*, 16(2), May 1: 161–70.

Wallendorf, Melanie and Russell W. Belk (1989) 'Assessing Trustworthiness in Naturalistic Consumer Research', in Elizabeth C. Hirschman (ed.), *Interpretive Consumer Research*. Provo, UT: Association for Consumer Research. pp. 69–84.

Walker Rettburg, Jill (2008) *Blogging*. Cambridge, UK and Malden, MA: Polity Press.

Walther, Joseph B. (1992) 'Interpersonal Effects in Mediated Interaction: a Relational Perspective', *Communication Research*, 19: 52–90.

Walther, Joseph B. (1995) 'Relational Aspects of Computer-Mediated Communication: Experimental Observations over Time', *Organization Science*, 6(2): 186–203.

Walther, Joseph (1997) 'Group and Interpersonal Effects in International Computer-Mediated Collaboration', *Human Communication Research*, 23(3), March: 342–69.

Walther, Joseph B. (2002), 'Research Ethics in Internet-Enabled Research: Human Subjects Issues and Methodological Myopia', *Ethics and Information Technology*, 4: 205–16.

Wasserman, Stanley and Katherine Faust (1994) *Social Network Analysis: Methods and Applications*. Cambridge: Cambridge University Press.

Watt, J.H. (1999) 'Internet Systems for Evaluation Research', in G. Gay and T.L. Bennington (eds), *Information Technologies in Evaluation: Social, Moral Epistemological and Practical Implications*. San Francisco, CA: Josey-Bass. pp. 23–44.

Weible, R. and J. Wallace, (1998) 'The Impact of the Internet on Data Collection', *Marketing Research*, 10(3): 19–23.

Weinberg, Bruce D. (2001) 'Research in Exploring the Online Consumer Experience', in Mary C. Gilly and Joan Meyers-Levy (eds), *Advances in Consumer Research*, Volume 28. Valdosta, GA: Association for Consumer Research. pp. 227–32.

Weinberger, David (2007) *Everything Is Miscellaneous: the Power of the New Digital Disorder*. New York: Times Books.

Weitzman, Eben A. and Matthew B. Miles (1995) *Computer Programs for Qualitative Data Analysis: A Software Sourcebook*. Thousand Oaks, CA: Sage.

Wellman, Barry (1988) 'Structural Analysis: from Method and Metaphor to Theory and Substance', in B. Wellman and S.D. Berkowitz (eds), *Social Structures: a Network Approach*. Cambridge, UK: Cambridge University Press. pp. 19–61.

Wellman, Barry (2001a) 'Computer Networks as Social Networks', *Science*, 293, September 14: 2031–4.

Wellman, Barry (2001b) 'Physical Place and Cyber Place: The Rise Of Networked Individualism', *International Journal of Urban and Regional Research*, 25(2) June: 227–52.

Wellman, Barry, Janet Salaff, Dimitrina Dimitrova, Laura Garton, Milena Gulia and Caroline Haythornthwaite (1996) 'Computer Networks as Social Networks: Collaborative Work, Telework, and Virtual Community', *Annual Review of Sociology*, 22: 213–38.

Welser, Howard T., Eric Gleave, Danyel Fisher and Marc Smith (2007) 'Visualizing the Signatures of Social Roles in Online Discussion Groups', *Journal of Social Structure*, 8, available online at: www.cmu.edu/joss/content/articles/volume8/Welser/

Whitty, Monica Therese (2003) 'Cyber-Flirting: Playing at Love on the Internet', *Theory & Psychology*, 13(3): 339–57.

Whitty, Monica Therese (2004) 'Cyber-Flirting: An Examination of Men's and Women's Flirting Behaviour both Offline and on the Internet', *Behaviour Change*, 21(2): 115–26.

Williams, J. Patrick and Heith Copes (2005) '"How Edge Are You?" Constructing Authentic Identities and Subcultural Boundaries in a Straightedge Internet Forum', *Symbolic Interaction*, 28(1): 67–89.

Williams, Raymond (1976) *Keywords: a Survey of Culture and Society*. London: Croom Helm.

Wikan, Unni (1992) 'Beyond Words: The Power of Resonance', *American Ethnologist*, 19 (August): 460–82.

Wittgenstein, Ludwig (1958 [1968]) *Philosophical Investigations*, 2nd edition, translated by G.E.M. Anscombe. New York: Macmillan.

Wolcott, Harry F. (1990) 'On Seeking and Rejecting Validity in Qualitative Research', in E.W. Eisner and A. Peshkin (eds), *Qualitative Inquiry in Education: The Continuing Debate*. New York: Teachers College Press. pp. 121–52.

Wolcott, Harry F. (1992) 'Posturing in Qualitative Inquiry', in M.D. LeCompte, W.L. Millroy and J. Preissle (eds), *The Handbook of Qualitative Research in Education*. New York: Academic Press. pp. 3–52.

Yun, Gi Woong and Craig W. Trumbo (2000) 'Comparative Response to a Survey Executed by Post, E-mail, & Web Form', *Journal of Computer-Mediated Communication*, September.

Zelwietro, Joseph (1998) 'The Politicization of Environmental Organizations through the Internet', *Information Society*, 14(1): 45–56.

Zwick, Detlev, Samuel K. Bonsu and Aron Darmody (2008) 'Putting Consumers to Work: "Co-creation" and New Marketing Govern-mentality', *Journal of Consumer Culture*, 8(2): 163–96.

INDEX

abstracting, 119, 188
accessibility, 70–1, 87–8, 178, 188
academic centres for cyberculture studies, 84
AIDS, 28
alcoholism, 28
Allen, Gove N. et al., 149, 150, 151
alteration, 68–70, 188
Alternative Reality Games (ARGs), 85
Altheide, David L. and Johnson, John M., 161
American Association for the Advancement of
    Science, 138, 141
American Psychological Association, 139
Andrews, Dorine et al., 43, 44
anonymity, 70, 111, 130, 178, 188
    and consent, 142–3
anthropology, 37, 62–3
anticipated interactions, 23–4
Apple PDA, 96
archiving, 71–2, 87, 90, 104–6, 188
Arnold, Stephen J. and Fischer, Eileen, 120, 135
Arnould, Eric J. and Wallendorf, Melanie, 12
Asia
    centres for cyberculture studies, 84
    Internet use, 16
Association of Internet Researchers Ethics Working
    Group, 138–9
Association of Internet Researchers (AoIR), 82
asynchronous media, 69, 188
    archives, 72
Atkinson, Paul A., 163
Atkinson, Paul A. et al., 62
ATLAS.ti 6.0, 128
audio/visual sites, 86, 188
Austria, 16
authenticity, 170
autonetnography, 181, 188

Bacon-Smith, Camille, 107
Bahktin, Mikhail, 168
Bakardjieva, Maria, 138, 142, 143
BarbieGirls, 85

Bassett, Elizabeth H. and O'Riordan, Kate, 141
Baym, Nancy K., 5, 29, 40, 46, 48, 64, 87, 157, 158,
    163, 173
Bazeley, Patricia, 128
Beaulieu, 2, 113, 165, 171, 172
Beaven, Zuleika and Laws, Chantal, 75
Bebo, 87, 177
Belk, Russell W., 184
Belmont report, 139
Beninger, J.R., 23
Benjamin, Walter, 99
Berkowitz, S.D., 49
Berners-Lee, Tim, 179
betweenness centrality, 52
blended ethnography/netnography, 65–8, 188–9
blogs, 32, 71, 86, 145, 177–8, 189
    netnography of, 179–80
Bodley, John, 11
body language, 130
Bonsu, Sammy and Darmody, Aron, 176
Bourdieu, Pierre, 124
Brazil, 16
Brown, Stephen et al., 75, 99
Brownlie, Douglas and Hewer, Paul, 75
Bruckman, Amy, 46, 77, 141, 144, 145, 147, 152,
    153, 156
Buchanan, Elizabeth, 138, 139, 156
bulletin boards, 5, 85, 189
Bulte, Christophe van den and Wuyts, Stefan, 52
Burglund Center for Internet Studies, 84
Burning Man festival, 38

Campbell, Alex, 37, 64
Campbell, John Edward, 39, 175–6
Campbell, John Edward and Carlson, M., 39
Carey, James W., 10, 11
Carter, Denise, 38
case studies, 59
Center for Computer Games Research, 84
Center for Digital Discourse and Culture, 84
Center for Women and Information Technology, 84

centrality, 52
CERN, 179
Chartier, Roger, 177
chat interviews, 111
chat-rooms, 85, 112, 145, 189
checking and refining of data, 119
Chenault, Brittney G., 117
Cherny, Lynn, 48, 69, 112, 169
    Conversation and Community, 29, 30
children and vulnerable adults, 152
Chile, 16
China, 44
Ciberpunk, 82
Clerc, Susan J., 24
Clifford, James, 165, 170
Clifford, James and Marcus, George E., 55, 160
closeness centrality, 52
Club Penguin, 85
coding, 119, 120, 122–3, 128, 129, 189
    example, 122–3
    manual, 122
'coding trap', 129
coherence, 163–4, 189
Cohn, Deborah Y. and Vaccaro, Valerie L., 2
commercial organizations and communities, 38,
    175–6
community: defined, 189
comparisons of data, 119
Computer Assisted Qualitative Data Analysis
    (CAQDAS), 79, 125–9, 189
    drawbacks, 129
    and manual data analysis, 125–7
    strengths, 128–9
computer conferences, 24
computer file storage, 129
computer-assisted data analysis, 125–9
computer-mediated communications (CMC):
    defined, 189
consent, 137–8, 142–3, 151–2
    form, 194–6
*Convergence: the Journal of Research into New Media
    Technologies,* 83
copyright, 142, 175, 176, 177
Correll, Shelley, 5, 31, 46, 64, 87, 174
Couper, M.P., 43
Cova, Bernard et al., 176
covert studies, 74
Creswell, John W., 42, 80, 81, 94
Crumlish, Christian, 14
Ctheory, 83
Cuba, 16
culture
    based on communication, 12
    definitions, 189
        anthropological view (Kluckhohn), 11
        cultivation/growth (Williams), 10
        society: total way of life (Bodley), 11

culture, definitions *cont.*
        in terms of semiotics (Geertz), 11
    learned systems of meanings/symbols, 12
    open-ended, 168
    specific cultures, 12
    state of flux, 12
culture of the 'Other', 170, 171
Cybercity, 38
cyberculture: definitions, 11–13, 189
*Cyberpsychology: Journal of Psychological Research on
    Cyberspace,* 83
Cyberpsychology and Behaviour, 83

Daft, Richard L. and Lengel, Robert H., 23
Dalli, Daniele and Corciolani, Matteo, 175
Danet, Brenda, 23, 30–1, 167
data analysis, 118–35
    coding, 119, 120, 122–3
    computer-assisted, 125–9
        compared with manual, 125–7
    example, 121–5
    hermeneutic interpretation, 120, 122, 123
    induction, 118–21
    manual or pen-and-paper techniques, 98, 99, 125–6
    netnographic data, 129–34
        falsification, 131–2
        generalizations, 134
        and identities, 130–1
        pragmatic-interactionist approach, 132–4
        textuality of, 130
    processes, 119
    software, 91–2
    three ways: interpretivism, social anthropology,
        social research, 119–20
data collection, 53–5, 95–116, 165
    accounting for data, 115–16
    archival data, 104–6, 188
        selection of data, 104–5
    capturing online data, 98–103
    classifying, 105
    and data analysis, 95–6
    downloading text as text files, 101–2
    fieldnotes, 5, 80, 113–15
    graphical data, 106
    image captures, 102–3
    interviews, 109, 110–13
        adapted to medium, 109, 111, 112
        e-mail, 111, 112–13
    pen-and-paper technique, 98, 99
    screen capture, 99, 100
    spam, 103–4
    tagging and sorting, 105
    types of data, 98
data as social acts, 133
Davis, Erik, 183
Davison, K.P. et al., 28
Dean, Howard, 53

del.icio.us, 86
Denzin, Norman K., 55, 171
Denzin, Norman K. and Lincoln, Yvonna S., 62,
    159–60, 161, 173
development of online community and culture, 7
DeviantArt, 112
dialogue, 169
Digg, 86, 89
Digital Ethnography at Kansas State University, 83
Digital Futures Project, 14–15, 44
Digital Games Research Association, 83
DiMaggio, Paul et al., 26
Douglas, Jack D., 168
Drucker, Peter, 21
Dubrovsky, Vitaly et al., 23
Dunbar, Robin, 9
Dungeons, 85, 86

e-mail, 7
e-Society, 84
eBay, 53
Ebr-electronic book review, 83
eigenvector centrality, 52
elderly people, 38
Ellis, Caroline, 168
embodiment, 30
Emerson, Robert M. et al., 114, 115, 117
emoticons, 23
emotion in fieldwork, 167–8
entrée, 190
Escobar, Arturo, 11
ethical netnography, 136–56
    consent, 137–8, 142–3, 151–2
        and implied consent, 143
    and criticism of community members, 144
    harm online, 143–4
    importance of ethics, 137–8
    Internet Research Ethics (IRE), 138–9, 191
    legal considerations, 145–6, 149
    procedures
        asking permission, 148–9
        children and vulnerable adults, 152
        commercial sites, 149
        concealing identities of community members,
            152–5
        disclosure of nature of research, 147
        disclosure of researcher's identity/intentions, 147
        gaining informed consent, 151–2
        information about researcher, 147–8
        interviews, 152
        member checks, 148, 191
    public *vs.* private, 140–2
    relevant questions, 139–40
    and resistance to being studied, 138
    risk/benefits balance, 144, 153–4
    stored communications, 144, 145, 146
    use of pseudonyms, 144–5, 146

ethnography
    adaptation, 59–60, 62
    application and definition, 55, 58–9
    applied to online culture, 5
    blending with netnography, 65–8, 188
        aspects of research, 66
    characterized by various theories/methods, 160
    compared with netnography, 55–6, 60–1
    definition, 190
    history and standards, 159–61
        1900–WWII (traditional), 159
        post-war to 1970 (modernist), 159
        1970–1986 (blurred genres), 160
        mid 80s–1990 (crisis of representation), 160
        1990–1995 (postmodern), 160
        1995–2000 (post-experimental enquiry), 160
        methodologically-contested present, 160
        fractured future, 160
    multiple methods, 59
    and netnography as incomplete
        ethnography, 62–3
    no single 'real' ethnography, 62–3
    origins of term, 4–5
    'realist', 163
    as science, 159, 163
Europe
    centres for cyberculture studies, 84
    Internet use, 16, 44
expansion of netnography, 181–2

face-to-face interactions
    developing from online communities, 14, 26
    difference from online communities, 130, 178
    and 'leanness' of online communities, 23
Facebook, 13, 39, 87, 89, 111, 180
    terms and conditions, 149–50
Facebook Netnography, 83
falsification, 131–2
Feedster, 181
Fernandez, James W., 167
Fetterman, David M., 62, 116
fibreculture, 84
fieldnotes, 5, 80, 113–15, 128
    and observation, 114–15
fieldwork, 62
51.com, 87
Finland, 16
First Monday, 83
Flickr, 86, 89, 111
focus groups, 48–9
    asynchronous methods, 48
    synchronous, 48–9
Fong, John and Burton, Susan, 175
Forrester Research, 24, 44
forums, 190
    see also bulletin boards
Fournier, Susan and Lee, Lara, 54

Fox, Richard G., 163
Frankel, Mark S. and Siang, Sanyin, 138, 141, 142
full-motion screen capture software, 190
Füller, Johann et al., 36, 75, 174, 175

Gaia Online, 85
Gaiser, Ted, 48
Game Studies, 83
games, 85
Games and Culture: A Journal of Interactive Media, 83
Garcia, Angela Cora et al., 2, 20, 66, 67, 133
Garton, Laura et al., 50, 51, 52, 57
gay and lesbian portals, 39
Geertz, Clifford, 11, 160, 173
gender roles, 37–8
generalizations, 119, 134, 190
German Society for Online Research, 82
Germany, 16
Giesler, Markus, 112
Gilder, George, 21
Glaser, Barney G. and Strauss, Anselm L., 116, 164
Google, 88
Gossett, Loril M. and Kilker, Julian, 38
govcom.org (Netherlands), 84
graphical data, 106
Greece, 16
Greenbaum, Thomas, 48
grounded theory, 119
    saturation principle, 116
groundedness, 166, 190
Guba, Egon G. and Lincoln, Yvonna S., 161, 170
Gubrium, Jaber F. and Holstein, A., 117, 168
Guild Wars, 85
Gumpert, Gary and Cathcart, Robert, 23

Habbo Hotel, 85
Hahn, Chris, 126
Hair, Neil and Clark, Moira, 153, 155
Hakken, David, 2, 11, 172
Hammersley, Martin, 161
Haythornthwaite, Caroline, 52–3
Haythornthwaite, Caroline et al., 50
Hemetsberger, Andrea and Reinhardt, Christian, 2, 36, 175
hermeneutic circle, 120
hermeneutic interpretation, 120, 122, 123
    example, 121–5
Herring, Susan, 144
Hiltz, Starr Roxanne, 8
Hiltz, Starr Roxanne and Turoff, Murray, 8
Hine, Christine, 5, 133–4, 163
    Virtual Ethnography, 62–3, 73
Hobbs, Dick, 59
Holeton, Richard, 69
Hookway, Nicholas, 184
hostile language, 23

Howard, P.E.M. et al., 26
Howard, Philip M., 59
Hudson, James and Bruckman, Amy, 138, 152
Hughes, Jerald and Lang, Karl R., 48, 49
Human Research Subjects Review Committee, 190
Human Subjects Research Ethics Committees, 91, 139
HypeRESEARCH 2.8, 128

iChat, 110
ICT (Information and Communications Technology), 190
identities, 66
    acceptance by others, 28–9
    and anonymity, 70, 111, 130, 132
    concealed by researchers, 152–5
        degrees of concealment, 154–5
    and falsification, 131–2
    fragmentation, 37
    of online researcher, 147–8
    and research, 130–1
    sharing, 28
illnesses with stigma and acceptance, 28
image captures, 102–3
importance of online communities to participants, 14, 15
India, 16
induction, 118–21, 190
Information, Communication & Society, 83
Information Society, The, 83
innovation, 166–7, 190
'inscription', 5
Institute of Network Cultures, 82, 84
Institute for New Media Studies, 84
Institutional Review Board, 91
intermix, 171–2, 190
International Center for New Media, 84
International Journal of Web-based Communities, 83
Internet
    expansion, 178–9
    as text or place, 141
Internet research, 1–2
Internet Research Ethics (IRE), 138–9, 191
Internet Studies Center, 84
Internet use, global, 2, 13, 15–17, 44
interpretivism, 160, 190
interviews, 45–7, 55–6, 109, 110–13, 192
    adapted to medium, 109, 111, 112
    anonymity, 111
    archiving, 111, 188
    chat interviews, 111
    'creative', 168
    in depth, 47, 110–11
    e-mail, 111, 112–13
    ethical considerations, 152
    face-to-face, 45–6, 110
    focus groups, 48–9, 55–6

interviews *cont.*
  graphical exchanges, 112
  and journals, 46–7
  limitations, 47
Italy, 16
iTunes, 86

Jackson, Sally, 164
Jacobson, David, 142
Japan, 16, 38, 44
Jenkins, Henry, 48, 87, 107, 134
Jeppesen, Lars Bo and Frederiksen, Lars, 175
Johns, M. et al., 138, 139
Jones, Steve, 69, 72
Jorgensen, D.L., 169
Journal of Business Research, 81
Journal of Computer-mediated
  Communication, 83
Journal of Virtual Worlds Research, 83

Kanayama, Tomoko, 38
Kavanaugh, A. and Patterson, S., 29
Kendall, Lori, 130
Kiesler, Sara et al., 23
King, Storm, 142
Kivits, Joëlle, 46
Kluckholm, Clyde, 11
Komito, Lee, 9
Kozinets, Robert V., 12, 26, 33, 35, 38, 46, 48, 73,
  85, 94, 97, 132, 135, 137, 144, 171, 175, 176,
  178–9, 184
Kozinets, Robert V. et al., 97, 175
Kozinets, Robert V. and Handelman, Jay M., 2,
  175, 176
Kozinets, Robert V. and Kedzior, Richard,
  97, 181, 184
Kozinets, Robert V. and Sherry, John F., 38
Kraut, R.S. et al., 26, 139
Krueger, R.A., 48

Lakoff, George and Johnson, Mark, 120
Langer, Roy and Beckman, Suzanne C., 74, 87
language, 12
  hostile, 23
  speech patterns in real-time chat, 30
language barriers, 71
language games, 132
Lather, Patti, 170, 171
Laurel, Brenda, 11
Lazar and Preece, 43
LeBesco, Kathleen, 138
'Lesbian Cafe', 31, 64
Lévy, Pierre, 11, 20
Lewins, Ann and Silver, Christina, 128, 135
Li, Charlene and Bernoff, Josh, 16, 24, 44
Lincoln, Yvonna and Guba, Egon G., 164, 166
LinkedIn Cyber & Web anthropology, 83

LinkedIn Netnography group, 83
Lipinski, Tomas, 145, 151, 156
lists, 86, 191
literacy, 165–6, 191
LiveJournal, 178, 180
local cultures and online communities, 39
LOL, 191
Lombardi, Jerry, 4
Lyman, Peter and Wakeford, Nina, 3, 113
Lysloff, René T.A., 37, 63

M/C: Media and Culture, 83
McArthur, Robert L., 142
McCracken, Grant, 110
McDougal, Robert, 39
Macek, Jakub, 11–12
McKay, H.G. et al., 28
McKenna, Karelyn and Seidman, Gwendolyn, 25–6,
  29, 40
McKenna, K.Y.A. and Bargh, J.A., 28
McLuhan, Marshall, 21
McMahan, Allison, 174
Madge, Clare and O'Connor, Henrietta,
  37–8, 167–8
Mann, Chris and Stewart, Fiona, 48, 49, 57
Marcus, George E. and Fischer, Michael, 171
marginalized and disenfranchized, 28–9
marketing and consumer research, 2, 6, 175
Markham, Annette N., 5, 29, 30, 46, 64, 69, 87, 97,
  111, 112, 163, 169
Markham, Annette N. and Baym, Nancy K., 73
Mason, Matt, 176
Matei, Sorin and Ball-Rokeach, Sandra, 26
Maulana, Amalia and Eckhardt, Giana M., 75
MAXqda2, 128
Mead, George Herbert, 132
member checks, 148, 191
memos, 119
Mexico, 16
Meyer, Gordon and Thomas, Jim, 24
microblogs, 86, 191
Miles, Matthew and Huberman, Michael, 6, 119,
  120, 135
Miller, Daniel and Slater, Don, 2, 171
Mitchell, William J., 113
MMOGs (massively multiplayer online games),
  85, 191
Molesworth, Mike and Denegri-Knott, Janice, 174
MOOs, 85
MSN, 88
MUDs (Multi-User Dungeons), 85
multiple selves, 37
Muñiz, Albert and Schau, Hope, 87, 96, 164, 174–5
Munt, Sally R., 141
Murray, Jeff B. and Ozanne, Julie L., 170
Myers, D., 24
MySpace, 13, 87, 89, 111

Naisbitt, John, 21
narrative, 167
naturalistic technique of netnography, 56
need for netnography, 4–7
Nelson, Michelle R. et al., 2
Nelson, Michelle R. and Otnes, Cele C., 2, 81, 94,
    149, 174
NetMeeting, 110
'netnography'
    definitions and application, 1–2, 74, 191
    need for term, 6–7
    origins of word, 6
New Media & Society, 83
New Yorker, 70
Newhagen, J.E. and Rafaeli, S., 71–2
Newton, 96
Nicaragua, 16
Niketalk forum, 36
Ning.com, 88
nonverbal communication, 23
North America
    Internet use, 16
Norway, 16
noting, 119, 191
numbers in online communities
    in America, 14
    growth, 14
    meeting face-to-face, 14
    world-wide, 2, 13
NVivo8, 128

Obama, Barack, 53
observation, 5
observational netnography, 75
observed and articulated behaviour, 66
Oceania
    centres for cyberculture studies, 84
Olaniran, Bolanle, 24, 39
OMG, 191
online behaviours
    liberated by anonymity, 70
    related to face-to-face interactions, 66–7
online communities
    anthropology and, 2–3
    defining features, 7–10, 191
        carrying culture, 7
        'discussions' or communications, 8
        'emerge from the net' (individual inter actions
            from Internet connections), 8
        'enough people' (minimum/maximum to
            make community), 8–9
        'long enough' (interactions over time), 9
        'public discussion', 9
        'social aggregations', 8
        'sufficient human feeling' (authentic contact
            with others), 9

online communities, defining features *cont.*
    'webs of personal relationships', 9
    global patterns in, 15–17
    not 'real', 130
    number of members, estimates, 2, 13
    types of, 13, 14, 35–6
online play, 70
    varieties of, 30–1
online relationships, 38
online social interaction
    blended with 'real life', 2
    divergence from 'real life', 5
    global use, 2, 13
    as social/language games, 132–3
online survey systems, 43
open-ended questions, 81
openness to presence of others, 169–70
Orkut, 87, 180
ownership of communities, 177
Oxford Internet Institute, 84
Ozanne, Julie and Saatcioglu, Bige, 134

Paccagnella, Luciano, 24
Parmentier, Mari-Agnes, 107
participation
    'consumption'/social relationships dimensions, 31–2
    geographically-dispersed, 71
    meaning of, 5
    open to all, 70–1
    progression of, 26–8
    styles of, 31–5
    types of, 32–5
participatory research
    data analysis software, 91–2
      and data collection, 96
      degree of involvement, 96–7
      ethics, 79, 91
    focus and research questions, 79, 80–2
      guidelines for, 81
    interaction with online communities, 92–3
    preparatory investigations, 75–80
      points to consider, 79–80
    reading written work of others, 81–2
      journals, 83
    search engines, 87–9
    selection of sites, 79, 81
      guidelines, 89–90
    value of, 74–5
    varieties of online interaction, 84–7
    work in related areas
      academic centres for cyberculture studies, 84
      communities of scholars, 82–3
    written guidelines, 91
    see also data collection
passive netnography, 75
Penley, Constance, 107

Penley, Constance and Ross, Andrew, 22
Pew Internet Report 2001, 13, 14, 20, 44
phenomenological, 192
playspaces, 85, 192
political/social activism, 39
polyphonic novels, 168
praxis, 170–1, 192
privacy, 142, 177
pseudonymity, 70, 192
public *vs.* private, 140–2, 177–8
Punch, Maurice, 169
pure netnography, 192

QDA Miner 3.1, 128
Qualrus, 128
questions
    clearly-worded, 109

RadioShackShucks.com, 38
Rabinow, Paul, 171
Rainbow Family, 77
'reality' of online communities, 130
reflexivity, 169–70, 192
Reid, Elizabeth, 24, 154
relationships and ties, 51, 52, 53
research on online interaction, 22–31, 192
    blending ethnography and netnography, 65–8
    choice of methods, 42–4
    developing nuanced understanding, 25–9
    ethnography and netnography, 55–6
    flow of research project, 61
    focus groups, 48–9
    initial research, 22–3
    interviews and journal methods, 45–7
    on new practices and systems of meaning, 29–31
    no single approach, 158
    on 'online communities' and 'communities
        online', 63–5
    qualitative/quantitative approaches, 42
    social network analysis, 49–55
    studies of online communities, 36–9
    surveys, 43–5
    testing assumptions, 23–5
    see also participatory research
research web pages, 106, 107
resonance, 167–8, 192
Resource Center for Cyberculture Studies, 84
Rettberg, Jill Walker, 32, 177, 179
Rheingold, Howard, 8–9, 20, 29
Rice and Rogers, 68
Rice, Ronald E., 23
Rice, Ronald E. and Love, G., 23
Richards, Lynn, 91, 92
richness of online communications, 25–6
rigour, 164, 192
rings, 86, 192

role-play, 70
Runescape, 85

Schaap, F., 113–14
Schau, Hope and Gilly, Mary, 2, 131, 174
Schivelbusch, Wolfgang, 69
Schouten, James and McAlexander, James H., 87
Schwandt, Thomas A., 160
science and rhetoric, separation of, 163
Scott, John, 50
Second Life, 31, 32, 85, 176
Second Life Research Listserv, 83
semiotics and culture, 11
Sharf, Barbara, 142
Sherry, John, 23, 24, 59
Shimanoff, Susan B., 24
Shoham, 112
Short, John et al., 23
Silver, David, 82, 94
Sims Online, 85
Singapore Internet Research Center, 84
Sirsi, Ajay K. et al., 59
skinhead culture, 37, 64
Slater, Don, 174
SmulWeb, 33
social activism, 53
social affiliation from information gathering, 26–7
social causes, involvement in, through Internet, 15
social class distinctions, 124
social content aggregators, 86, 192
social and family life
    effects by Internet use, 26
social inclusiveness, 70–1
social network analysis, 49–55, 193
    centrality, 52
    collecting data, 53–5
    limitations, 54–5
    relationships and ties, 51, 52, 53
    uses, 54
    whole network approach, 51
social networking sites, 32, 86–7, 193
    netnography of, 180–1
social sciences
    incorporating computer studies, 2, 3
    use of word 'ethnography', 6
social structures in online communities,
        23, 24, 70–1
Social Technographics Profile, 44
social/emotional support from online
        communities, 15
software
    data analysis, 91–2, 127–9
    focus group interviews, 48
    social network analysis, 53–4
Sohn, Changsoo, 44
Sony Pictures website, 150

South America
    Internet use, 16
South Korea, 16, 44
Spain, 16
spam, 103–4, 193
Spiggle, Susan, 120, 135, 166
'Spore', 31
Sproull, Lee and Kiesler, Sara, 23
standards, 157–9, 161–3
    criteria, 161–72
        coherence, 163–4, 189
        groundedness, 166, 190
        innovation, 166–7, 190
        intermix, 171–2, 190
        literacy, 165–6, 191
        praxis, 170–1, 192
        reflexivity, 169–70, 192
        resonance, 167–8, 192
        rigour, 164, 192
        verisimilitude, 168–9, 193
    lack of qualitative standards, 157–8
    positivist position, 161–3
    post-positivist position, 161–3
    post-structural position, 161–3
    postmodern position, 161–3
    validity, 161, 162, 170
Star Trek community, 64
Star Trek Research Web page, 106–7, 109
Steiner, Peter, 70
still-image screen capture software, 193
Stone, Allucquère Rosanne, 113
stored communications, 144, 145, 146
storing text, 128
Strauss, Anselm and Corbin, Julie, 119
StumbleUpon, 86
Sudweeks, Fay and Simoff, Simeon J., 42
Sunderland, Patricia L. and Denny Rita M., 6, 56
Surveillance and Society, 83
SurveyMonkey.com, 43
surveys, 43–5
    costs, 44
    general online surveys, 43–4
    on online communities, 44–5
symbols/signs, 12
synchronous media, 69, 193
    archives, 72
Synthetic Worlds Initiative at Indiana University, 83

Tacchi, J. et al., 170
TAMS/TamsAnalyser, 128
Tapscott, Don and Williams, Anthony D., 36, 175, 176
Taylor, T.L., 181
technoculture, 21–2, 171, 193
technological change
    merging with 'social mechanisms', 53
    and perceptions of communication, 69
    shaping culture and communities, 21–2, 68–70

technosociality, 171
Tedlock, Barbara, 131
Teknocultura, 83
telephone interviews, 69
TerraNova, 83
Tesch, R., 6
text
    culturally situated, 163
    interpretation, 120
    open or closed, 170
    storing, 128
textuality of data, 130
theorizing, 119
Thomas, Jane Boyd et al., 175
Thompson, Craig J., 164
Thompson, Craig J. et al., 120
Thorseth, May, 139
Tielhard de Chardin, Pierre, 183
time lag, 69
Toffler, Alvin, 21
Transana 2, 128
Turkle, Sherry, 29, 70, 174
Twitter, 86, 87
types of online communities, 13, 14, 35–6

unobtrusiveness of netnography, 56, 143
USA
    centres for cyberculture studies, 84
    Institutional Review Boards (IRBs),
        139, 144, 191
    numbers in online communities, 14, 44
Usenet groups, 14

Valck, Kristine de, 32–3, 174
validity, 161, 162, 170
Van Maanen, John, 62, 163, 168, 169
verisimilitude, 168–9, 193
'virtual community', 8, 193
virtual worlds, 31, 32, 71, 85, 193
    netnography of, 181, 193
    persistence, 71–2
visualization techniques, 54
Vroman, Kerryellen and Kovacich, Joann, 25

Walker Rettburg, Jill, 86
Wallendorf, Melanie and Belk, Russell W., 164, 166
Walther, Joseph B., 4, 23–4, 26, 40, 141, 142, 143,
        144, 153, 156
Wasserman, Stanley and Faust, Katherine, 52
Watt, James H., 44
web-pages of researchers, 147–8
Weber, Max, 11
Webkinz, 85
websites, number of, 2
Weft QDA, 128
Weible, R. and Wallace, J., 44
Weinberg, Bruce, 97

Weinberger, David, 105, 117
Weitzman, Eben and Miles, Matthew, 128
WELL, 14, 29
Wellman, Barry, 24, 49, 50
Wellman, Barry et al., 50
Welser, Howard T. et al., 54, 57
Whitty, Monica Therese, 38, 131
Wikan, Unni, 167
Wikiasearch, 88
Wikipedia, 86, 89
wikis, 86, 169, 193
Williams, J. Patrick and Copes, Heith, 28, 37
Williams, Raymond, 10

Wittgenstein, Ludwig, 132
Wolcott, Harry, 161
work-based frustrations, 38
World of Warcraft, 85
writing, 167

Yahoo!, 88
YouTube, 39, 86, 89, 111
Yun, Gi Woong and Trumbo, Craig W., 44

Zelwietro, Joseph, 39
Zwick, Detlev et al., 176

Research Methods Books from SAGE

INTERPRETING QUALITATIVE DATA — THIRD EDITION

DAVID SILVERMAN

Qualitative Research & Evaluation Methods

3 EDITION

Michael Quinn Patton

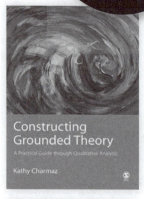

Constructing Grounded Theory

A Practical Guide through Qualitative Analysis

Kathy Charmaz

EVALUATION
A Systematic Approach
SEVENTH EDITION

PETER H. ROSSI
MARK W. LIPSEY
HOWARD E. FREEMAN

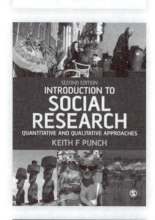

SECOND EDITION
INTRODUCTION TO SOCIAL RESEARCH
QUANTITATIVE AND QUALITATIVE APPROACHES
KEITH F PUNCH

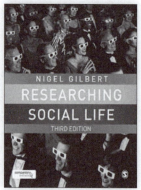

NIGEL GILBERT
RESEARCHING SOCIAL LIFE
THIRD EDITION

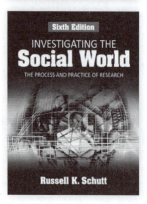

Sixth Edition
INVESTIGATING THE Social World
THE PROCESS AND PRACTICE OF RESEARCH

Russell K. Schutt

AN INTRODUCTION TO QUALITATIVE RESEARCH
UWE FLICK
EDITION 4

DEVELOPING EFFECTIVE RESEARCH PROPOSALS

Keith F Punch

SECOND EDITION

www.sagepub.co.uk

SAGE